TIME FOR KIDS

WORLD ATLAS

Keep your world knowledge up-to-the-minute
with news from around the globe at
timeforkids.com.

Continue your travel adventures online with
TIME FOR KIDS Around the World. Explore countries, test
your knowledge, and learn words in other languages at
timeforkids.com/TFK/kids/hh/goplaces.

TIME For Kids World Atlas
PUBLISHER: Bob Der
MANAGING EDITOR, TIME For Kids MAGAZINE: Nellie Gonzalez Cutler
EDITOR, TIME LEARNING VENTURES: Jonathan Rosenbloom
MAPS: Joe LeMonnier **Additional maps:** Joe Lertola
FIRST EDITION RESEARCH: Kathleen Adams
ORIGINAL CONTRIBUTORS: Claudia Atticot, David Bjerklie, Jeremy Caplan, Borden Elniff, Jennifer Marino, Butch Phelps, Lisa Jo Rudy, Kathryn R. Satterfield, Tiffany Sommers, Elizabeth Winchester
ORIGINAL ART DIRECTION AND DESIGN: Raúl Rodriguez/Rebecca Tachna for R studio T, NYC
COVER DESIGN TEMPLATE: Elliot Kreloff

Time HOME ENTERTAINMENT

PUBLISHER: Richard Fraiman
GENERAL MANAGER: Steven Sandonato
EXECUTIVE DIRECTOR, MARKETING SERVICES: Carol Pittard
EXECUTIVE DIRECTOR, RETAIL & SPECIAL SALES: Tom Mifsud
EXECUTIVE DIRECTOR, NEW PRODUCT DEVELOPMENT: Peter Harper
DIRECTOR, BOOKAZINE DEVELOPMENT & MARKETING: Laura Adam
PUBLISHING DIRECTOR: Joy Butts
ASSISTANT GENERAL COUNSEL: Helen Wan
BOOK PRODUCTION MANAGER: Susan Chodakiewicz
DESIGN & PREPRESS MANAGER: Anne-Michelle Gallero
ASSOCIATE MARKETING MANAGER: Jonathan White
ASSOCIATE PREPRESS MANAGER: Alex Voznesenskiy
SPECIAL THANKS: Christine Austin, Jeremy Biloon, Glenn Buonocore, Malati Chavali, Jim Childs, Rose Cirrincione, Jacqueline Fitzgerald, Christine Font, Lauren Hall, Carrie Hertan, Suzanne Janso, Raphael Joa, Malena Jones, Mona Li, Robert Marasco, Kimberly Marshall, Amy Migliaccio, Nina Mistry, Dave Rozzelle, Ilene Schreider, Adriana Tierno, Vanessa Wu, Time Imaging

For information on TIME For Kids magazine for the classroom or home, go to TIMEFORKIDS.COM or call 1-800-777-8600.

For subscriptions to SI Kids, go to SIKIDS.COM or call 1-800-889-6007.

DOWNTOWN BOOKWORKS INC.

PRODUCED BY DOWNTOWN BOOKWORKS
PRESIDENT: Julie Merberg
EDITORIAL DIRECTOR: Sarah Parvis
MANAGING EDITOR: LeeAnn Pemberton
PRODUCTION DESIGNER: Brian Michael Thomas/Our Hero Productions
SPECIAL THANKS: Patty Brown, Mike DeCapite, Kathy Gordon, Lynn Messina, Stephen Callahan

PUBLISHED BY TIME For Kids BOOKS
AN IMPRINT OF TIME HOME ENTERTAINMENT INC.
135 West 50th Street
New York, New York 10020

ISBN 10: 1-60320-884-4
ISBN 13: 978-1-60320-884-0

We welcome your comments and suggestions about TIME For Kids Books. Please write to us at:
TIME For Kids Books
Attention: Book Editors
P.O. Box 11016
Des Moines, IA 50336-1016

If you would like to order any TIME For Kids or Sports Illustrated Kids hardcover Collector's Edition books, please call us at 1-800-327-6388. (Monday through Friday, 7:00 a.m.–8:00 p.m. or Saturday, 7:00 a.m.–6:00 p.m. Central Time).

Contents

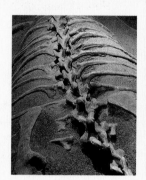

The Arctic 12

North America 14

1 CWP 11

World Guide

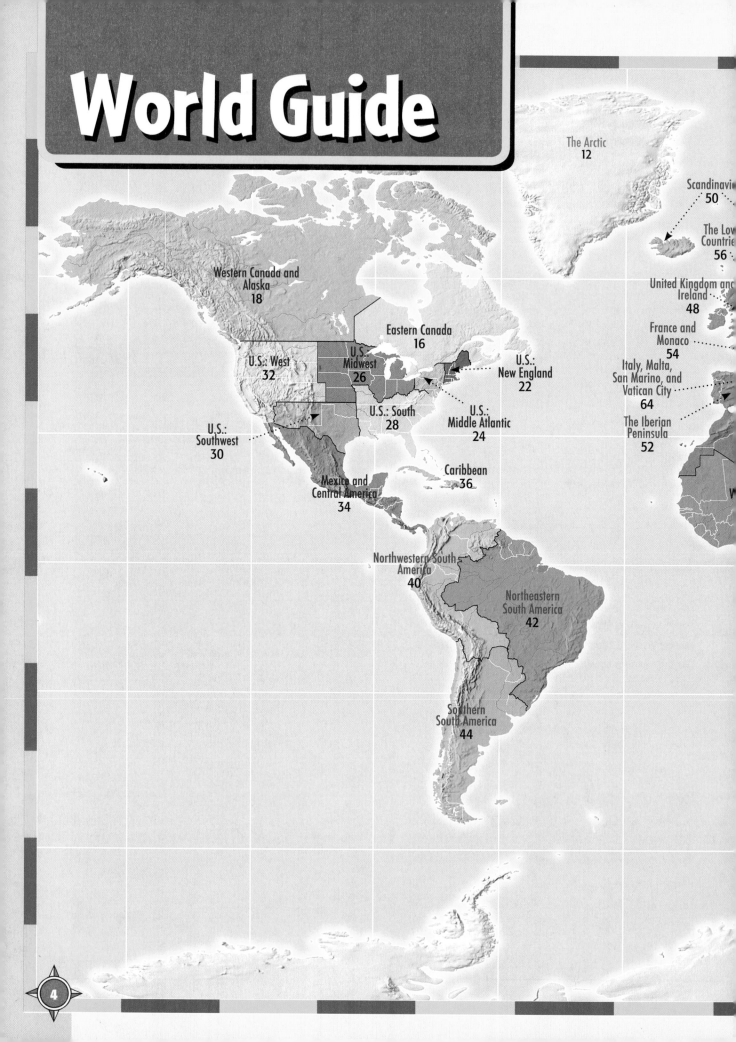

The Arctic
12

Scandinavi
50

The Low
Countrie
56

United Kingdom and
Ireland
48

France and
Monaco
54

Italy, Malta,
San Marino, and
Vatican City
64

The Iberian
Peninsula
52

Western Canada and
Alaska
18

Eastern Canada
16

U.S.:
New England
22

U.S.:
Midwest
26

U.S.: West
32

U.S.:
Middle Atlantic
24

U.S.: South
28

U.S.:
Southwest
30

Mexico and
Central America
34

Caribbean
36

Northwestern South
America
40

Northeastern
South America
42

Southern
South America
44

Austria, Liechtenstein, and Switzerland
60

Central Europe
62

Ukraine, Moldova, and the Caucasus Republics
72

The Baltic States and Belarus
70

Western Russia
74

Eastern Russia
78

Central Asia
86

China, Mongolia, and Taiwan
92

The Balkans
66

Turkey and Cyprus
80

Southeastern Europe
68

Israel, Jordan, Lebanon, and Syria
82

Afghanistan, Iran, and Pakistan
88

Indian Subcontinent
90

Japan, North Korea, and South Korea
94

tern Africa
04

The Arabian Peninsula
84

Northeastern Africa
102

Southeast Asia
96

Central Africa
108

Maritime Southeast Asia
98

East Central Africa
110

Southern Africa
112

Australia and Papua New Guinea
116

New Zealand and the Pacific Islands
118

Antarctica
120

How to Use the TFK World Atlas

Take a trip around the world with the TIME FOR KIDS World Atlas. This book divides the world into continents, regions, and countries. Each of the book's sections begins with a map of the continent and an explanation of the continent's features. "Wow Zone!" and "Did You Know?" features will introduce interesting information about the people, places, and landmarks within a country or region. The "World-at-a-Glance" chapter at the end of the book gives vital statistics for every country in the world. But before you begin to explore the world, take a few moments to find out about planet Earth by reading pages 8 through 11.

Abbreviations

E.U.	European Union
ft	feet
g	gallon
kg	kilogram
L	liter
lb	pound
m	meter
mi	mile
Mt.	Mount
Mtns.	Mountains
NA	not available
oz	ounce
St.	Saint
sq km	square kilometer
sq mi	square mile
U.K.	United Kingdom

Key to Map Symbols

- ✪ Country capital
- ✪ State, province, or territory capital
- ● City
- ▲ Mountain or volcano

Introduction
These paragraphs give a brief overview of the continent's geographic features.

Color Tabs
Each continent has a different color tab, so you can easily locate the pages that are about each continent.

Lines of Longitude and Latitude
Lines of longitude run in a north-south direction. Lines of latitude run in an east-west direction.

Continent

[Map of Europe with Eiffel Tower, Continent Facts, Wow Zone! sections]

Continent Facts
Here you will find the size of the continent, a list of its countries, and other information.

Scale
Use the scale to measure distances. The scale is given in miles and kilometers.

Wow Zone!
This is where you will find amazing facts about the continent.

Locator Globe
The globe shows the continent's location in the world.

Introduction
These paragraphs give a brief overview of states, provinces, territories, or countries.

Compass Rose
The compass rose will help you locate north, south, east, west, and points in between.

Country/Region

Map Grid
A grid surrounds the country and regional maps. Use it to quickly locate places.

Data Bank
Each section has a Data Bank with important information about area, population, capital city, and languages.

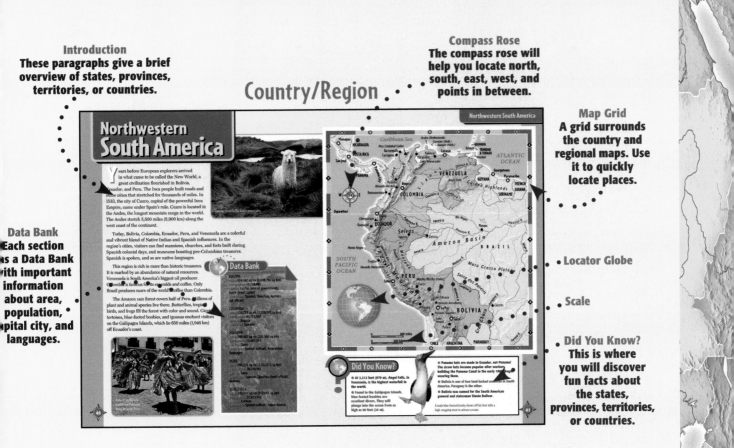

Northwestern South America

Northwestern South America

Years before European explorers arrived in what came to be called the New World, a great civilization flourished in Bolivia, Ecuador, and Peru. The Inca people built roads and stone cities that stretched for thousands of miles. In 1533, the city of Cuzco, capital of the powerful Inca Empire, came under Spain's rule. Cuzco is located in the Andes, the longest mountain range in the world. The Andes stretch 5,500 miles (8,900 km) along the west coast of the continent.

Today, Bolivia, Colombia, Ecuador, Peru, and Venezuela are a colorful and vibrant blend of Native Indian and Spanish influences. In the region's cities, visitors can find mansions, churches, and forts built during Spanish colonial days, and museums boasting pre-Columbian treasures. Spanish is spoken, and so are native languages.

This region is rich in more than historic treasures. It is marked by an abundance of natural resources. Venezuela is South America's biggest oil producer. Colombia is famous for its emeralds and coffee. Only Brazil produces more of the world's coffee than Colombia.

The Amazon rain forest covers half of Peru. Millions of plant and animal species live there. Butterflies, tropical birds, and frogs fill the forest with color and sound. Giant tortoises, blue-footed boobies, and iguanas enchant visitors on the Galápagos Islands, which lie 650 miles (1,046 km) off Ecuador's coast.

Data Bank

Did You Know?

Locator Globe

Scale

Did You Know?
This is where you will discover fun facts about the states, provinces, territories, or countries.

World-at-a-Glance
Turn to pages 122–136 for information about every country in the world. Here you will find a country's flag, area, population, capital, languages, government, religions, literacy rate, currency, and main exports.

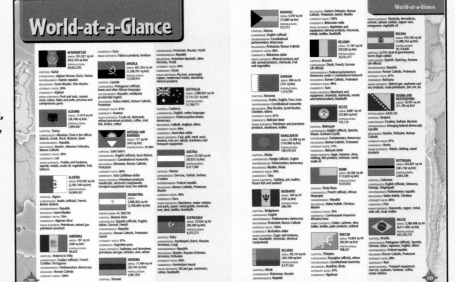

World-at-a-Glance

World-at-a-Glance

The Living Earth

When did life on Earth begin, and how? What were the conditions that made life possible? Did life arise only once? For centuries, scientists have struggled with these difficult questions.

We know from studying tiny microfossils of simple marine bacteria that life on Earth began at least 3.5 billion years ago. For the first 1.5 billion years of Earth's history, bacteria were the only life on the planet. Some types of marine bacteria formed large colonies, and their fossil remains, called stromatolites, can be found along the coasts of South Africa and Australia.

Gradually, more complex animals began to evolve in the sea. An explosion in the diversity of animals took place between 550 million and 500 million years ago. This was followed by the appearance of the first creatures with backbones: fish. The next 100 million years saw the first plants, animals, and insects to live on land. Dinosaurs appeared nearly 250 million years ago. They ruled Earth until 65 million years ago, when they disappeared. Some scientists believe that an asteroid hit Earth and caused mass extinctions.

Today, life is present in every nook and cranny of the globe, from the coldest, darkest depths of the ocean to the hot, arid climate of the Sahara to desolate Himalayan mountaintops.

Biologists categorize the amazing diversity of the world's plant and animal life by habitat. The Arctic tundra, for example, with its polar bears and seals, is one habitat. The tropical rain forest along the Amazon River is another. Habitats range from the grasslands of bison and prairie dogs to the coral reefs of clown fish and moray eels. As the number of human beings on the planet grows larger and larger, it is our responsibility to make sure that these habitats and the precious creatures that depend on them are kept healthy and safe.

Major Events in Earth's History

4.5 billion years ago
Earth forms.

3.5 billion years ago
The oldest forms of life, such as bacteria, appear.

2 billion years ago
Simple microbes called protists emerge.

1 billion years ago
Plants and fungi begin to grow.

Atmosphere

Lithosphere

Hydrosphere

Biosphere

Did You Know?

● Earth is made up of four spheres. The atmosphere includes the gases that surround Earth. The biosphere includes all the living organisms. The hydrosphere contains all the planet's water. The lithosphere is Earth's hard crust, which includes the tallest craggy mountains and the dirt in our gardens.

● There have been periods in Earth's history when many plants and animals have died all at once. Scientists have found fossils and bones (left) from these mass extinctions, which they believe were caused by climate change or something like an asteroid hitting Earth.

● Bacteria, the first living things on Earth, are still the most plentiful organisms on the planet. They are found on land, in water, and in the air.

● Each type of plant and animal is called a species. Biologists use the word *biodiversity* to describe the many different species on Earth. Scientists have identified fewer than 2 million species, but there may be as many as 30 million in the world.

600 million years ago
More-complex, soft-bodied animals come into existence.

500 million years ago
Animals with backbones (jawless fish) emerge.

7 million years ago
Human ancestors appear.

Weather and Climate

Category F0 tornadoes, with winds 65–85 miles per hour (105–137 kmph), are the least destructive. An F5 twister, with winds stronger than 200 miles per hour (322 kmph), is the most destructive.

When it comes to the day's forecast, climate is what you expect and weather is what you get. You can *expect* that it will be hot in Dallas, Texas, in July and cold in Minneapolis, Minnesota, in January. It's impossible to know for sure whether it will be sunny or raining or exactly what the temperature will be.

The sun is the ultimate climate-and-weather machine for our planet. The sun's energy doesn't fall evenly on Earth—and that makes all the difference. The tilt of our planet as it orbits the sun causes the four seasons and contributes to the patterns of air circulation that create wet and dry seasons. Because Earth is round, the sun's rays hit the planet at different angles. Places located near the equator get more direct sunlight and more intense heat. The sun also drives the weather on a daily basis. The collision of warm and cold air can produce a spring shower or a swarm of tornadoes. The circulation of water in oceans also plays a role in creating weather conditions. Some ocean currents keep northern Europe warm. Other currents fuel hurricanes and monsoons.

Climate is stable from year to year. But over long periods of time, climate can change dramatically. Fifteen thousand years ago, large parts of Europe, Canada, and the United States were stuck in a long, deep freeze called the Ice Age. Scientists are now busy taking the planet's temperature and measuring polar ice caps and mountaintop glaciers. They're trying to determine how much our climate is changing, because global warming affects all life on Earth. They have found that temperatures are rising, Arctic habitats are melting, coral reefs are dying off, and the number of extreme weather events—such as tropical storms, wildfires, and heat waves—has increased. Scientists believe that the burning of fossil fuels is causing global warming.

Due to global warming, polar bears in the Arctic are losing their habitat.

Did You Know?

● The end of the Ice Age, about 10,000 years ago, was the time of mammals such as the mastodon, the woolly mammoth, and the saber-toothed tiger. We know from fossils that Ice Age peoples used stone spears to hunt animals. Did these animals disappear because of overhunting or because the climate was getting warmer? Scientists don't know.

● In the past million years, ice ages have been common. It is the warm periods between them, such as the one we are in now, that are unusual.

Some scientists believe that the next ice age is right around the corner. Don't worry—that could be 10,000 years away!

● Is Earth getting warmer? The average worldwide surface temperature has been above normal for the past 30 years. The 10 warmest years on record for at least a century also occurred during that time. This warming trend is a concern for a lot of scientists—and for polar bears, too!

The Changing Planet

E arth is 4.5 billion years old. Like all other planets, it was formed from dust and debris by the powerful pull of the sun's gravity. Scientists believe a smaller planet crashed into Earth when Earth was still a ball of molten rock. This collision created our moon. Gradually, the surface of Earth cooled and hardened. But most of the planet is still molten. What we think of as solid ground is only the outer layer, or the crust, less than 50 miles (80 km) thick. In some places it is only a couple of miles (kilometers) thick.

The Earth's crust is on the move. Think of it as a giant jigsaw puzzle floating on a hot lava ball that is nearly 8,000 miles (12,785 km) across! The slowly shifting pieces of crust are called tectonic plates. Scientists believe that 220 million years ago, our seven continents were actually joined in a single supercontinent called Pangaea (pan-*jee*-uh). Right now, the plates that meet in the middle of the Atlantic Ocean are pulling apart. That movement widens the Atlantic by 1 inch (2.5 cm) each year.

Even though shifting plates move as slowly as snails, the shifts create dramatic results. Mountains are formed by plates crashing into one another. Earthquakes happen when two plates grinding against each other suddenly slip. Volcanoes are spots where the molten rock beneath the crust leaks out, sometimes explosively. And although we can't see them, many of the most spectacular formations on Earth—from the biggest mountains to the deepest canyons—are under the oceans, which cover two-thirds of the planet.

Mt. Bromo, in Indonesia, is an active volcano.

Did You Know?

● In 1999, a team of scientists used satellite equipment to calculate a more accurate height for Mount Everest. They concluded that the new height was 29,035 feet (8,850 m) above sea level. That is 7 feet (2 m) higher than before.

● Volcanoes can form where two plates meet. They can also form as a sea-floor plate passes over a "hot spot," an area where the crust is thin and the molten rock below has broken through. As the moving crust passes over the hot spot, volcanoes form, sometimes one after another. This is how the Hawaiian Islands were formed.

The devastating earthquake that hit Haiti in January 2010 measured 7 on the Richter scale.

● There are thousands of volcanic eruptions each year. Most of them are minor. Many occur underwater. In 1963, an underwater eruption created a new island near Iceland.

● The Richter scale measures the strength of earthquakes. The scale goes from magnitude 0 to 9, with 9 as the strongest quake. An earthquake measuring 8 on the Richter scale is 10 times more powerful than a quake measuring 7. In 1908, a magnitude-8 earthquake nearly destroyed San Francisco, California.

The Arctic

Walrus tusks can be as long as 3 feet (1 m). Walruses use their tusks to help pull their giant bodies out of the cold Arctic water.

The Arctic region is the northernmost place on the planet. Strictly speaking, it is the area that falls inside the Arctic Circle. But many scientists define the Arctic as the area centered around the North Pole, including everything north of the tree line (the point beyond which no trees can grow). That region includes parts of Alaska, Canada, Greenland, Iceland, Norway, and Russia.

The Arctic climate is cold and harsh. Winter at the North Pole lasts six months, during which the sun never rises. The average winter temperature is about –22°F (–30°C). Summer at the top of the world is nearly opposite, with six months of constant daylight and relatively mild temperatures of around 32°F (0°C).

Despite the forbidding environment, some hardy animals—including humans!—thrive in the frozen north. Giant polar bears, walruses, seals, and some 23 other animal species survive year-round in the polar climate. The people of the Arctic, including the Inuit of North America, the Lapps (Sami) of Scandinavia, and the Nenets and Chukchis of Russia, have also adapted to their surroundings. It is not possible to grow food, so nourishment must come from land and sea animals. In the past, native Arctic communities were isolated from the rest of the world. But in recent years, tourism and the discovery of oil and mineral deposits have brought more outsiders to the region.

The aurora borealis, or nothern lights, can be seen in the Arctic night sky. The appearance of colorful patterns of light is caused by solar winds interacting with Earth's atmosphere.

Regional Facts

ARCTIC CIRCLE AREA: 5,400,000 sq mi (13,985,936 sq km)
ARCTIC OCEAN AREA: 5,406,000 sq mi (14,001,476 sq km)
AVERAGE ARCTIC OCEAN DEPTH: 3,450 feet (1,052 m)
LOWEST POINT: Fram Basin, 15,305 feet (4,665 m)
LARGEST ISLAND: Greenland, 836,222 sq mi (2,165,805 sq km)

NORTH AMERICA

UNITED STATES
OF AMERICA

PACIFIC OCEAN

Gulf of
Alaska

Aleutian Islands

CANADA

Anchorage

ALASKA

Washington, D.C.

Ottawa

Arctic Circle

Fairbanks

Bering Sea

New York City

St. Lawrence I.

Victoria I.

Barrow

Banks I.

Beaufort Sea

Bering
Strait

Anadyr

Wrangel I.

Baffin I.

ARCTIC
OCEAN

Sea of Okhotsk

Baffin Bay

Ellesmere I.

Permanent Ice cap

Barbeau Peak

New
Siberian Is.

JAPAN

Nuuk

Alert

Greenland
(Denmark)

North
Pole

Laptev Sea

Severnaya
Zemlya Is.

Greenland Sea

Svalbard
(Norway)

Franz Josef
Land Is.

Tiksi

ATLANTIC OCEAN

ICELAND

Jan Mayen I.
(Norway)

Siberia

Norwegian Sea

Novaya
Zemlya Is.

Kara Sea

IRELAND

U.K.

London

NORWAY

Hammerfest

Barents Sea

Oslo

SWEDEN

Murmansk

RUSSIA

FINLAND

MONGOLIA

EUROPE

Archangelsk

Moscow

CHINA

KAZAKHSTAN

ASIA

AFRICA

Wow Zone!

● A common problem for people in the Arctic is snow blindness, a temporary loss of vision due to the sun's reflection off snow or ice.

● The word *Arctic* comes from the Greek word *arktos*, which means "bear." It probably refers to the northern constellation of stars Ursa Major, or Great Bear.

● The Arctic Ocean is the smallest ocean in the world.

● Dogsledding is not only an Arctic mode of transportation, it is also a popular sport.

Most sled dogs run an average of about 20 miles per hour (32 kmph) in races more than 25 miles (40 km) long.

North America

Niagara Falls, on the U.S.–Canada border, is a major source of hydroelectric power.

Stretching 9 million square miles (23 million sq km), North America is the world's third biggest continent. The region extends from the icy Arctic Ocean in the north to the warm, turquoise waters of the Caribbean Sea. In between lies nearly every landscape imaginable: massive glaciers, snow-covered mountains, vast canyons, scorched deserts, fertile plains, and tropical rain forests.

North America is made up of 23 nations, including Canada, the world's second largest country, and the United States, the world's third largest country. The continent is rich in natural resources—abundant water, minerals, and fertile soil—and has one of the world's most developed economies.

North America is also known for its dynamic cities. Those hungry for cultural and intellectual experiences can find world-class museums, universities, and concert halls in cities all over the continent, including New York City; Los Angeles, California; Mexico City, Mexico; and Vancouver, Canada.

Continent Facts

NUMBER OF COUNTRIES AND TERRITORIES: 36—Anguilla (U.K.), Antigua and Barbuda, Aruba (Netherlands), Bahamas, Barbados, Belize, Bermuda (U.K.), Canada, Cayman Islands (U.K.), Costa Rica, Cuba, Dominica, Dominican Republic, El Salvador, Greenland (Denmark), Grenada, Guadeloupe (France), Guatemala, Haiti, Honduras, Jamaica, Martinique (France), Mexico, Montserrat (U.K.), Nicaragua, Panama, Puerto Rico (U.S.), Saint Barthelemy (France), Saint Kitts and Nevis, Saint Lucia, Saint Maarten/Saint Martin (Netherlands/France), Saint Vincent and the Grenadines, Trinidad and Tobago, Turks and Caicos (U.K), United States, Virgin Islands (U.S. and U.K.)

AREA: 9,361,791 sq mi (24,247,039 sq km)

HIGHEST POINT: Mount McKinley (Denali), Alaska, U.S., 20,320 ft (6,194 m)

LOWEST POINT: Death Valley, California, U.S., 282 ft (86 m) below sea level

LARGEST LAKE: Lake Superior, Canada/U.S., 31,700 sq mi (82,103 sq km)

LONGEST RIVER: Missouri-Mississippi river system, U.S., 3,710 mi (5,971 km)

LARGEST COUNTRY: Canada, 3,855,085 sq mi (9,984,670 sq km)

SMALLEST COUNTRY: Saint Kitts and Nevis, 101 sq mi (261 sq km)

Wow Zone!

- The national sports of Canada are hockey and lacrosse.
- Greenland is the world's largest island. It is nearly covered with ice.
- North America includes two of the world's most populous cities, New York City and Mexico City, Mexico. Both have populations in excess of 8 million.
- Everglades National Park covers about 1.5 million acres (607,028 hectares) in southwestern Florida. It is home to more than 350 species of birds, including flamingos (right); 40 species of mammals; 50 species of reptiles; and 300 species of fish.
- Lake Superior, on the U.S.–Canada border, is the world's largest freshwater lake.

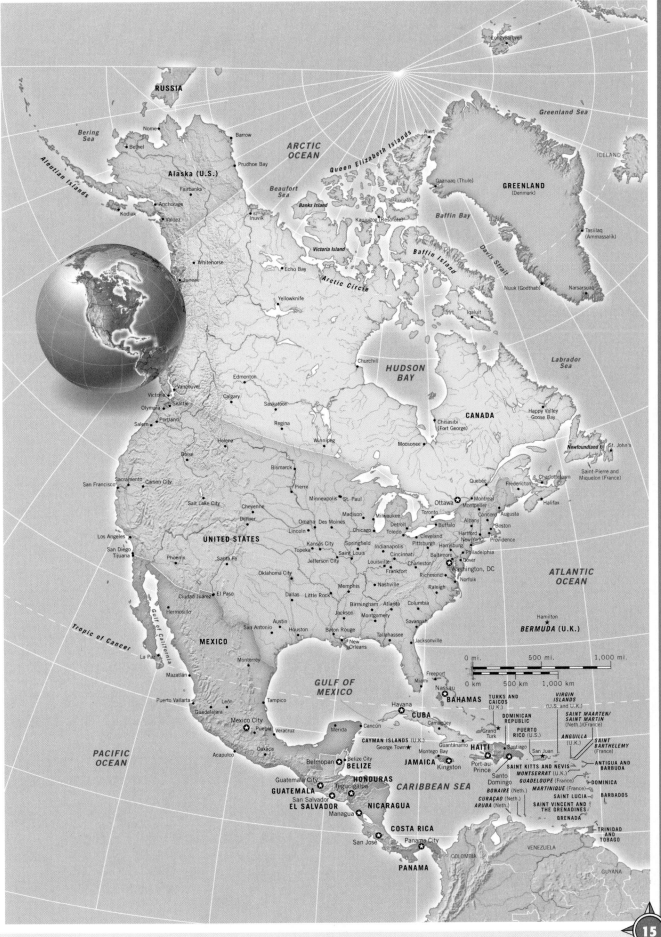

RUSSIA

*Bering
Sea*

Aleutian Islands

Nome
Bethel

Barrow

Prudhoe Bay

**ARCTIC
OCEAN**

Queen Elizabeth Islands

Alert

Greenland Sea

ICELAND

Alaska (U.S.)

*Beaufort
Sea*

Banks Island

Qaanaaq (Thule)

GREENLAND
(Denmark)

Fairbanks
Anchorage
Valdez

Inuvik

Kugluktuk (Resolute)

Victoria Island

Baffin Bay

Kodiak

Baffin Island

Tasiilaq
(Ammassalik)

Whitehorse

Echo Bay

Arctic Circle

Davis Strait

Nuuk (Godthab)

Narsarsuaq

Juneau

Yellowknife

Iqaluit

Churchill

**HUDSON
BAY**

*Labrador
Sea*

Edmonton

CANADA

Happy Valley
Goose Bay

Vancouver

Calgary

Saskatoon

Chisasibi
(Fort George)

Newfoundland I.   St. John's

Victoria
Olympia   Seattle
Salem   Portland

Regina

Winnipeg

Moosonee

Québec

Charlottetown

Saint-Pierre and
Miquelon (France)

Helena

Fredericton

Boise

Bismarck

Pierre

Minneapolis   St. Paul

Montréal
Ottawa   Montpelier

Halifax

San Francisco
Sacramento   Carson City

Salt Lake City
Cheyenne

Madison
Milwaukee

Toronto

Albany   Concord
Buffalo   Boston

Augusta

Los Angeles

Denver

Omaha   Des Moines

Detroit
Chicago   Toledo

Cleveland

Hartford   Providence
New York

UNITED STATES

Lincoln

Topeka   Kansas City

Springfield
Indianapolis

Pittsburgh   Harrisburg
Philadelphia

San Diego
Tijuana

Phoenix

Santa Fe

Jefferson City

St. Louis
Louisville

Cincinnati

Baltimore
Dover

**ATLANTIC
OCEAN**

Charleston
Frankfort

Richmond   Washington, DC

Oklahoma City

Memphis   Nashville

Norfolk

Ciudad Juárez   El Paso

Dallas   Little Rock

Raleigh

Hermosillo

Birmingham   Atlanta   Columbia

Austin

Jackson
Montgomery

Savannah

Hamilton

San Antonio   Houston

Baton Rouge
New
Orleans

Tallahassee

BERMUDA (U.K.)

Tropic of Cancer

MEXICO

Gulf of California

Jacksonville

0 mi.   500 mi.   1,000 mi.

La Paz

Monterrey

Miami

0 km   500 km   1,000 km

Freeport
Nassau

Mazatlán

**GULF OF
MEXICO**

Havana

BAHAMAS

*TURKS AND
CAICOS
(U.K.)*

*VIRGIN
ISLANDS
(U.S. and U.K.)*

Puerto Vallarta

Tampico

León

CUBA

Camagüey

*DOMINICAN
REPUBLIC*

*SAINT MAARTEN/
SAINT MARTIN
(Neth.)(France)*

Guadalajara

Cancún

**PUERTO
RICO (U.S.)**

Mexico City

Puebla   Veracruz

Mérida

Grand
Turk

*ANGUILLA
(U.K.)*

*SAINT
BARTHELEMY
(France)*

Acapulco

Oaxaca

CAYMAN ISLANDS (U.K.)

George Town

Guantánamo

Santiago

San Juan

**PACIFIC
OCEAN**

Belmopan   Belize City

Montego Bay

HAITI

Port-au-
Prince

*ANTIGUA AND
BARBUDA*

BELIZE

JAMAICA

Kingston

SAINT KITTS AND NEVIS
MONTSERRAT (U.K.)

Guatemala City

Santo
Domingo

GUADELOUPE (France)

DOMINICA

GUATEMALA

HONDURAS

Tegucigalpa

CARIBBEAN SEA

BONAIRE (Neth.)

MARTINIQUE (France)

CURAÇAO (Neth.)

SAINT LUCIA

ARUBA (Neth.)

*SAINT VINCENT AND
THE GRENADINES*

BARBADOS

San Salvador

NICARAGUA

EL SALVADOR

Managua

GRENADA

COSTA RICA

*TRINIDAD
AND
TOBAGO*

San José

Panama City

VENEZUELA

COLOMBIA

PANAMA

GUYANA

Longyearbyen

15

Eastern Canada

Measuring nearly 4 million square miles (10 million sq km), Canada is the world's second largest country. Only Russia is larger. Canada is divided into 10 provinces and three territories. It stretches from the Atlantic Ocean in the east to the Pacific Ocean in the west. The east is the location of the country's capital, Ottawa, and its two largest cities, Montreal and Toronto. Many of Canada's early settlers were from France and Britain. Both countries believed that Canada should belong to them, which led to years of war and conflict. In 1763, at the end of the Seven Years' War, France was forced to give its Canadian territory to Britain. In 1867, Canada's colonies joined to form the Dominion of Canada. The country's government included a governor general, who represented Britain's monarch.

In winter, the Rideau Canal, in Ottawa, becomes the world's longest skating rink. It is 4.8 miles (7.7 km) long.

Canadians today are proud of their freedom, but they have not forgotten their heritage. French is spoken by about one-third of the population; Britain's Queen is still pictured on some Canadian money; and the customs and traditions of native people are valued and respected.

Data Bank

CANADA
AREA: 3,855,085 sq mi (9,984,624 sq km)
POPULATION: 34,030,589
CAPITAL: Ottawa
LANGUAGES: English, French (both official), others

Eastern Canada's Provinces

NEW BRUNSWICK
AREA: 28,345 sq mi (73,413 sq km)
POPULATION: 751,800
CAPITAL: Fredericton

NEWFOUNDLAND AND LABRADOR
AREA: 156,185 sq mi (404,517 sq km)
POPULATION: 509,700
CAPITAL: St. John's

NOVA SCOTIA
AREA: 21,425 sq mi (55,490 sq km)
POPULATION: 942,500
CAPITAL: Halifax

ONTARIO
AREA: 412,582 sq mi (1,068,582 sq km)
POPULATION: 13,210,700
CAPITAL: Toronto

PRINCE EDWARD ISLAND
AREA: 2,184 sq mi (5,657 sq km)
POPULATION: 142,300
CAPITAL: Charlottetown

QUEBEC
AREA: 594,860 sq mi (1,540,680 sq km)
POPULATION: 7,907,400
CAPITAL: Québec

There are about 480 active lighthouses along Canada's coastline. Cape Spear Lighthouse is the oldest surviving lighthouse in Newfoundland and Labrador.

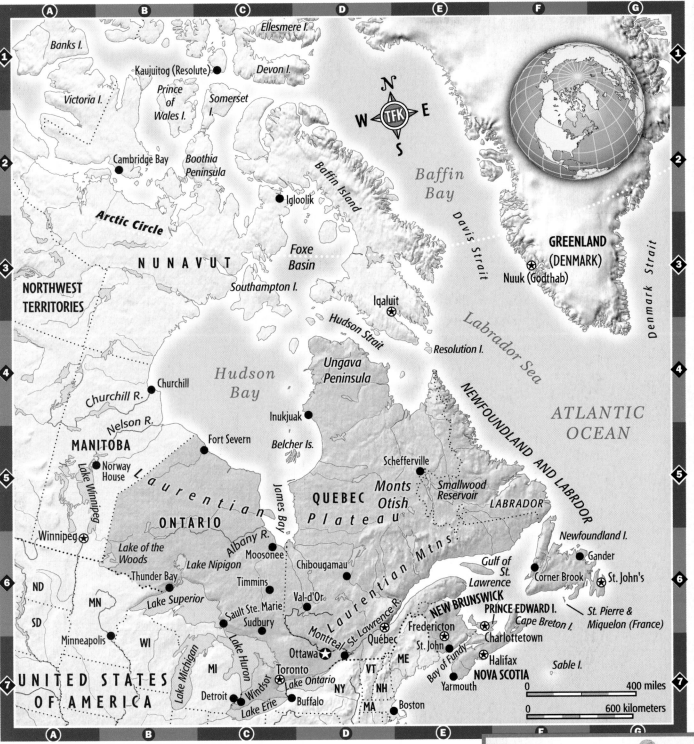

Map labels:

A B C D E F G

1 Banks I. · Kaujuitog (Resolute) · Ellesmere I. · Devon I.

Victoria I. · Prince of Wales I. · Somerset I.

2 Cambridge Bay · Boothia Peninsula · Baffin Island · Baffin Bay · GREENLAND (DENMARK)

Igloolik · Nuuk (Godthab)

Arctic Circle · Davis Strait

3 NUNAVUT · Foxe Basin · Denmark Strait

NORTHWEST TERRITORIES · Southampton I. · Iqaluit · Labrador Sea

Hudson Strait · Resolution I.

4 Hudson Bay · Ungava Peninsula · ATLANTIC OCEAN

Churchill · Churchill R.

Nelson R. · Inukjuak · NEWFOUNDLAND AND LABRADOR

5 MANITOBA · Fort Severn · Belcher Is. · Schefferville · Smallwood Reservoir · LABRADOR

Norway House · Monts Otish · Newfoundland I.

Lake Winnipeg · Laurentian · James Bay · QUEBEC Plateau

6 Winnipeg · ONTARIO · Albany R. · Moosonee · Gander

Lake of the Woods · Lake Nipigon · Chibougamau · Gulf of St. Lawrence · Corner Brook · St. John's

ND · Thunder Bay · Timmins · Val-d'Or · Laurentian Mtns · NEW BRUNSWICK · PRINCE EDWARD I. · St. Pierre & Miquelon (France)

MN · Lake Superior · Sault Ste. Marie · Montreal St. Lawrence R. · Cape Breton I.

7 SD · Sudbury · Québec · Fredericton · Charlottetown

Minneapolis · WI · MI · Ottawa · St. John · Halifax · Sable I.

UNITED STATES OF AMERICA · Toronto · VT · ME · Bay of Fundy · NOVA SCOTIA

Lake Michigan · Lake Huron · Detroit · Windsor · Lake Ontario · NY · NH · Yarmouth

Lake Erie · Buffalo · MA · Boston

0 400 miles
0 600 kilometers

Did You Know?

● Canada has the world's longest coastline. Its length of 151,019 miles (243,042 km) would circle the Earth more than six times!

● Ice fishing is a popular hobby in parts of Canada, but only about one-third of the fish caught under the ice are kept and eaten.

● Canada is considered the birthplace of ice hockey. More than half the players in the U.S. National Hockey League are Canadian.

● Niagara Falls has two sides, one in Canada and one in the United States. The Canadian Falls, or Horseshoe Falls, is 180 feet (55 m) high. As much as 6 million cubic feet (168,000 cubic m) of water rushes over the rim of Niagara Falls each minute.

● The word *Canada* is from an Iroquois word that means "community."

Ice fishermen use drills and chisels to create holes in the ice.

17

Western Canada and Alaska

S nowcapped mountains, icy glaciers, grassy prairies, and fertile farmland are the landscapes that cover the vast area that makes up western Canada. This region has four provinces and three territories. Nunavut—a sprawling region of tundra, Arctic islands, and frozen fjords—was carved out of the Northwest Territories in 1999.

Vancouver, British Columbia, is the third largest city in Canada.

Most of western Canada's residents live near the country's southern border, where temperatures are milder. Alberta, Saskatchewan, and Manitoba are known for their agriculture and bison. British Columbia, which is Canada's westernmost province, features the beautiful city of Vancouver.

West of Canada lies Alaska. It is the largest state in the United States but has the fewest people per square mile. In 1867, the U.S. bought Alaska from Russia for $7.2 million. Many people thought it was a foolish purchase. But they changed their minds when gold was discovered in 1896. Today, oil is Alaska's largest industry.

Data Bank

Western Canada's Provinces

ALBERTA
AREA: 255,285 sq mi (661,185 sq km)
POPULATION: 3,720,900
CAPITAL: Edmonton

BRITISH COLUMBIA
AREA: 366,255 sq mi (948,596 sq km)
POPULATION: 4,351,000
CAPITAL: Victoria

MANITOBA
AREA: 250,934 sq mi (649,916 sq km)
POPULATION: 1,235,400
CAPITAL: Winnipeg

NORTHWEST TERRITORIES
AREA: 532,643 sq mi (1,379,539 sq km)
POPULATION: 43,800
CAPITAL: Yellowknife

NUNAVUT
AREA: 772,260 sq mi (2,000,144 sq km)
POPULATION: 33,200
CAPITAL: Iqaluit

SASKATCHEWAN
AREA: 251,700 sq mi (651,900 sq km)
POPULATION: 1,045,600
CAPITAL: Regina

YUKON TERRITORY
AREA: 207,076 sq mi (536,324 sq km)
POPULATION: 34,500
CAPITAL: Whitehorse

U.S. State

ALASKA
AREA: 656,424 sq mi (1,700,130 sq km)
POPULATION: 708,862
CAPITAL: Juneau
MOTTO: North to the future

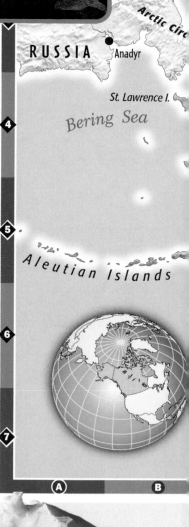

RUSSIA   Anadyr

Arctic Circle

St. Lawrence I.

Bering Sea

Aleutian Islands

Icebergs float in the waters around Nunavut.

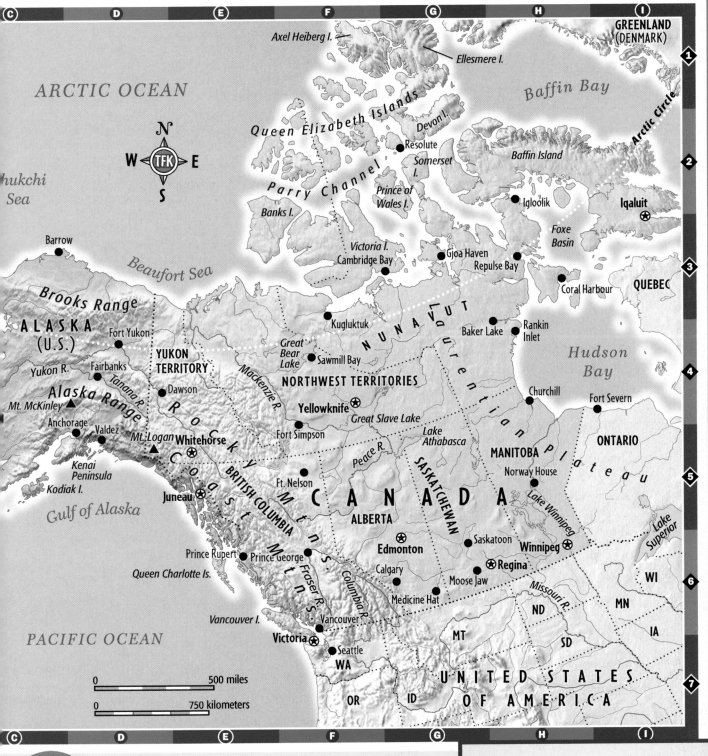

ARCTIC OCEAN

Axel Heiberg I.

Ellesmere I.

GREENLAND (DENMARK)

Baffin Bay

Arctic Circle

Queen Elizabeth Islands

Devon I.

Chukchi Sea

Parry Channel

Resolute

Somerset I.

Baffin Island

Igloolik

Iqaluit

Banks I.

Prince of Wales I.

Foxe Basin

Barrow

Beaufort Sea

Victoria I.
Cambridge Bay

Gjoa Haven

Repulse Bay

Coral Harbour

QUEBEC

Brooks Range

ALASKA (U.S.)

Fort Yukon

YUKON TERRITORY

Kugluktuk

NUNAVUT

Baker Lake

Rankin Inlet

Hudson Bay

Yukon R.

Fairbanks

Tanana R.

Dawson

Great Bear Lake

Sawmill Bay

Laurentian

Churchill

Fort Severn

Alaska Range

Mt. McKinley

Anchorage

Valdez

Mt. Logan

Whitehorse

NORTHWEST TERRITORIES

Yellowknife

Mackenzie R.

Fort Simpson

Great Slave Lake

Lake Athabasca

MANITOBA

Plateau

ONTARIO

Kenai Peninsula

Kodiak I.

Gulf of Alaska

Rocky

BRITISH COLUMBIA

Ft. Nelson

Peace R.

CANADA

SASKATCHEWAN

Norway House

Lake Winnipeg

Lake Superior

Juneau

Coast

Mtns.

ALBERTA

Edmonton

Saskatoon

Winnipeg

WI

Prince Rupert

Prince George

Fraser R.

Calgary

Regina

MN

Queen Charlotte Is.

Columbia R.

Medicine Hat

Moose Jaw

Missouri R.

ND

IA

Vancouver I.

Vancouver

MT

SD

PACIFIC OCEAN

Victoria

Seattle

WA

UNITED STATES OF AMERICA

OR

ID

0   500 miles

0   750 kilometers

N W E S TFK

Did You Know?

● Bald eagles (right) live throughout Alaska. Admiralty Island, in southeast Alaska's Tongass National Forest, is thought to have the largest nesting population of bald eagles in the U.S.

● There are about 100,000 glaciers in Alaska. The largest, the Malaspina, stretches across 1,500 square miles (3,885 sq km).

● Elbow and Eyebrow are the names of two towns in Saskatchewan.

● The magnetic north pole is located in Nunavut.

● Alaska's nickname is the Last Frontier.

United States of America

The United States of America stretches across the North American continent and beyond. It includes a vast range of climates and geographic regions, from temperate forests to arid deserts. In 1776, the 13 original colonies revolted against the British and formed a new nation. Since the Revolution, the United States has grown to 50 states and become a destination for emmigrants from around the world. Over the centuries, these very diverse cultures have found a means to coexist in a democracy. For this reason, the population of the United States is often referred to as a "melting pot" of people.

The United States includes 49 states on the North American continent, one state in the Pacific Ocean, and a number of possessions. Puerto Rico and the Virgin Islands are in the Caribbean Sea, and American Samoa and Guam are in the Pacific Ocean. The nation is governed by an elected President and a Congress, made up of the Senate and the House of Representatives. Washington, D.C., is the nation's capital. In addition to the President and Congress, each state has its own elected government. Although an American national culture exists, each region has its own particular accent, customs, and cuisines. Among the regions are New England, the Middle Atlantic, the South, the Midwest, the Southwest, and the West.

Since its founding, the United States has steadily increased in physical size and political power. Today, as a superpower, the nation wields a great deal of economic and cultural influence around the world.

Cherry blossoms bloom near the Washington Monument in Washington, D. C.

Data Bank

UNITED STATES OF AMERICA
AREA: 3,794,100 sq mi (9,826,675 sq km)
POPULATION: 313,232,044
CAPITAL: Washington, D.C.
LANGUAGES: English, Spanish

Hollywood, California, is the hub of moviemaking in the United States.

HOLLYWOOD

CANADA

Edmonton
Nelson R.
Saskatchewan R.
Lake Winnipeg
Hudson Bay
James Bay

Regina
Lake Manitoba
Lake of the Woods
Lake Nipigon

Helena
MONTANA
Billings
NORTH DAKOTA
Bismarck
MINNESOTA
Lake Superior
St. Lawrence R.
MAINE
Augusta
Montreal
Ottawa
VERMONT
NEW HAMPSHIRE
Concord
Montpelier
MASSACHUSETTS

SOUTH DAKOTA
Pierre
St. Paul
Minneapolis
WISCONSIN
Madison
Milwaukee
MICHIGAN
Lake Huron
Lansing
Detroit
Lake Ontario
Toronto
NEW YORK
Niagara Falls
Albany
Boston
Providence
RHODE ISLAND
Hartford
CONNECTICUT
New York City

WYOMING
Cheyenne
NEBRASKA
Omaha
IOWA
Des Moines
Lake Michigan
Chicago
Lake Erie
PENNSYLVANIA
Harrisburg
Trenton
NEW JERSEY
Philadelphia
Dover
DELAWARE

Lake City
Salt Lake City
Missouri R.
N. Platte R.
Lincoln
ILLINOIS
INDIANA
Indianapolis
Columbus
OHIO
WEST VIRGINIA
Charleston
Annapolis
Washington, D.C.
MARYLAND

Denver
COLORADO
Topeka
Kansas City
KANSAS
Springfield
St. Louis
Jefferson City
MISSOURI
Ohio R.
Frankfort
KENTUCKY
Richmond
VIRGINIA
Cape Hatteras

Santa Fe
Tulsa
Nashville
TENNESSEE
Raleigh
NORTH CAROLINA

NEW MEXICO
Oklahoma City
OKLAHOMA
ARKANSAS
Little Rock
Memphis
Mississippi R.
Columbia
SOUTH CAROLINA

Fort Worth
Dallas
MISSISSIPPI
Jackson
ALABAMA
Montgomery
Atlanta
GEORGIA
Charleston
Savannah

TEXAS
Austin
Houston
LOUISIANA
Baton Rouge
Mobile
Tallahassee

Rio Grande
New Orleans
Gulf of Mexico
FLORIDA
ATLANTIC OCEAN

MEXICO
Miami
BAHAMAS

Key West
Havana
CUBA

Appalachian Mtns.
Great Plains
Rocky Mtns.

PACIFIC OCEAN
Honolulu
HAWAII
Mauna Kea (volcano)
Hilo
100 miles

0   500 miles
0   750 kilometers

● In 1814, during the bombardment of Fort McHenry, Francis Scott Key wrote the poem that would become "The Star-Spangled Banner," the U.S. national anthem.

● The bald eagle is the national bird of the United States. With its 7-foot (2 m) wingspan and powerful beak and talons, the eagle is an impressive bird of prey. Still, not all the Founding Fathers wanted the eagle to represent the country. Benjamin Franklin thought the wild turkey would be a more appropriate symbol!

● Mount Rushmore National Memorial (left) is an enormous sculpture carved into the side of a mountain in the Black Hills of South Dakota. Completed in 1941, the monument depicts Presidents George Washington, Thomas Jefferson, Theodore Roosevelt, and Abraham Lincoln.

● The motto of the United States is *E pluribus unum*, which means "From many, one."

United States of America
New England

Founded in 1701, Yale University, in New Haven, Connecticut, is one of America's oldest universities

Nestled between Canada, New York, and the Atlantic Ocean are the six states that make up New England. Each state has its own special identity. But they share many features, including snowcapped mountains that beckon skiers during the winter; miles of scenic coastline; marshy bogs where cranberries grow; spectacular fall foliage; and bustling cities and towns.

The Atlantic Ocean forms the eastern border of all but Vermont, which is landlocked. Connecticut, Massachusetts, Maine, New Hampshire, and Rhode Island touch the ocean.

Much of America's colonial history is anchored in New England. Plymouth Colony, in Massachusetts, was the first permanent European settlement in New England. The first battles of the American Revolution took place in Concord, Massachusetts, near Boston. Historically, trade, fishing, and shipbuilding were important revenue sources for the region. But tourism, banking, and industry have emerged as the major moneymakers for these Northeastern states.

The black-capped chickadee is the state bird of both Maine and Massachusetts.

Tourists known as leaf peepers flock to New England during the autumn to see the leaves change colors.

Data Bank

CONNECTICUT
AREA: 4,845 sq mi (12,548 sq km)
POPULATION: 3,526,937
CAPITAL: Hartford
MOTTO: *Qui transtulit sustinet.* (He who transplanted still sustains.)

MAINE
AREA: 30,865 sq mi (79,940 sq km)
POPULATION: 1,312,939
CAPITAL: Augusta
MOTTO: *Dirigo.* (I lead.)

MASSACHUSETTS
AREA: 7,838 sq mi (20,300 sq km)
POPULATION: 6,631,280
CAPITAL: Boston
MOTTO: *Ense petit placidam sub libertate quietem.* (By the sword we seek peace, but peace only under liberty.)

NEW HAMPSHIRE
AREA: 8,969 sq mi (23,231 sq km)
POPULATION: 1,323,530
CAPITAL: Concord
MOTTO: Live free or die.

RHODE ISLAND
AREA: 1,045 sq mi (2,707 sq km)
POPULATION: 1,056,870
CAPITAL: Providence
MOTTO: Hope

VERMONT
AREA: 9,249 sq mi (23,955 sq km)
POPULATION: 622,433
CAPITAL: Montpelier
MOTTO: Freedom and unity

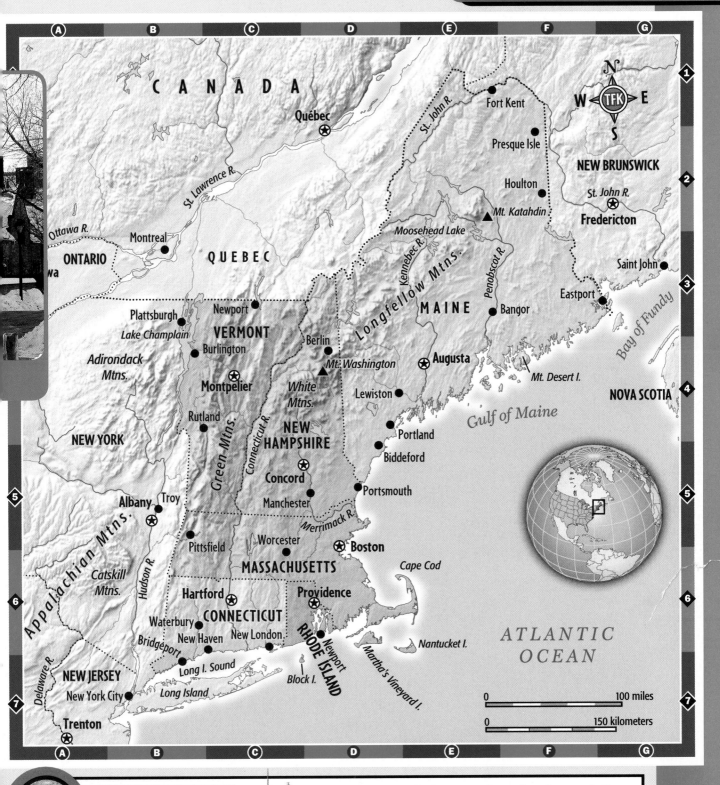

CANADA

Québec

ONTARIO

Ottawa R.

Montreal

QUEBEC

St. Lawrence R.

Plattsburgh

Lake Champlain

VERMONT

Adirondack Mtns.

Burlington

Newport

Berlin

Montpelier

NEW YORK

Rutland

Green Mtns.

Connecticut R.

White Mtns.

Mt. Washington

NEW HAMPSHIRE

Concord

Manchester

Albany

Troy

Pittsfield

Worcester

MASSACHUSETTS

Merrimack R.

Appalachian Mtns.

Catskill Mtns.

Hudson R.

Hartford

CONNECTICUT

Waterbury

New Haven

New London

Bridgeport

Long I. Sound

Long Island

NEW JERSEY

New York City

Delaware R.

Trenton

St. John R.

Fort Kent

Presque Isle

Houlton

Mt. Katahdin

Moosehead Lake

Kennebec R.

Longfellow Mtns.

MAINE

Penobscot R.

Bangor

Augusta

Lewiston

Portland

Biddeford

Portsmouth

Boston

Cape Cod

Providence

RHODE ISLAND

Newport

Block I.

Martha's Vineyard I.

Nantucket I.

NEW BRUNSWICK

St. John R.

Fredericton

Saint John

Eastport

Bay of Fundy

Mt. Desert I.

NOVA SCOTIA

Gulf of Maine

ATLANTIC OCEAN

0   100 miles

0   150 kilometers

N W E S TFK

Did You Know?

● In 1826, the first American railroad was built in Quincy, Massachusetts.

● Built in 1713, the Old State House is Boston's oldest public building. The Declaration of Independence was read from its balcony in 1776.

● Vermont is the largest producer of maple syrup in the country. More than 500,000 gallons (1,892,706 L) are made in the state every year.

● Rhode Island is the smallest state in the United States.

● The Wadsworth Atheneum Museum, in Hartford, Connecticut, was the first public art museum in the country.

● West Quoddy Head Light (left), a lighthouse in Lubec, Maine, marks the easternmost point in the United States.

United States of America
Middle Atlantic

The Middle Atlantic region is the most ethnically diverse, densely populated area of the United States. From New York to Maryland, people of every race and religion live in a colorful cultural mix.

New York City is the nation's largest city, with more than 8 million residents. It is home to the United Nations and many international companies and organizations. It is also the country's financial capital. Philadelphia, the sixth largest city in the United States, is the birthplace of the nation. It was there that the Declaration of Independence was drafted in 1776 and the U.S. Constitution was written in 1787. Washington, D.C., the nation's capital, lies on the Potomac River, nestled between Maryland and Virginia. Washington, D.C., is a federal city rather than a state; it belongs to the entire nation.

More than 12 million immigrants to the United States entered through Ellis Island, in New York Harbor, between 1892 and 1954.

Outside the big cities, the Middle Atlantic region has fertile farmland. Pennsylvania has the largest rural population in the United States, and is a major producer of milk, eggs, and poultry. Farmland covers about 20% of New Jersey.

Industry and tourism are equally important to the region. New Jersey and Delaware are major pharmaceutical and chemical manufacturers. Maryland, famous for its delicious fresh crabs and shellfish, also produces many electronic goods and metals. New York City, with its theaters and museums, draws many visitors.

The peach blossom is the state flower of Delaware.

Data Bank

DELAWARE
AREA: 1,955 sq mi (5,063 sq km)
POPULATION: 891,464
CAPITAL: Dover
MOTTO: Liberty and independence

MARYLAND
AREA: 9,775 sq mi (25,317 sq km)
POPULATION: 5,737,274
CAPITAL: Annapolis
MOTTO: *Fatti maschii, parole femine* (Manly deeds, womanly words)

NEW JERSEY
AREA: 7,419 sq mi (19,215 sq km)
POPULATION: 8,732,811
CAPITAL: Trenton
MOTTO: Liberty and prosperity

NEW YORK
AREA: 47,224 sq mi (122,310 sq km)
POPULATION: 17,577,730
CAPITAL: Albany
MOTTO: *Excelsior* (Ever upward)

PENNSYLVANIA
AREA: 44,820 sq mi (116,083 sq km)
POPULATION: 12,632,780
CAPITAL: Harrisburg
MOTTO: Virtue, liberty, and independence

WASHINGTON, D.C.
AREA: 68 sq mi (176 sq km)
POPULATION: 610,589
MOTTO: *Justitia omnibus* (Justice for all)

The slightly salty water of the Chesapeake Bay provides an ideal habitat for the blue crab, Maryland's state crustacean.

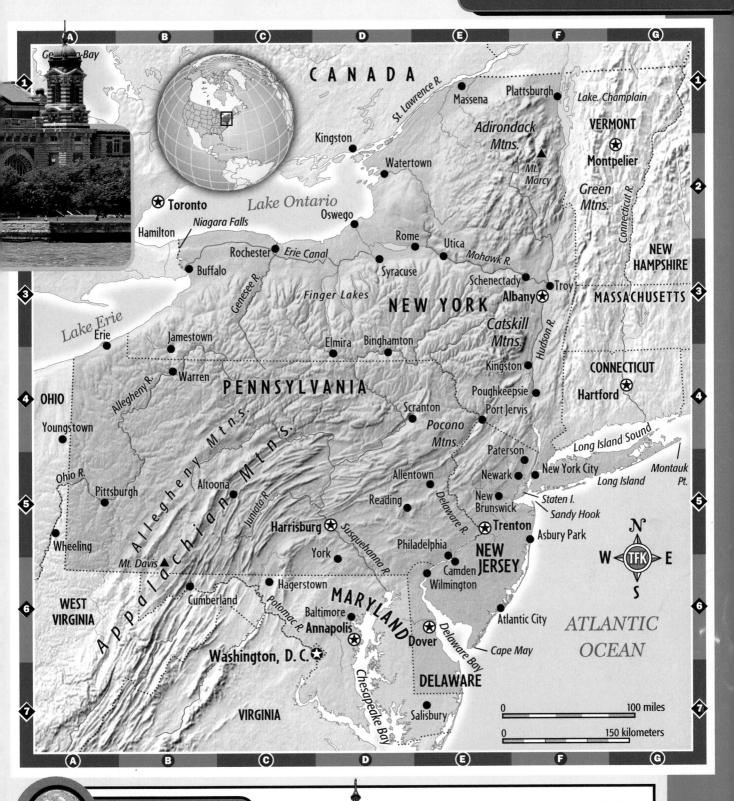

CANADA

Georgian Bay

Massena
Plattsburgh
Lake Champlain

VERMONT
⊛
Montpelier

Kingston

Adirondack Mtns.
▲ *Mt. Marcy*

Watertown

Green Mtns.

Connecticut R.

NEW HAMPSHIRE

Toronto ⊛

Lake Ontario

Oswego

Rome

Utica

Mohawk R.

Niagara Falls

Hamilton

Rochester
Erie Canal

Syracuse

Schenectady

Troy

MASSACHUSETTS

Buffalo

Genesee R.

Finger Lakes

NEW YORK

Albany ⊛

Catskill Mtns.

Hudson R.

Lake Erie

Erie

Jamestown

Elmira

Binghamton

Kingston

CONNECTICUT
⊛
Hartford

Warren

Allegheny R.

PENNSYLVANIA

Poughkeepsie

Port Jervis

Scranton

Pocono Mtns.

OHIO

Youngstown

Appalachian Mtns.

Allegheny Mtns.

Paterson

Long Island Sound

Montauk Pt.

Newark

New York City

Long Island

Ohio R.

Pittsburgh

Altoona

Allentown

Juniata R.

Reading

Delaware R.

New Brunswick

Staten I.

Sandy Hook

Wheeling

Susquehanna R.

Harrisburg ⊛

York

Philadelphia

Trenton ⊛

NEW JERSEY

Asbury Park

▲ *Mt. Davis*

Camden

Hagerstown

Wilmington

WEST VIRGINIA

Cumberland

Potomac R.

MARYLAND

Baltimore

Annapolis ⊛

Dover ⊛

Atlantic City

ATLANTIC OCEAN

Washington, D.C. ⊛

Delaware Bay

Cape May

DELAWARE

VIRGINIA

Chesapeake Bay

Salisbury

N
W ⊕ TFK E
S

0 — 100 miles

0 — 150 kilometers

Did You Know?

● Opened in 1825, the Erie Canal connects the waters of Lake Erie to the Hudson River. It made transportation of goods across New York easier, and helped make New York City into the trading center it is today.

● New Jersey is known as the Garden State.

● Delaware, the second smallest state, was the first to ratify the U.S. Constitution, in 1787.

● Both the Declaration of Independence and the U.S. Constitution were written in Independence Hall (left) in Philadelphia, Pennsylvania.

● The places and properties featured in the board game Monopoly are based on streets in Atlantic City, New Jersey.

● Annapolis, Maryland, is home to the U.S. Naval Academy, founded in 1845.

United States of America
Midwest

Ancient mammals once roamed South Dakota's Badlands National Park.

Tucked in the middle of the United States between the eastern and the western states are the 12 states that make up the Midwest. Much of the terrain in the Midwest is flat. Rich, fertile soil and an abundance of crops have earned the region its nickname, the Nation's Breadbasket. Farmers here grow wheat, oats, corn, and potatoes, among other crops.

The population of the Midwest grew dramatically in the 19th century. People from the eastern states moved there, as well as immigrants from Germany, Sweden, and Norway. Today, the population, especially in large urban centers, is ethnically and culturally diverse.

Chicago is the biggest city in the Midwest and the nation's third largest. The city serves as a major hub for train and airline passengers. One of the country's tallest buildings, the Willis Tower (formerly the Sears Tower), looms over Chicago's imposing skyline. Other large cities contribute to the vitality of the region. The U.S. automobile industry is based in Detroit, Michigan. Each year, Indianapolis, Indiana, hosts the Indianapolis 500, a car race.

Data Bank

ILLINOIS
AREA: 55,593 sq mi (143,985 sq km)
POPULATION: 12,944,410
CAPITAL: Springfield
MOTTO: State sovereignty, national union

INDIANA
AREA: 35,870 sq mi (92,903 sq km)
POPULATION: 6,445,295
CAPITAL: Indianapolis
MOTTO: The crossroads of America

IOWA
AREA: 55,875 sq mi (144,716 sq km)
POPULATION: 3,023,081
CAPITAL: Des Moines
MOTTO: Our liberties we prize and our rights we will maintain.

KANSAS
AREA: 81,823 sq mi (211,921 sq km)
POPULATION: 2,841,121
CAPITAL: Topeka
MOTTO: Ad astra per aspera (To the stars through difficulties)

MICHIGAN
AREA: 56,809 sq mi (147,135 sq km)
POPULATION: 9,931,235
CAPITAL: Lansing
MOTTO: Si quaeris peninsulam amoenam circumspice. (If you seek a pleasant peninsula, look around you.)

MINNESOTA
AREA: 79,617 sq mi (206,207 sq km)
POPULATION: 5,290,467
CAPITAL: Saint Paul
MOTTO: L'Etoile du nord (The north star)

NEBRASKA
AREA: 76,878 sq mi (199,113 sq km)
POPULATION: 1,811,072
CAPITAL: Lincoln
MOTTO: Equality before the law

NORTH DAKOTA
AREA: 70,704 sq mi (183,123 sq km)
POPULATION: 653,778
CAPITAL: Bismarck
MOTTO: Liberty and union, now and forever, one and inseparable

OHIO
AREA: 40,953 sq mi (106,068 sq km)
POPULATION: 11,532,111
CAPITAL: Columbus
MOTTO: With God all things are possible.

SOUTH DAKOTA
AREA: 75,898 sq mi (196,575 sq km)
POPULATION: 820,077
CAPITAL: Pierre
MOTTO: Under God the people rule.

WISCONSIN
AREA: 97,105 sq mi (251,501 sq km)
POPULATION: 5,668,519
CAPITAL: Madison
MOTTO: Forward

Corn is grown throughout Iowa.

WYOMING

Harney Peak ▲
● Rapid City
Black Hills

North Platte R.

Cheyenne ✪

South Platte R.

✪ Denver

COLORADO

NOR

SOU

WAN

B

TXAS

miles
meters

B

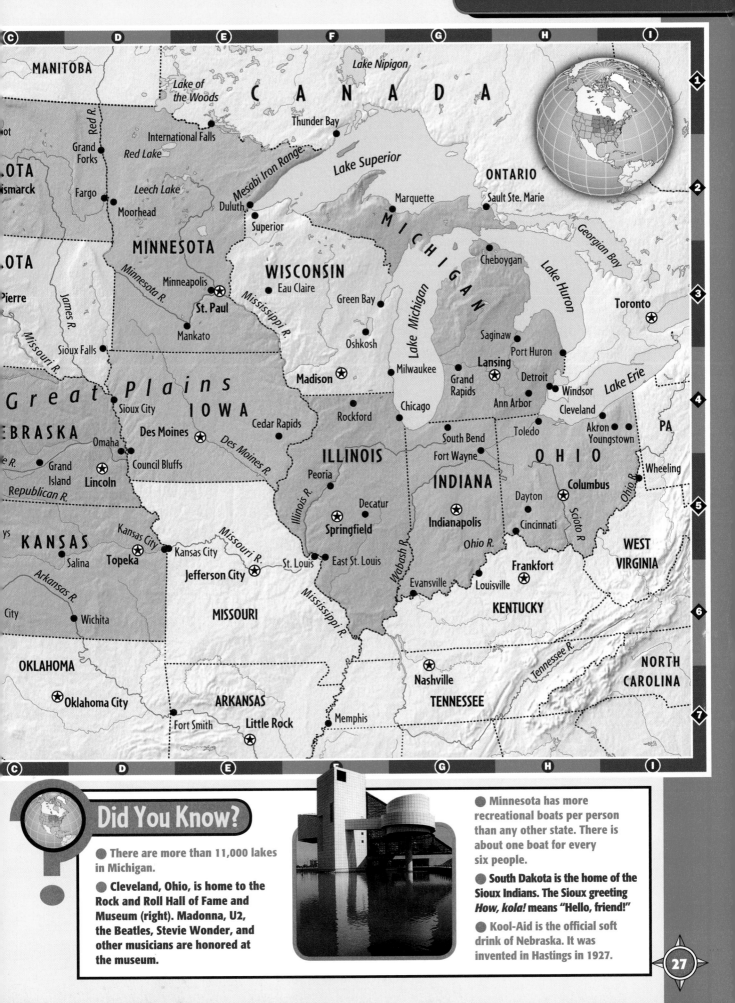

MANITOBA

CANADA

Lake Nipigon
Lake of the Woods
Thunder Bay
International Falls
Red R.
Red Lake
Grand Forks
Fargo
Leech Lake
Moorhead
Mesabi Iron Range
Duluth
Superior
Lake Superior

ONTARIO

Marquette
Sault Ste. Marie
Georgian Bay

MINNESOTA

WISCONSIN
Eau Claire
Minneapolis
St. Paul
Mankato
Mississippi R.
Minnesota R.

MICHIGAN
Cheboygan
Lake Huron
Toronto

Green Bay
Oshkosh
Saginaw
Lake Michigan
Lansing
Port Huron
Detroit
Windsor
Lake Erie
Madison
Milwaukee
Grand Rapids
Ann Arbor
Cleveland
Akron
Youngstown

PA

Great Plains
Sioux Falls
Sioux City

IOWA
Cedar Rapids
Des Moines
Rockford
Chicago
South Bend
Fort Wayne

OHIO
Wheeling
Columbus
Ohio R.

NEBRASKA
Omaha
Council Bluffs
Grand Island
Lincoln
Republican R.
Missouri R.
James R.
Pierre

ILLINOIS
Peoria
Illinois R.
Decatur
Springfield

INDIANA
Indianapolis
Dayton
Cincinnati
Scioto R.

WEST VIRGINIA

KANSAS
Kansas City
Salina
Topeka
Wichita
Arkansas R.
Kansas City
Jefferson City
Missouri R.
St. Louis
East St. Louis
Wabash R.
Ohio R.
Evansville
Louisville
Frankfort

MISSOURI
Mississippi R.

KENTUCKY

OKLAHOMA
Oklahoma City
Fort Smith

ARKANSAS
Little Rock
Memphis
Nashville
Tennessee R.

TENNESSEE

NORTH CAROLINA

United States of America
South

Great Smoky Mountains National Park is America's most-visited national park.

At one time, the states that make up the southern part of the United States were best known for their rolling fields of cotton, tobacco, soybeans, and other crops. In the 1800s, cotton was king. Plantation owners relied on slave labor to grow and harvest the crop. From 1861 to 1865, the southern states fought the northern states in the bloody and destructive Civil War.

Today, agriculture is still an important industry. But southern cities such as Atlanta, Georgia, and Miami, Florida, are commercial, industrial, and cultural centers. In Miami as well as in New Orleans, Louisiana, and Nashville, Tennessee, the sounds of music set the rhythm and pace.

Southerners are proud of their region's scenic beauty. The Great Smoky Mountains National Park, in North Carolina and Tennessee, attracts more than 9 million visitors each year. The park has more than 800 miles (1,287 km) of trails. Everglades National Park, in Florida, is the only subtropical preserve in North America. It is the only place in the world where alligators and crocodiles live side by side.

Bayous and other marshy bodies of water are found throughout Lousiana.

Data Bank

ALABAMA
AREA: 50,750 sq mi (131,442 sq km)
POPULATION: 4,729,656
CAPITAL: Montgomery
MOTTO: *Audemus jura nostra defendere.*
(We dare defend our rights.)

ARKANSAS
AREA: 52,075 sq mi (134,874 sq km)
POPULATION: 2,910,236
CAPITAL: Little Rock
MOTTO: *Regnat populus.* (The people rule.)

FLORIDA
AREA: 54,153 sq mi (140,256 sq km)
POPULATION: 18,678,049
CAPITAL: Tallahassee
MOTTO: In God we trust.

GEORGIA
AREA: 57,919 sq mi (150,010 sq km)
POPULATION: 9,908,357
CAPITAL: Atlanta
MOTTO: Wisdom, justice, and moderation

KENTUCKY
AREA: 39,732 sq mi (102,905 sq km)
POPULATION: 4,339,435
CAPITAL: Frankfort
MOTTO: United we stand, divided we fall.

LOUISIANA
AREA: 43,566 sq mi (112,835 sq km)
POPULATION: 4,529,426
CAPITAL: Baton Rouge
MOTTO: Union, justice, and confidence

MISSISSIPPI
AREA: 46,914 sq mi (121,507 sq km)
POPULATION: 2,960,467
CAPITAL: Jackson
MOTTO: *Virtute et armis* (By valor and arms)

MISSOURI
AREA: 68,898 sq mi (178,445 sq km)
POPULATION: 6,011,741
CAPITAL: Jefferson City
MOTTO: *Salu populi suprema lex esto.*
(The welfare of the people shall be the supreme law.)

NORTH CAROLINA
AREA: 48,718 sq mi (126,179 sq km)
POPULATION: 9,458,888
CAPITAL: Raleigh
MOTTO: *Esse quam videri* (To be rather than to seem)

SOUTH CAROLINA
AREA: 30,111 sq mi (77,987 sq km)
POPULATION: 4,596,958
CAPITAL: Columbia
MOTTO: *Animis opibusque parati*
(Prepared in mind and resources) and
Dum spiro spero. (While I breathe, I hope.)

TENNESSEE
AREA: 41,220 sq mi (106,759 sq km)
POPULATION: 6,338,112
CAPITAL: Nashville
MOTTO: Agriculture and commerce

VIRGINIA
AREA: 39,598 sq mi (102,558 sq km)
POPULATION: 7,952,119
CAPITAL: Richmond
MOTTO: *Sic semper tyrannis* (Thus always to tyrants)

WEST VIRGINIA
AREA: 24,087 sq mi (62,385 sq km)
POPULATION: 1,825,513
CAPITAL: Charleston
MOTTO: *Montani semper liberi.*
(Mountaineers are always free.)

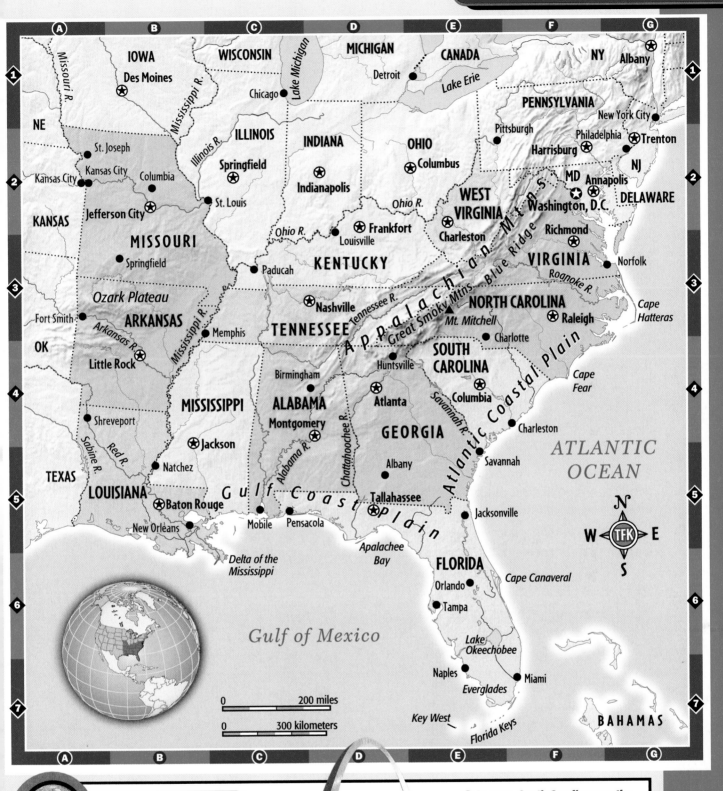

IOWA — Des Moines
WISCONSIN
MICHIGAN — Detroit
CANADA
Lake Erie
NY — Albany
PENNSYLVANIA — Pittsburgh, Harrisburg
New York City
Philadelphia, Trenton
NJ
Chicago
Lake Michigan
NE
Missouri R.
St. Joseph
ILLINOIS — Springfield
INDIANA — Indianapolis
OHIO — Columbus
WEST VIRGINIA — Charleston
MD — Annapolis
DELAWARE
Washington, D.C.
Kansas City
KANSAS — Kansas City
Columbia
Mississippi R.
Illinois R.
St. Louis
Ohio R.
Frankfort
Louisville
Richmond
Jefferson City
MISSOURI — Springfield
Paducah
KENTUCKY
Ohio R.
Tennessee R.
Blue Ridge
Appalachian Mtns.
VIRGINIA — Norfolk
Roanoke R.
Ozark Plateau
Fort Smith
ARKANSAS
Nashville
TENNESSEE
Memphis
Great Smoky Mtns.
Mt. Mitchell
NORTH CAROLINA — Raleigh
Cape Hatteras
OK
Arkansas R.
Little Rock
Mississippi R.
Huntsville
Charlotte
SOUTH CAROLINA — Columbia
Atlantic Coastal Plain
Cape Fear
MISSISSIPPI
Birmingham
ALABAMA — Montgomery
Atlanta
GEORGIA — Albany
Charleston
Savannah
ATLANTIC OCEAN
TEXAS
Shreveport
Sabine R.
Red R.
Jackson
Natchez
Chattahoochee R.
Alabama R.
Savannah R.
LOUISIANA — Baton Rouge
New Orleans
Gulf Coast Plain
Mobile
Pensacola
Tallahassee
Jacksonville
Delta of the Mississippi
Apalachee Bay
FLORIDA — Orlando, Tampa
Cape Canaveral
Gulf of Mexico
Lake Okeechobee
Naples — Miami
Everglades
Key West
Florida Keys
BAHAMAS

N W TFK E S

0 — 200 miles
0 — 300 kilometers

Did You Know?

● *The Grand Ole Opry*, performed in Nashville, Tennessee, is the world's longest-running live radio show.

● The St. Louis Gateway Arch, in Missouri (right), was designed to sway up to 18 inches (46 cm), to help it withstand earthquakes.

● In 1860, South Carolina was the first state to secede from the Union. Mississippi, Florida, Alabama, Georgia, Louisiana, Texas, Virginia, Arkansas, Tennessee, and North Carolina joined it to form the Confederacy that fought against the North in the Civil War.

● The famous horse race the Kentucky Derby is run every year at Churchill Downs, in Louisville.

United States of America
Southwest

Arizona's Grand Canyon is 277 miles (365 km) long, and about 1 mile (1.6 km) deep. About 5 million people visit the gorge each year!

The Southwest is a region of dry desert and high plains. It is rich in Native American and Hispanic culture. Geographically, the region is dominated by Texas. Known as the Lone Star State, Texas is the second largest state in the United States and an industrial giant. When it comes to oil production and cattle ranching, Texas leads the nation. It is also tops in farmland and in the production of cotton and cottonseed oil. The Johnson Space Center, which is the home of astronaut training and Mission Control for NASA, is in Houston.

To the north of Texas lies Oklahoma, another state that struck it rich with oil. Farming and cattle ranching are also vital to the state's economy. Wheat is Oklahoma's main crop.

In New Mexico and Arizona, pueblos (flat-roofed stone or adobe dwellings) still dot the desert landscape, along with giant saguaro cacti. Many Native Americans live in the area, including people belonging to the Hopi, Zuni, and Navajo tribes. Arizona is perhaps best known for the Grand Canyon, the world's largest gorge. Carved by the Colorado River beginning 6 million years ago, the etched rocky walls turn brilliant shades of red, orange, and yellow at sunset each day.

The saguaro cactus can grow as tall as 50 feet (15 m) and live more than 150 years. It is the largest cactus in the United States.

Data Bank

ARIZONA
AREA: 113,642 sq mi (294,331 sq km)
POPULATION: 6,676,627
CAPITAL: Phoenix
MOTTO: *Ditat deus.* (God enriches.)

NEW MEXICO
AREA: 121,365 sq mi (314,334 sq km)
POPULATION: 2,033,875
CAPITAL: Santa Fe
MOTTO: *Crescit eundo.* (It grows as it goes.)

OKLAHOMA
AREA: 68,679 sq mi (177,878 sq km)
POPULATION: 3,724,447
CAPITAL: Oklahoma City
MOTTO: *Labor omnia vincit.* (Labor conquers all things.)

TEXAS
AREA: 261,914 sq mi (678,354 sq km)
POPULATION: 25,213,445
CAPITAL: Austin
MOTTO: Friendship

OREG

NEVAD

Carson Cit

Nevada

CALIFORNIA

Los Angeles

San Diego
Tijuana

PACIFIC
OCEAN

IDAHO
WYOMING
NEBRASKA
IOWA
Missouri R.
North Platte R.
Cheyenne ⊛
Great Salt Lake
Salt Lake City ★
UTAH
Denver ⊛
Lincoln ⊛
Topeka ⊛
Kansas City
Missouri R.
Kansas City
eat Basin
KANSAS
MISSOURI
COLORADO
Arkansas R.
ARKANSAS
Great Plains
Colorado R.
Rocky Mountains
Grand Canyon
Colorado Plateau
Santa Fe ★
Canadian R.
Oklahoma City ⊛
Tulsa
Humphreys Peak ▲
Gallup
Amarillo
OKLAHOMA
Ouachita Mtns.
Flagstaff
Albuquerque
NEW MEXICO
Lawton
Red R.
ARIZONA
Sacramento Mtns.
Lubbock
Dallas
Sabine R.
LA
Phoenix ⊛
Black Range
Sierra Blanca ▲
Fort Worth
Tyler
Yuma
Gila R.
Llano Estacado
Waco
Tucson
TEXAS
Douglas
El Paso
Colorado R.
Brazos R.
Davis Mtns.
Pecos R.
Edwards Plateau
Austin ⊛
Houston
Gulf Coastal Plain
Galveston
Sierra Madre Occidental
Chihuahua
San Antonio
Rio Grande
Corpus Christi
Hermosillo
Nueces R.
Laredo
Baja California
Gulf of California
MEXICO
Sierra Madre Oriental
Gulf of Mexico
Monterrey
Matamoros

N W E S TFK

0 ——— 300 miles
0 ——— 450 kilometers

Did You Know?

● There are more man-made lakes in Oklahoma than in any other U.S. state.

● The northern part of the state of Texas that juts toward Oklahoma is known as the Texas Panhandle.

● More than 600 historic shipwrecks have been documented along Texas's coastline.

● The Chapel of San Miguel, built in Santa Fe, New Mexico, in the 17th century, is known as the oldest church in the United States.

● In the 1830s, what is now Oklahoma was set aside for Native Americans and was referred to as the Indian Territory. The state is still home to about 60 tribes.

There are more than 110 limestone caves in New Mexico's Carlsbad Caverns National Park.

United States of America
West

Crater Lake, in Oregon, is the deepest lake in the United States at 1,943 feet (592 m).

The Mississippi River forms a natural boundary between the American East and the American West. Before the 1840s, very few pioneers ventured beyond the Mississippi. By 1900, settlers had built cities all across the West, and were laying claim to Indian territories. The Gold Rush of 1849 brought an influx of miners to California. The following year, California became the first state west of the Mississippi.

Stories of the Old West are part of the heritage of the United States. So, too, are the natural wonders of the region. The area's towering mountains, wide deserts, canyons, and waterfalls inspired the creation of the U.S. national park system, which includes Yellowstone, in Wyoming, Montana, and Idaho; and Yosemite, in California.

The westernmost state, Hawaii, did not become a state until 1959. Located in the South Pacific, Hawaii is a string of volcanic islands with its own history and culture.

Hawaii's state flower is the hibiscus.

PACIFIC OCEAN

0 — 300 m
0 — 450 kilomet

Kauai
Oahu
Molokai
Honolulu
Lanai

HAWAII

PACIFIC OCEAN

50 miles

Data Bank

CALIFORNIA
AREA: 155,973 sq mi (403,968 sq km)
POPULATION: 37,266,600
CAPITAL: Sacramento
MOTTO: *Eureka.* (I have found it.)

COLORADO
AREA: 103,730 sq mi (268,659 sq km)
POPULATION: 5,095,309
CAPITAL: Denver
MOTTO: *Nil sine numine* (Nothing without providence)

HAWAII
AREA: 6,423 sq mi (16,635 sq km)
POPULATION: 1,300,086
CAPITAL: Honolulu
MOTTO: *Ua mau ke ea o ka aina i ka pono.* (The life of the land is perpetuated in righteousness.)

IDAHO
AREA: 82,751 sq mi (214,324 sq km)
POPULATION: 1,559,796
CAPITAL: Boise
MOTTO: *Esto perpetua.* (Let it be perpetual.)

MONTANA
AREA: 145,556 sq mi (376,988 sq km)
POPULATION: 980,152
CAPITAL: Helena
MOTTO: *Oro y plata* (Gold and silver)

NEVADA
AREA: 109,806 sq mi (284,396 sq km)
POPULATION: 2,654,751
CAPITAL: Carson City
MOTTO: All for our country

OREGON
AREA: 96,003 sq mi (248,647 sq km)
POPULATION: 2,744,425
CAPITAL: Salem
MOTTO: *Alis volat propriis.* (She flies with her own wings.)

UTAH
AREA: 82,168 sq mi (212,814 sq km)
POPULATION: 2,830,753
CAPITAL: Salt Lake City
MOTTO: Industry

WASHINGTON
AREA: 66,582 sq mi (172,447 sq km)
POPULATION: 6,746,199
CAPITAL: Olympia
MOTTO: *Al-ki* (By and by)

WYOMING
AREA: 97,105 sq mi (251,501 sq km)
POPULATION: 547,637
CAPITAL: Cheyenne
MOTTO: Equal rights

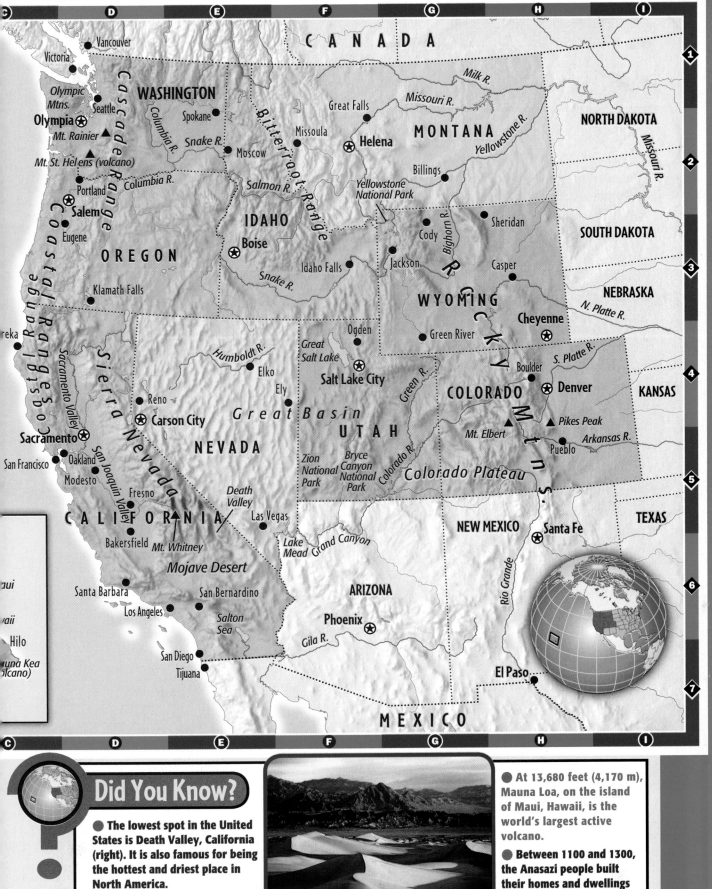

CANADA

Vancouver

Victoria

Olympic Mtns.
WASHINGTON
Seattle
Spokane
Olympia ⊛
Mt. Rainier ▲
Columbia R.
Moscow
Mt. St. Helens (volcano) ▲
Columbia R.
Portland
Salem ⊛
Eugene
Cascade Range

Bitterroot Range

Great Falls
Missoula
Helena ⊛
MONTANA
Milk R.
Missouri R.
Yellowstone R.
Billings

Salmon R.
IDAHO
Boise ⊛
Snake R.
Idaho Falls
Snake R.
Klamath Falls
OREGON

Yellowstone National Park

Cody
Jackson
Bighorn R.
Sheridan
Casper
WYOMING

NORTH DAKOTA

SOUTH DAKOTA

NEBRASKA
N. Platte R.

Eureka

Coastal Ranges
Coastal Range
Sacramento Valley

Humboldt R.
Elko
Ely
Reno
Carson City ⊛
Great Basin
NEVADA

Sierra Nevada

Sacramento ⊛
San Francisco
Oakland
Modesto
San Joaquin Valley
Fresno
CALIFORNIA
Bakersfield
Mt. Whitney ▲
Death Valley
Las Vegas
Mojave Desert
Santa Barbara
San Bernardino
Los Angeles
Salton Sea
San Diego
Tijuana

Great Salt Lake
Ogden
Salt Lake City ⊛
Green R.
UTAH
Zion National Park
Bryce Canyon National Park
Colorado R.

Green River
Cheyenne ⊛
Boulder
S. Platte R.
COLORADO
Denver ⊛
Mt. Elbert ▲
▲ Pikes Peak
Pueblo
Arkansas R.
Colorado Plateau

Rocky Mtns.

KANSAS

Lake Mead
Grand Canyon
Gila R.
Phoenix ⊛
ARIZONA

NEW MEXICO
Santa Fe ⊛
Rio Grande
El Paso

TEXAS

MEXICO

aui

aii

Hilo

una Kea lcano)

Did You Know?

● The lowest spot in the United States is Death Valley, California (right). It is also famous for being the hottest and driest place in North America.

● The 11 national forests in Idaho cover 20.4 million acres (8.2 million hectares).

● At 13,680 feet (4,170 m), Mauna Loa, on the island of Maui, Hawaii, is the world's largest active volcano.

● Between 1100 and 1300, the Anasazi people built their homes and dwellings directly into cliffs in southwestern Colorado. These dwellings still exist.

33

Mexico and Central America

Just south of the United States lie Mexico and Central America, on a narrow landmass that connects North America and South America. From Mexico's dry plateaus to Costa Rica's tropical rain forests, this is an area of varied terrain and climate.

The spider monkey is one of the four species of primates that live in Costa Rica.

Archaeological excavations have uncovered ruins of the ancient Mayan city Ek Balam in Mexico.

Mexico was once home to several great civilizations, including the Maya and the Aztec. Today, Mexico's language, food, culture, and architecture reflect its rich history: magnificent temples and pyramids mix with sleek skyscrapers and luxurious beachfront resorts. Mexico City, the nation's capital, is the oldest continuously inhabited city in the Western Hemisphere.

To the south of Mexico sit the seven small countries that make up Central America: Belize, Costa Rica, El Salvador, Guatemala, Honduras, Nicaragua, and Panama. Combined, they are less than half the size of Mexico. Rare and exotic wildlife can be found throughout the region. In tiny Costa Rica alone, there are about 850 species of birds, 136 species of snakes, and 1,500 species of orchids.

Data Bank

MEXICO
AREA: 758,449 sq mi (1,964,374 sq km)
POPULATION: 113,724,226
CAPITAL: Mexico City
LANGUAGES: Spanish, Mayan, Nahuatl, other native languages

BELIZE
AREA: 8,867 sq mi (22,965 sq km)
POPULATION: 321,115
CAPITAL: Belmopan
LANGUAGES: English (official), Spanish, Mayan, Garifuna (Carib)

COSTA RICA
AREA: 19,730 sq mi (51,100 sq km)
POPULATION: 4,576,562
CAPITAL: San José
LANGUAGES: Spanish (official)

EL SALVADOR
AREA: 8,124 sq mi (21,041 sq km)
POPULATION: 6,071,774
CAPITAL: San Salvador
LANGUAGES: Spanish, Nahuatl

GUATEMALA
AREA: 42,042 sq mi (108,888 sq km)
POPULATION: 13,824,463
CAPITAL: Guatemala City
LANGUAGES: Spanish, Amerindian languages

HONDURAS
AREA: 43,278 sq mi (112,090 sq km)
POPULATION: 8,143,564
CAPITAL: Tegucigalpa
LANGUAGES: Spanish, Amerindian dialects

NICARAGUA
AREA: 50,306 sq mi (130,292 sq km)
POPULATION: 5,666,301
CAPITAL: Managua
LANGUAGES: Spanish (official), English and native languages on Atlantic coast

PANAMA
AREA: 29,120 sq mi (75,420 sq km)
POPULATION: 3,460,462
CAPITAL: Panama City
LANGUAGES: Spanish (official), English

Belize's barrier reef is the second largest coral reef system in the world and stretches across 185 miles (297 km).

CA
AZ
T
San Diego
Tijuana
Mexicali
Nogales
Ciudad
Hermosillo
Baja California
Gulf of California
Yaqui R.
Sierra
M
Cabo San Lucas
Islas Ma
Islas Revillagigedo (Mexico)

Map labels:

C | D | E | F | G | H | I

UNITED STATES OF AMERICA

OK | AR | TN | NC | SC | GA | AL | MS | LA | TX

Mississippi R.

Houston
New Orleans
Miami

FL

ATLANTIC OCEAN

Gulf of Mexico

Río Grande
uahua
M
I
C
O
Laredo
Nuevo Laredo
Monterrey
Matamoros
Sierra Madre Oriental
Mexican Plateau
urango
rango
Tampico
dalajara
León
Santiago R.
Mexico City
Paricutín
Citlaltépetl
Puebla
Sierra Madre del Sur
Veracruz
Bay of Campeche
Oaxaca
Acapulco

Mérida
Cancún
Yucatán Channel
Yucatán Peninsula
Chichén Itzá (ruin)
Campeche

Havana
CUBA

Caribbean Sea

JAMAICA
Kingston

PACIFIC OCEAN

Gulf of Tehuantepec
Tajumulco Volcano
GUATEMALA
Guatemala City
San
EL SALVADOR

Belize City
Gulf of Honduras
Belmopan
BELIZE
Cobán
San Pedro Sula
HONDURAS
Tegucigalpa
NICARAGUA
León
Managua
Lake Nicaragua
Granada
Puerto Cabezas
Bluefields
Puerto Limón
San José
Puntarenas
COSTA RICA
David
Colón
Panama Canal
Panama City
PANAMA

0 — 400 miles
0 — 600 kilometers

N W E S — TFK

Did You Know?

● More than 1,250 kinds of butterflies live in Costa Rica.

● The Panama Canal (right), which connects the Atlantic and Pacific Oceans, took about 56,000 workers more than 10 years to build. The United States controlled the canal from 1914 until December 31, 1999, when control was returned to the Panamanians.

● At its narrowest point, in Panama, Central America is just 50 miles (80 km) wide.

● Some of the largest and possibly oldest Mayan ruins can be found in Tikal, Guatemala. The ancient site has thousands of structures, including spectacular temples and pyramids that were used in the first *Star Wars* movie.

● Central America's two largest forest reserves are in Nicaragua. They help protect the country's diverse ecosystems, and its plant and animal species.

Caribbean

Magen's Bay on St. Thomas is one of the most popular tourist destinations in the U.S. Virgin Islands.

The Caribbean islands, also called the West Indies, are known for their sparkling blue waters, white sand beaches, and gentle tropical breezes. The multiethnic people of the Caribbean are proud of their contributions to the fields of literature, dance, and music.

There are thousands of islands in the Caribbean, including 13 nations and many colonial dependencies, territories, and possessions. Just 90 miles (145 km) off the coast of Florida lies the Caribbean's largest island, Cuba. Since 1960, relations between the governments of Cuba and the United States have been strained.

FLORIDA (U.S.)

Miami

Strai Flor

Havana

Pinar del Río

Cienfuegos

Isla De La Juventad

Cayman Is. (U.K.)

Data Bank

The West Indies

AREA: The islands of the West Indies are an archipelago approximately 2,000 miles (3,218 km) long. There are four island chains in the West Indies: the Bahamas, the Greater Antilles, and the eastern and southern islands of the Lesser Antilles.
POPULATION: 39.8 million
LANGUAGES: Spanish, French, English, Dutch, Creole, local dialects

Countries

ANTIGUA AND BARBUDA
AREA: 171 sq mi (443 sq km)
POPULATION: 87,884
CAPITAL: Saint John's
LANGUAGES: English (official), local dialects

BAHAMAS
AREA: 5,359 sq mi (13,880 sq km)
POPULATION: 313,312
CAPITAL: Nassau
LANGUAGE: English (official)

BARBADOS
AREA: 166 sq mi (430 sq km)
POPULATION: 286,705
CAPITAL: Bridgetown
LANGUAGE: English

CUBA
AREA: 42,803 sq mi (110,859 sq km)
POPULATION: 11,087,330
CAPITAL: Havana
LANGUAGE: Spanish

DOMINICA
AREA: 290 sq mi (751 sq km)
POPULATION: 72,969
CAPITAL: Roseau
LANGUAGES: English (official), French patois

DOMINICAN REPUBLIC
AREA: 18,792 sq mi (48,671 sq km)
POPULATION: 9,956,648
CAPITAL: Santo Domingo
LANGUAGE: Spanish

GRENADA
AREA: 133 sq mi (344 sq km)
POPULATION: 108,419
CAPITAL: Saint George's
LANGUAGES: English (official), French patois

HAITI
AREA: 10,714 sq mi (27,749 sq km)
POPULATION: 9,719,932
CAPITAL: Port-au-Prince
LANGUAGES: French, Creole (both official)

JAMAICA
AREA: 4,244 sq mi (10,992 sq km)
POPULATION: 2,868,380
CAPITAL: Kingston
LANGUAGES: English, English patois

SAINT KITTS AND NEVIS
AREA: 101 sq mi (262 sq km)
POPULATION: 50,314
CAPITAL: Basseterre
LANGUAGE: English

SAINT LUCIA
AREA: 238 sq mi (616 sq km)
POPULATION: 161,557
CAPITAL: Castries
LANGUAGES: English (official), French patois

SAINT VINCENT AND THE GRENADINES
AREA: 150 sq mi (388 sq km)
POPULATION: 103,869
CAPITAL: Kingstown
LANGUAGES: English, French patois

TRINIDAD AND TOBAGO
AREA: 5,384 sq mi (13,945 sq km)
POPULATION: 1,227,505
CAPITAL: Port-of-Spain
LANGUAGES: English (official), Hindi, French, Spanish, Chinese (Mandarin)

U.S. Territories

PUERTO RICO (Commonwealth)
AREA: 5,384 sq mi (13,944 sq km)
POPULATION: 3,791,913
CAPITAL: San Juan
LANGUAGES: Spanish, English

VIRGIN ISLANDS (Unincorporated territory)
AREA: 737 sq mi (1,908 sq km)
POPULATION: 109,666
CAPITAL: Charlotte Amalie
LANGUAGES: English, French, Creole, Spanish

Mona monkeys were found only in southwest Africa until the 1600s, when they were introduced to Grenada. Monas carry food inside their cheek pouches, which are almost as large as their stomachs.

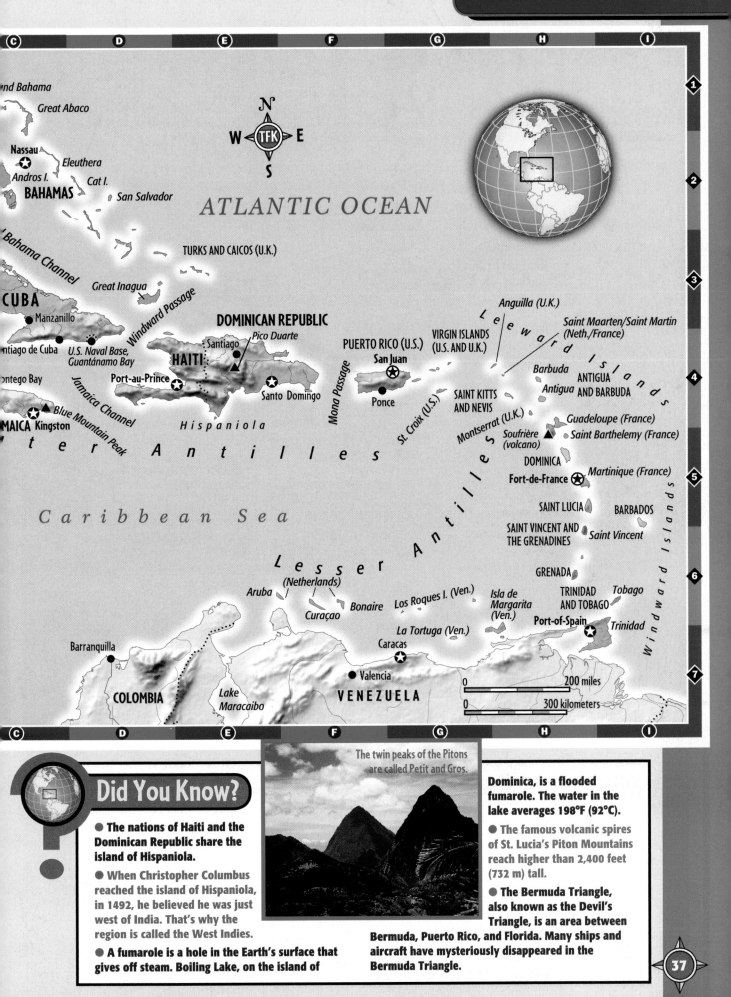

C   D   E   F   G   H   I

Grand Bahama

Great Abaco

N
W TFK E
S

Nassau
Eleuthera
Andros I.   Cat I.
BAHAMAS   San Salvador

ATLANTIC OCEAN

Old Bahama Channel

TURKS AND CAICOS (U.K.)

Great Inagua

CUBA
Manzanillo

Windward Passage

Santiago de Cuba
U.S. Naval Base,
Guantánamo Bay

Montego Bay

DOMINICAN REPUBLIC
Santiago   Pico Duarte
HAITI
Port-au-Prince
Santo Domingo

PUERTO RICO (U.S.)   **VIRGIN ISLANDS**
San Juan   (U.S. AND U.K.)

Anguilla (U.K.)

L e e w a r d

Saint Maarten/Saint Martin
(Neth./France)

Barbuda   **ANTIGUA**
Antigua   **AND BARBUDA**

I s l a n d s

Jamaica Channel
Blue Mountain Peak
JAMAICA Kingston

G r e a t e r   A n t i l l e s

Hispaniola

Mona Passage

Ponce

St. Croix (U.S.)

**SAINT KITTS
AND NEVIS**

Montserrat (U.K.)

Soufrière
(volcano)

Guadeloupe (France)
Saint Barthelemy (France)

DOMINICA
Fort-de-France   Martinique (France)

SAINT LUCIA   **BARBADOS**

**SAINT VINCENT AND
THE GRENADINES**   Saint Vincent

C a r i b b e a n   S e a

L e s s e r   A n t i l l e s

L e s s e r   A n t i l l e s

(Netherlands)
Aruba
Curaçao   Bonaire

Los Roques I. (Ven.)

La Tortuga (Ven.)

Isla de
Margarita
(Ven.)

GRENADA

**TRINIDAD
AND TOBAGO**   Tobago

Port-of-Spain   Trinidad

W i n d w a r d   I s l a n d s

Barranquilla

Caracas

Valencia

COLOMBIA   Lake
Maracaibo

VENEZUELA

0   200 miles
0   300 kilometers

C   D   E   F   G   H   I

1
2
3
4
5
6
7

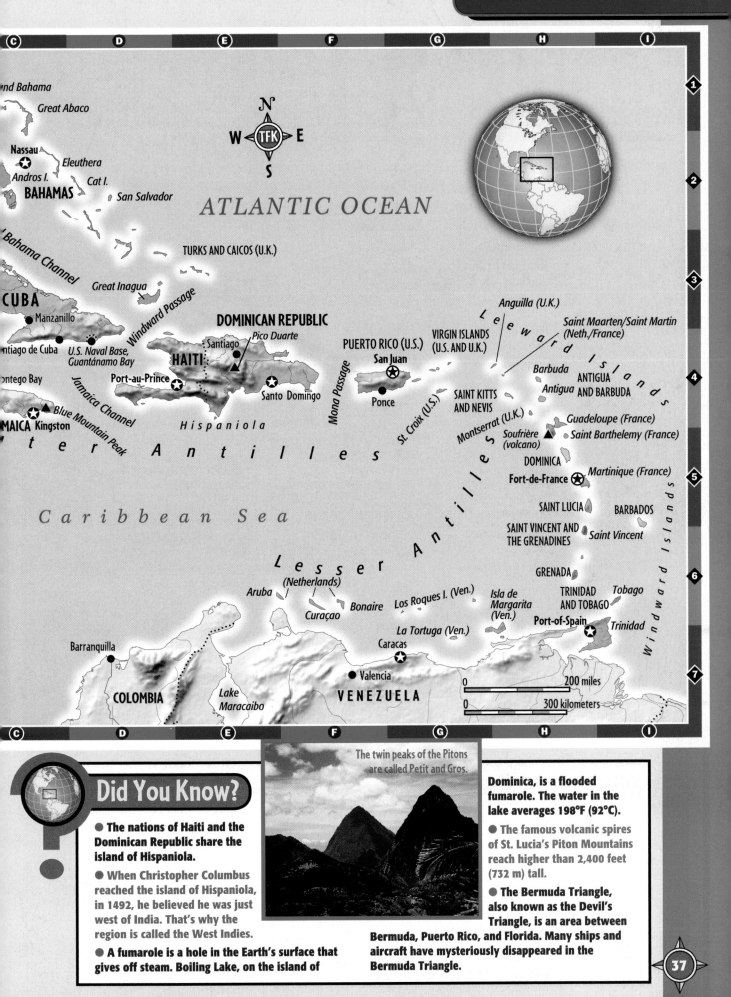

The twin peaks of the Pitons
are called Petit and Gros.

Did You Know?

● The nations of Haiti and the Dominican Republic share the island of Hispaniola.

● When Christopher Columbus reached the island of Hispaniola, in 1492, he believed he was just west of India. That's why the region is called the West Indies.

● A fumarole is a hole in the Earth's surface that gives off steam. Boiling Lake, on the island of

Dominica, is a flooded fumarole. The water in the lake averages 198°F (92°C).

● The famous volcanic spires of St. Lucia's Piton Mountains reach higher than 2,400 feet (732 m) tall.

● The Bermuda Triangle, also known as the Devil's Triangle, is an area between Bermuda, Puerto Rico, and Florida. Many ships and aircraft have mysteriously disappeared in the Bermuda Triangle.

South America

South America, the world's fourth largest continent, is a region of contrasts and extremes. The world's longest mountain range, the Andes, stretches along the continent's western coast. Even though the equator crosses South America and four-fifths of the continent is located in the tropics, the tall peaks of the Andes remain cold and snow-covered year-round. To the east of the Andes lies the world's largest tropical rain forest. The waters of the mighty Amazon River have their source in the mountains of Peru. The river flows across Peru and into Brazil. The Amazon River basin is hot, humid, and rainy. The Atacama Desert, in northern Chile, is cold and extremely dry.

Patagonia is a small expanse of unspoiled land located in southern Argentina and Chile. The Perito Moreno Glacier (above) is part of Argentine Patagonia.

South America's varying climate and terrain offer ideal conditions for a wide variety of plant and animal life. Colorful birds, giant snakes, monkeys, and jaguars are among the many creatures that make their home in the lush rain forest. At the southern tip of the continent, seals, penguins, and whales swim in the waters of the Southern Ocean. Animals that are found nowhere else on Earth, such as Darwin finches and giant tortoises, can be seen on Ecuador's Galápagos Islands.

Continent Facts

NUMBER OF COUNTRIES AND TERRITORIES: 12 countries—Argentina, Bolivia, Brazil, Chile, Colombia, Ecuador, Guyana, Paraguay, Peru, Suriname, Uruguay, Venezuela; three territories— Falkland Islands (U.K.), French Guiana (France), South Georgia and the South Sandwich Islands (U.K.)

AREA: 6,878,000 sq mi (17,813,928 sq km)

LONGEST RIVER: Amazon River, 4,195 mi (6,751 km)

LONGEST MOUNTAIN RANGE: Andes mountains, 5,500 mi (8,851 km)

HIGHEST PEAK: Mount Aconcagua in Argentina, 22,834 ft (6,960 m)

The endangered Galápagos tortoises can reach a weight of 573 pounds (260 kg).

The Amazon River is about 4,195 miles (6,751 km) long.

Wow Zone!

● At a length of about 2,700 miles (4,345 km) and an average width of 110 miles (177 km), Chile is the world's longest, narrowest country.

● The Atacama Desert, in Chile, is one of the driest places in the world. In some parts of the desert, rain has never been recorded!

● Ushuaia (oo-*swy*-ah), at the southern tip of Argentina, is the southernmost city in the world. It is just 745 miles (1,199 km) from Antarctica.

● The Amazon River basin is home to a third of the world's plant and animal species.

● Lake Titicaca, located 12,500 feet (3,810 m) above sea level between Bolivia and Peru, is the largest freshwater lake in South America.

● Most of the world's coffee comes from Brazil and Colombia.

CARIBBEAN SEA

DOMINICAN REPUBLIC
CUBA
Puerto Rico (U.S.)
JAMAICA
HAITI
ANTIGUA AND BARBUDA
SAINT KITTS AND NEVIS
GUADELOUPE
BELIZE
DOMINICA
HONDURAS
SAINT LUCIA
BARBADOS
NICARAGUA
GRENADA
SAINT VINCENT AND THE GRENADINES
ATLANTIC OCEAN
COSTA RICA
PANAMA
TRINIDAD AND TOBAGO

Aruba
Barranquilla
Cartagena
Maracaibo
Lake Maracaibo
Caracas
Georgetown
Orinoco River
Ciudad Guayana
Paramaribo
Medellín
VENEZUELA
GUYANA
Cayenne
Cali
Bogotá
SURINAME
FRENCH GUIANA
COLOMBIA
Negro River
Macapá
Esmeraldas
Belém
Equator
Quito
Putumayo River
Amazon River
São Luís
ECUADOR
Manaus
Santarém
Parnaíba
Guayaquil
Benjamin Constant
Fortaleza
Iquitos
AMAZON BASIN
Piura
Amazon River
Madeira River
Xingu River
Tocantins River
Natal
PERU
Selvas
Marañón River
Cruzeiro do Sul
Recife
Ucayali River
Pôrto Velho
BRAZIL
Maceió
Trujillo
Cobija
Riberalta
São Francisco River
Araguaia River
Salvador
Lima
Cuzco
Lake Titicaca
Brasília
Arequipa
La Paz
BOLIVIA
Cochabamba
Brazilian Highlands
Belo Horizonte
Arica
Santa Cruz
Sucre
Iquique
PACIFIC OCEAN
Paraguay River
São Paulo
Rio de Janeiro
Antofagasta
PARAGUAY
Asunción
Curitiba
Formosa
Ciudad del Este
Paraná River
San Miguel de Tucumán
Resistencia
Encarnación
Andes Mts.
Pôrto Alegre
CHILE
Córdoba
URUGUAY
Salto
Valparaíso
Rosario
ATLANTIC OCEAN
Santiago
Buenos Aires
Montevideo
ARGENTINA
Rio de la Plata
Concepción
Mar del Plata
Bahía Blanca
Puerto Montt
Comodoro Rivadavia
Strait of Magellan
Río Gallegos
Stanley
Punta Arenas
Falkland Is. (Islas Malvinas)
Ushuaia
(Administered by U.K.; claimed by Argentina)
Cape Horn

0 mi.   500 mi.   1,000 mi.

0 km   500 km   1,000 km

Northwestern South America

Llamas thrive in the Andes mountains.

Years before European explorers arrived in what came to be called the New World, a great civilization flourished in Bolivia, Ecuador, and Peru. The Inca people built roads and stone cities that stretched for thousands of miles. In 1533, the city of Cuzco, capital of the powerful Inca Empire, came under Spain's rule. Cuzco is located in the Andes, the longest mountain range in the world. The Andes stretch 5,500 miles (8,900 km) along the west coast of the continent.

Today, Bolivia, Colombia, Ecuador, Peru, and Venezuela are a colorful and vibrant blend of Native Indian and Spanish influences. In the region's cities, visitors can find mansions, churches, and forts built during Spanish colonial days, and museums boasting pre-Columbian treasures. Spanish is spoken, and so are native languages.

This region is rich in more than historic treasures. It is marked by an abundance of natural resources. Venezuela is South America's biggest oil producer. Colombia is famous for its emeralds and coffee. Only Brazil produces more of the world's coffee than Colombia.

The Amazon rain forest covers half of Peru. Millions of plant and animal species live there. Butterflies, tropical birds, and frogs fill the forest with color and sound. Giant tortoises, blue-footed boobies, and iguanas enchant visitors on the Galápagos Islands, which lie 650 miles (1,046 km) off Ecuador's coast.

Data Bank

BOLIVIA
AREA: 424,162 sq mi (1,098,754 sq km)
POPULATION: 10,118,683
CAPITAL: La Paz (seat of government), Sucre (legal capital)
LANGUAGES: Spanish, Quechua, Aymara (all official)

COLOMBIA
AREA: 439,733 sq mi (1,138,903 sq km)
POPULATION: 44,725,543
CAPITAL: Bogotá
LANGUAGE: Spanish

ECUADOR
AREA: 109,483 sq mi (283,560 sq km)
POPULATION: 15,007,343
CAPITAL: Quito
LANGUAGES: Spanish (official), Amerindian languages

PERU
AREA: 496,223 sq mi (1,285,212 sq km)
POPULATION: 29,248,943
CAPITAL: Lima
LANGUAGES: Spanish, Quechua (both official), Aymara

VENEZUELA
AREA: 352,141 sq mi (912,041 sq km)
POPULATION: 27,635,743
CAPITAL: Caracas
LANGUAGES: Spanish (official), native dialects

Dancers perform in traditional Peruvian dress in Cuzco, Peru.

Caribbean Sea

Aruba (Netherlands)
Curaçao (Neth.)
Bonaire (Neth.)

GRENADA

TRINIDAD & TOBAGO

Tobago
Trinidad

ATLANTIC OCEAN

NICARAGUA
Managua

COSTA RICA
San José

PANAMA
Panama City

Pico Cristóbal Colón
Barranquilla
Cartagena

Cauca R.
Magdalena R.

Valencia
Maracaibo
Lake Maracaibo
Caracas

VENEZUELA

Angel Falls

Llanos

Orinoco R.

Georgetown
Paramaribo

GUYANA

SURINAME

FRENCH GUIANA

N
W E
S
TFK

Medellín
Nevado del Ruiz
Buenaventura
Cali

Bogotá

COLOMBIA

Guaviare R.

Orinoco R.

Guiana Highlands

Equator

Chimborazo
Guayaquil

Quito

ECUADOR

Putumayo R.

Japurá R.

Río Negro

Amazon R.

Selvas
Iquitos

Leticia

Amazon R.

Manaus

Amazon Basin

BRAZIL

SOUTH PACIFIC OCEAN

Punta Negra

Andes Mountains

Marañón R.
Ucayali R.
La Montaña

Juruá R.

Madeira R.

Xingu R.

Mato Grosso Plateau

Trujillo
Nevado Huascarán

PERU

Lima

Machu Picchu (ruins)
Cuzco

Beni R.

Mamoré R.

Guaporé R.

Serra dos Parecis

Arequipa

Lake Titicaca
Nevado Ancohuma
La Paz
Nevado Sajama
Lake Poopó
Sucre
Potosí

BOLIVIA

Gran Chaco

Paraguai R.

Cáceres

Paraná R.

CHILE   ARGENTINA   PARAGUAY

0   400 miles
0   600 kilometers

Northeastern South America

Every spring, the people of Rio de Janeiro, in Brazil, throw the world's biggest party, called Carnival. It is a four-day extravaganza that brings together people from all backgrounds and cultures. Brazil is the fifth most populous nation on Earth and South America's biggest country. But more than 75% of Brazil's people are crowded into six large cities: São Paulo, Rio de Janeiro, Salvador, Brasília, Fortaleza, and Belo Horizonte. Brazil is one of the world's top producers of steel, iron ore, tin, gold, emeralds, motor vehicles, coffee, and sugar.

Much of Brazil is untamed wilderness. The Amazon jungle is home to millions of rare plants and animals, including 1,600 kinds of birds. Sadly, in the past 100 years, about 20% of the original forest has been destroyed.

The agouti, which lives in parts of northern South America, can crack open Brazil nuts with its powerful teeth. No other animal can do that!

Brazil shares a border with every nation in South America except Chile and Ecuador. To Brazil's north are the small countries of Suriname and Guyana and the territory of French Guiana. Guyana, the only English-speaking nation on the continent, gained its independence from Britain in 1966. Nine years later, neighboring Suriname gained its independence from the Netherlands. Most of French Guiana, which is a department of France, is unsettled wilderness.

The Potaro River, in Guyana, comes to a sheer 741-foot (225 m) drop at Kaieteur Falls.

Brazil's most famous monument is Christ the Redeemer, which sits atop Corcovado Mountain in Rio de Janeiro.

Data Bank

BRAZIL
AREA: 3,286,488 sq mi (8,511,965 sq km)
POPULATION: 203,429,773
CAPITAL: Brasília
LANGUAGES: Portuguese (official), Spanish, German, Italian, Japanese, English, others

FRENCH GUIANA (Department of France)
AREA: 35,135 sq mi (91,000 sq km)
POPULATION: 199,509
CAPITAL: Cayenne
LANGUAGE: French

GUYANA
AREA: 83,000 sq mi (214,969 sq km)
POPULATION: 744,768
CAPITAL: Georgetown
LANGUAGES: English, Amerindian dialects, Creole, Hindi, Urdu

SURINAME
AREA: 63,251 sq mi (163,819 sq km)
POPULATION: 491,989
CAPITAL: Paramaribo
LANGUAGES: Dutch (official), Surinamese, English

A B C D E F G

1

Orinoco R.
VENEZUELA
GUYANA
Georgetown
SURINAME
Paramaribo
FRENCH GUIANA
COLOMBIA
Kaieteur Falls
Cayenne
Guiana Highlands
Lethem

2
Equator
Pico da Neblina
Canal do Norte
Canal do Sul-Perigoso
Japurá R.
Río Negro
Marajó I.
Amazon R.
Amazon Basin
Manaus
Belém
São Luis
Fortaleza

3
Benjamin Constant
Amazon R.
S e l v a s
Borba
Tapajós R.
Juruá R.
Madeira R.
B R A Z I L
C a t i n g a s
São Francisco R.
Recife
Porto Velho
Xingu R.
Tocantins R.

4
PERU
Serra dos Parecis
Guaporé R.
Araguaia R.
C a m p o s
Brazilian Highlands
Salvador

5
Lake Titicaca
BOLIVIA
Mato Grosso Plateau
Brasília
La Paz
Lake Poopó
Sucre
Campo Grande
Serra de Amambaí
Belo Horizonte
Pico da Bandeira

6
G r a n C h a c o
PARAGUAY
Paraná R.
Iguazú Falls
São Paulo
Paraíba R.
Rio de Janeiro
Asunción
Curitiba
Serra do Mar
ATLANTIC OCEAN

7
CHILE
ARGENTINA
Paraná R.
Uruguay R.
Pôrto Alegre
URUGUAY

PACIFIC OCEAN

La Montaña
A n d e s M o u n t a i n s

N
W TFK E
S

0 — 500 miles
0 — 750 kilometers

A B C D E F G

Did You Know?

● More people speak Portuguese than Spanish in South America, largely because it is the official language of Brazil, which has a huge population.

● More than 80% of Guyana is covered in tropical rain forests.

● More than 80 kinds of monkeys live in the Amazon jungle. Brazil has more primate species than any other country.

● Until 1938, France sent prisoners to colonies in French Guiana. Devil's Island, in the Atlantic Ocean, housed the most notorious prison.

● It has been estimated that there are between 10 million and 15 million species of insects in Brazil.

● The blue poison arrow frog (right) is found only in southern Suriname. It would take about only two micrograms of its poison to kill a human being.

Southern South America

The countries of southern South America—Argentina, Chile, Paraguay, and Uruguay—form a long, geographically diverse triangle stretching from Chile's hot, dry Atacama Desert across Argentina's rolling grasslands (called pampas) to the frigid lands of Tierra del Fuego, near Antarctica. Much of the region is abundant in natural resources.

About 275 waterfalls make up Iguazú Falls, on the border of Argentina and Brazil.

At the top of the triangle is the landlocked country of Paraguay. The people of Paraguay take great pride in their heritage. Many are more comfortable speaking the native language Guarani than they are speaking Spanish.

Millions of immigrants from Spain, Italy, France, and other European nations settled in Argentina, Chile, and Uruguay. The wide boulevards of Argentina's capital, Buenos Aires, and the cosmopolitan flair of Uruguay's capital, Montevideo, show a strong European influence.

Polynesians were the first inhabitants of Easter Island, which is located in the Pacific Ocean 2,300 miles (3,701 km) west of Chile's capital, Santiago. The remote Chilean island is famous for its giant stone statues called *moai*.

Easter Island *moai* weigh about 14 tons (13 metric tons), and most stand about 13 feet (4 m) high.

Did You Know?

● The Perito Moreno Glacier, at the southern tip of Argentina, is 20 miles (32 km) long.

● Easter Island is one of the most isolated places on Earth. It is equidistant from Chile and Tahiti.

● More copper comes from Chile than from any other country. There are large copper deposits in the Atacama Desert.

● Argentines call the Falkland Islands the Malvinas. In 1982, Argentina went to war against Britain over ownership of the islands and lost.

Data Bank

ARGENTINA
AREA: 1,068,302 sq mi (2,766,889 sq km)
POPULATION: 41,769,726
CAPITAL: Buenos Aires
LANGUAGES: Spanish (official), English, Italian, German, French

CHILE
AREA: 291,933 sq mi (756,103 sq km)
POPULATION: 16,888,760
CAPITAL: Santiago
LANGUAGE: Spanish, Mapudungun, German, English

PARAGUAY
AREA: 157,046 sq mi (406,747 sq km)
POPULATION: 6,459,058
CAPITAL: Asunción
LANGUAGES: Spanish, Guarani (both official)

URUGUAY
AREA: 68,038 sq mi (176,218 sq km)
POPULATION: 3,308,535
CAPITAL: Montevideo
LANGUAGES: Spanish, Portunol, Brazilero

The Falkland Islands are an important breeding ground for penguins.

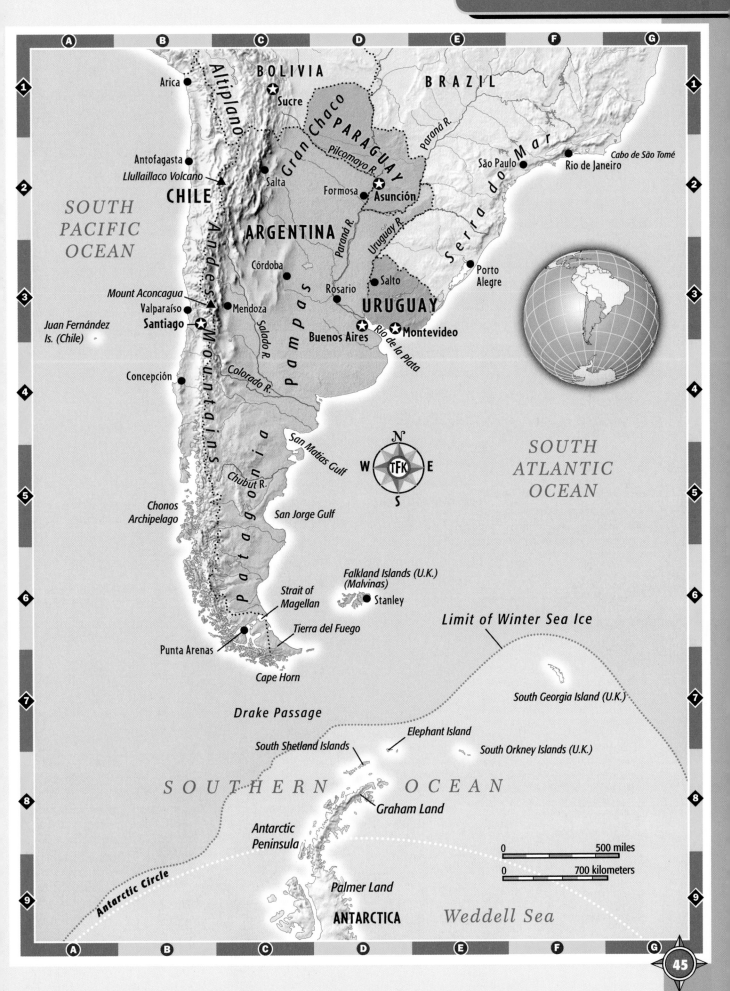

SOUTH
PACIFIC
OCEAN

BOLIVIA
Sucre
BRAZIL
Arica
Altiplano
Gran Chaco
PARAGUAY
Paraná R.
Antofagasta
Pilcomayo R.
Llullaillaco Volcano
São Paulo
Cabo de São Tomé
Salta
Rio de Janeiro
CHILE
Formosa
Asunción
Serra do Mar
ARGENTINA
Paraná R.
Uruguay R.
Córdoba
Andes
Rosario
Porto Alegre
Mount Aconcagua
Salto
Valparaíso
Mendoza
Pampas
URUGUAY
Santiago
Juan Fernández
Is. (Chile)
Buenos Aires
Montevideo
Rio de la Plata
Salado R.
Concepción
Colorado R.

SOUTH
ATLANTIC
OCEAN

San Matias Gulf
Patagonia
Chubut R.
N
W E
TFK
S
Chonos
Archipelago
San Jorge Gulf

Falkland Islands (U.K.)
(Malvinas)
Strait of
Magellan
Stanley
Limit of Winter Sea Ice
Tierra del Fuego
Punta Arenas
South Georgia Island (U.K.)
Cape Horn
Drake Passage
Elephant Island
South Shetland Islands
South Orkney Islands (U.K.)

S O U T H E R N   O C E A N
Graham Land
Antarctic
Peninsula
0   500 miles
0   700 kilometers
Antarctic Circle
Palmer Land
ANTARCTICA
Weddell Sea

Europe

Edinburgh Castle, in Scotland, is nearly 900 years old.

Technically, Europe is not a continent. Most geographers consider Europe to be part of a larger area called Eurasia. The Ural and the Caucasus mountains separate Europe from Asia. The countries to the west of the mountains are part of Europe, and the countries to the east of the mountains make up Asia. Russia and Turkey are considered part of both Europe and Asia. A tiny portion of Azerbaijan also lies in Europe.

By area, Europe is the second smallest of the continents. But by population, it is the third largest. It is also one of the richest economically.

Europe is also rich in natural resources and beauty. From Scandinavia's frozen fjords to Greece's sun-drenched islands, Europeans enjoy breathtaking surroundings. Large, bustling cities such as Athens, Greece; Berlin, Germany; London, England; Madrid, Spain; Paris, France; Rome, Italy; and Vienna, Austria, are cultural and industrial centers.

The central figure of the famous Trevi Fountain, in Rome, Italy, is Neptune, the god of the sea.

Continent Facts

NUMBER OF COUNTRIES: 45 countries—Albania, Andorra, Austria, Belarus, Belgium, Bosnia and Herzegovina, Bulgaria, Croatia, Czech Republic, Denmark, Estonia, Finland, France, Germany, Greece, Hungary, Iceland, Ireland, Italy, Kosovo, Latvia, Liechtenstein, Lithuania, Luxembourg, Macedonia, Malta, Moldova, Monaco, Montenegro, Netherlands, Norway, Poland, Portugal, Romania, Russia, San Marino, Serbia, Slovakia, Slovenia, Spain, Sweden, Switzerland, Ukraine, United Kingdom, Vatican City (Holy See)

AREA: 3,997,929 sq mi (10,354,589 sq km)

HIGHEST PEAK: Mount Elbrus, in Russia, 18,481 ft (5,633 m)

LONGEST RIVER: Volga River, in Russia, 2,293 mi (3,690 km)

LARGEST COUNTRY: Russia

SMALLEST COUNTRY: Vatican City (Holy See), .17 sq mi (.44 sq km)

At 1,063 feet (324 m) tall, the Eiffel Tower, in Paris, France, was the world's tallest building for 43 years until 1930, when the Chrysler Building, in New York City, was built.

eykjavik

0 mi.   300 mi.   6
0 km   300 km   600 km

IRELA

GUERN
JERSE

ATLANTIC OCEAN

BAY
BISC

Porto
Bilbao

Lisbon
Madrid

PORTUGAL
SPAIN

Faro
Seville

Málaga
Gibraltar

MOROCCO

AFRICA

Arctic Circle

ASIA

RUSSIA

Tromso
Murmansk
Pechora
Kiruna
Arkhangel'sk
Lulea
Oulu
Umea
FINLAND
Izhevsk
Trondheim
Tampere
Turku Helsinki
Nizhniy Novgorod
Kazan
NORWAY
St. Petersburg
Samara
Bergen
Gävle
Oslo
SWEDEN Stockholm Tallinn
ESTONIA
Moscow
Stavanger
Aberdeen
Göteborg
Riga LATVIA
dinburgh
DENMARK
LITHUANIA
Smolensk
Lipetsk
Saratov
UNITED
INGDOM NORTH
SEA Ålborg Copenhagen BALTIC
SEA Vilnius
Kaliningrad Minsk Homyel' Voronezh
Leeds
Malmö RUSSIA BELARUS
KAZAKHSTAN
heffield
NETHERLANDS Hamburg Gdansk
Brest
don Amsterdam Bremen Berlin POLAND
The Hague Warsaw Kiev Kharkiv
Volgograd
Rotterdam Poznan Lodz Voroshilovgrad
Calais Antwerp Essen GERMANY Wroclaw Lviv Gorlovka
Brussels Düsseldorf Cologne Derazhnya Makeyevka
BELGIUM Bonn Frankfurt Krakow UKRAINE Zhdanov Rostov
Havre
LUXEMBOURG Prague Brno
aris Luxembourg Stuttgart CZECH SLOVAKIA Chisinau Mykolayiv Grozny
REPUBLIC Iasi Odessa
Strasbourg LIECHTENSTEIN Munich Vienna Bratislava Simferopol' Kerch'
ANCE Dijon Zürich Vaduz AUSTRIA Budapest MOLDOVA Sevastopol'
Bern Geneva SWITZERLAND Ljubljana HUNGARY Arad ROMANIA
Lyon Milan SLOVENIA Zagreb Belgrade Bucharest BLACK SEA
Turin Trieste CROATIA Craiova Constanta
Genoa BOSNIA AND SERBIA
Marseille ITALY HERZEGOVINA Varna
MONACO Florence SAN MARINO Sarajevo Sofia
ANDORRA Bastia ADRIATIC Nis Pristina BULGARIA
Corsica SEA MONTENEGRO KOSOVO Skopje Istanbul
Vatican Rome Podgorica MACEDONIA
City Bari Tirane TURKEY
Sardinia Naples Korce Thessaloniki IRAN
ALBANIA
EAN SEA Cagliari Volos
Palermo Messina Kerkira GREECE Izmir
Sicily
Athens
Crete SYRIA
Valletta IRAQ
TUNISIA MALTA CYPRUS
LEBANON

Wow Zone!

● At 15,771 feet (4,807 m), Mont Blanc, in the French Alps, is the highest mountain in Western Europe.

● In 1896, the Millennium Underground, in Budapest, Hungary, was the first subway system to be built in continental Europe.

● There are no snakes in Ireland. You won't find any snakes in New Zealand or at the North and South Poles, either!

● Ninth-century boats are on display at the Viking Ship Museum, in Oslo, Norway.

● There are about 1,300 bridges in Amsterdam (left), in the Netherlands.

United Kingdom and Ireland

Ireland is often called the Emerald Isle. The English sing of "England's green and pleasant shores." Both lands have a wet, temperate climate, which makes the soil fertile—and green! Over the centuries, these lands have been farmed and mined for coal and minerals. The lush farms, gardens, and forests of the region continue to impress visitors.

Britain, Northern Ireland, and several smaller islands are all part of a nation called the United Kingdom. England, Scotland, and Wales are located on the island of Britain,

The Cliffs of Moher in County Clare, Ireland, rise 702 feet (214 m) above the Atlantic O

which is the eighth largest island in the world. Ireland is a separate island. While England, Scotland, Wales, and Northern Ireland are all governed by one democratic system, the southern part of Ireland, called the Republic of Ireland, is a separate nation.

Huge stone structures like Stonehenge, barrows (burial mounds), ruined castles, and crumbling stone walls tell some of the area's history. The islands were first inhabited 7,000 years ago. Ancient peoples, including Druids and Celts, built mysterious stone circles that fascinate us today. Roman Emperor Julius Caesar invaded the region in 54 B.C., and the Romans ruled until 410 A.D. They too built structures. Then came the Middle Ages, the time of knights and castles. Dozens of little kingdoms fought each other, forming and breaking alliance after alliance. It was not until 1707 that England, Scotland, and Wales joined together to form the United Kingdom. By the 19th century, a huge British Empire circled the globe. Today, that empire is nearly gone. But the United Kingdom and Ireland are both part of the European Union, which is made up of 27 countries.

At 3,560 feet (1,085 m), Mt. Snowdon (above), in Wales, is the second highest point in Britain. Ben Nevis, in Scotland, is the highest.

Data Bank

UNITED KINGDOM
AREA: 94,058 sq mi (243,609 sq km)
POPULATION: 62,698,362
CAPITAL: London
LANGUAGES: English, Welsh, Scottish Gaelic

IRELAND
AREA: 27,136 sq mi (70,282 sq km)
POPULATION: 4,670,976
CAPITAL: Dublin
LANGUAGES: English, Irish Gaelic (both official)

ATLANTIC OCEAN

North Sea

NORWAY
Stavanger

Shetland Is.

Fair Isle

Orkney Is.

Isle of Lewis
Ben Hope

Outer Hebrides
Inner Hebrides

Moray Firth
Loch Ness
Spey R.
Ben Nevis
Grampian Mtns.
Aberdeen
Dundee
Glasgow
Clyde R.
Edinburgh

Islay

North Channel

SCOTLAND

Tyne R.

UNITED KINGDOM

NORTHERN IRELAND (U.K.)
Lake Neagh
Belfast

Isle of Man

Donegal Bay

Central Plain
Galway
REPUBLIC OF IRELAND
Shannon R.
Dublin

Irish Sea

Leeds
Liverpool
Manchester
Trent R.
Eastern Plain
The Wash

Aran Is.

Limerick
Blackwater R.
Waterford
Carrantuohill
Cork

St. George's Channel

Cambrian Mtns.
Severn R.
Midland Plain
Birmingham
Norwich

WALES
Cardiff
Swansea
Bristol
Bristol Channel

ENGLAND
London
Thames R.
Southampton
Dover
Strait of Dover
Calais

Isle of Wight

Amsterdam
NETHERLANDS

BELGIUM
Brussels

Land's End
Plymouth
English Channel

Is. of Scilly

Channel Islands (U.K.)
Guernsey
Jersey

Cherbourg

Seine R.

FRANCE

0   150 miles
0   200 kilometers

N W TFK E S

ATLANTIC OCEAN

Did You Know?

● At its height, in the 19th century, the British Empire covered one-fourth of the Earth's surface.

● Bagpipes were actually brought to Scotland by the Romans, who discovered them in the Middle East.

● Many people think that the nickname Big Ben refers to the famous clock tower in London, England. In fact, Big Ben is the huge bell inside the clock tower.

● As cell phone use increases, London's iconic red telephone booths (left), in use since the 1920s, are slowly disappearing from the city's streets.

Scandinavia

In the far north of Europe are the seafaring nations of Denmark, Finland, Iceland, Norway, and Sweden. All five share a similar history, culture, and climate. Only Norway and Sweden form the Scandinavian Peninsula, but all are grouped under the heading Scandinavia or the Nordic nations.

Though winters are harsh where Scandinavia overlaps the Arctic Circle, the climate in the rest of the region is less severe. Surrounding waters keep temperatures from becoming bitterly cold. Because Scandinavia is so far north, the region can have summer daylight almost around the clock. In winter, darkness often falls after only a few hours of light.

Although each of the Scandinavian countries has its own history and language, all of Scandinavia shares the legacy of the Vikings. Beginning in about 800 A.D., these warrior-sailors from Denmark, Sweden, and Norway built open sailing ships that ventured as far as what is known today as North America. They also visited Finland, and laid claim to some of its islands. As the Vikings traveled the seas, they conquered and claimed other lands, including Russia, Holland, Belgium, Britain, France, Iceland, and Greenland. Gradually, the Vikings became part of the communities they conquered.

There are about 130 volcanic mountains in Iceland, a country that was created by volcanic activity.

Today, all the Scandinavian nations are members of the European Union, and all enjoy a high standard of living. Cities such as Copenhagen, Denmark; Oslo, Norway; and Stockholm, Sweden, are international cultural centers.

Data Bank

DENMARK
AREA: 16,639 sq mi (43,095 sq km)
POPULATION: 5,529,888
CAPITAL: Copenhagen
LANGUAGES: Danish, Faroese, Greenlandic, German

FINLAND
AREA: 130,559 sq mi (338,146 sq km)
POPULATION: 5,259,250
CAPITAL: Helsinki
LANGUAGES: Finnish, Swedish (both official)

ICELAND
AREA: 39,768 sq mi (102,999 sq km)
POPULATION: 311,058
CAPITAL: Reykjavik
LANGUAGES: Icelandic, English, Nordic languages, German

NORWAY
AREA: 125,021 sq mi (323,803 sq km)
POPULATION: 4,691,849
CAPITAL: Oslo
LANGUAGE: Norwegian (official)

SWEDEN
AREA: 173,731 sq mi (449,961 sq km)
POPULATION: 9,088,728
CAPITAL: Stockholm
LANGUAGE: Swedish

This statue of Hans Christian Andersen sits near City Hall in Copenhagen, Denmark. The beloved storyteller wrote "The Little Mermaid," and other stories.

Arctic Circle

Horn
Grimsey I.
Fontur
Hüna Bay
Akureyri
ICELAND
Hvítá R.
Faxa Bay
Keflavik
Reykjavik
Vatnajökull
Hvannadalshnúkur
Hekla (volcano)
Surtsey I.
100 miles

North Cape
Hammerfest
Barents Sea
Norwegian Sea
Tana
Tromso
Finnmark Plateau
Lake Inari
Mt. Haltia
Murmansk
Narvik
Muonio R.
LAPLAND
Arctic Circle
Vest Fjord
Mt. Kebnekaise
Lule R.
Kemi R.
ATLANTIC OCEAN
Lulea
Oulu
Skelleftea
Oulu R.
Faroe Is.
(Denmark)
Trondheim Fjord
Angerman R.
FINLAND
N
W   E
TFK
S
Alesund
Trondheim
SWEDEN
Östersund
Vaasa
Lake Saimaa
Shetland Is. (U.K.)
NORWAY
Tampere
Lake Ladoga
Glittertind Peak
Gulf of Bothnia
Bergen
Turku
Helsinki
St. Petersburg
Hardanger Fjord
Drammen
Oslo
Klar R.
Dal R.
Aland Is.
Gulf of Finland
Tallinn
North Sea
Stavanger
Karlstad
Uppsala
ESTONIA
RUSSIA
SCOTLAND
Otra R.
Lake Vänern
Stockholm
Arendal
Kristiansand
Lake Vättern
Norrköping
Gulf of Riga
Skagerrak
Kattegat
Göteborg
Baltic Sea
LATVIA
Alborg
Gotland I.
Riga
DENMARK
Öland I.
LITHUANIA
Esbjerg
Odense
Malmö
Bornholm (Denmark)
Vilnius
BELARUS
Kristiansand
Copenhagen
Kaliningrad
RUSSIA
0   300 miles
Kiel
Gdansk
0   450 kilometers
ENGLAND
GERMANY
POLAND

Did You Know?

- There are more than 180,000 lakes in Finland.

- Reykjavik, the capital of Iceland, is the northernmost national capital in the world.

- In his will, Swedish inventor and businessman Alfred Nobel established the Nobel Prizes. They were first awarded in 1901. The prizes reward leaders in the fields of physics, chemistry, medicine, literature, economics, and peace.

- Iceland is home to the Icelandic horse (left), a small but hardy breed. And because Iceland is an isolated island, Icelandics are some of the purest-bred horses in the world.

- Sweden is famous for the smorgasbord, a buffet including all kinds of foods, such as pickled and smoked fish.

- Wild reindeer can still be found in Norway.

The Iberian Peninsula

Flamenco dancing is a traditional art form popular in Spain.

Poets and writers have often likened Spain to a fortress. The snowcapped Pyrenees Mountains have protected Spain, as well as its smaller neighbors on Europe's Iberian Peninsula—Portugal and Andorra. But the mountains have also separated the countries from the rest of the European continent.

The geography of the peninsula, which ranges from high plateaus and mountains to Mediterranean and Atlantic coastlines, presents varying climates. The north is the wettest; the central region, home to Spain's capital and largest city, Madrid, is dry and, in the winter, cold. The coasts experience mild winter temperatures. Summer is hot almost everywhere. The sunny beaches and resorts are popular tourist destinations.

At the peninsula's southern tip is the British territory of Gibraltar. It is only about 8 miles (13 km) from Africa. The influence of Moors from North Africa, who conquered the Iberian Peninsula in the 8th century, is reflected in some of the region's architecture. Throughout the area, great works of art adorn magnificent cathedrals and museums.

Fiestas occur at intervals all year. The lively celebrations, which honor everything from saints to the changing seasons, often include parades and fireworks. Spain is also known for flamenco dancing and for bullfighting, one of the country's most popular sporting events.

The Andorran village of Ordino, in the Pyrenees, is popular with skiers.

Bullfighting dates back to 711 A.D. in Spain, when it was performed for nobles. Many regions have outlawed the sport because of concerns over animal rights.

Data Bank

ANDORRA
AREA: 181 sq mi (469 sq km)
POPULATION: 84,825
CAPITAL: Andorra la Vella
LANGUAGES: Catalan (official), French, Castilian, Portuguese

PORTUGAL
AREA: 35,556 sq mi (92,090 sq km)
POPULATION: 10,760,305
CAPITAL: Lisbon
LANGUAGES: Portuguese, Mirandese

SPAIN
AREA: 195,124 sq mi (505,369 sq km)
POPULATION: 46,754,784
CAPITAL: Madrid
LANGUAGES: Castilian Spanish, Catalan, Galician, Basque

ATLANTIC OCEAN

N
W · E
S
TFK

Bay of Biscay

FRANCE

Bordeaux

Toulouse

Costa Verde

La Coruña

Biarritz

Bilbao

Andorra la Vella (capital)

Narbonne

Santiago de Compostela

Cantabrian Mtns.

ANDORRA

Pyrenees Mtns.

Ebro R.

Aneto Peak

Costa Brava

Braga

Valladolid

Duero R.

Iberian Cordillera

Saragossa

Porto

Douro R.

Salamanca

Segovia

S P A I N

Barcelona

PORTUGAL

Coimbra

Madrid

Minorca I.

Majorca I.

Tagus R.

Tagus R.

Toledo

Valencia

Palma

Lisbon

Guadiana R.

La Mancha Plain

Júcar R.

Gulf of Valencia

Ibiza I.

Balearic Isands

Setúbal

Mérida

Cape Nao

Sierra Morena

Guadalquivir R.

B a e t i c   M t n s .

Murcia

Mediterranean Sea

Córdoba

Cape St. Vincent

Faro

Sevilla

Granada

Mulhacén

Algiers

Málaga

Almería

Cádiz

Costa del Sol

Strait of Gibraltar

Gibraltar (U.K.)

Ceuta (Spain)

Tangier

Melilla (Spain)

Oran

ALGERIA

ATLANTIC OCEAN

MOROCCO

0   200 miles

0   300 kilometers

Did You Know?

- Spanish-born Pablo Picasso is considered the founder of modern art.

- *Don Quixote*, written by Spanish author Miguel de Cervantes in the early 1600s, is considered to be the first modern novel.

- During the 15th and 16th centuries, explorers like Christopher Columbus, Vasco da Gama, and Ferdinand Magellan set sail from Lisbon, Portugal.

- About one-third of the world's cork oak trees (right) grow in Portugal. The country produces about half the world's cork.

- Spain is the world's leading producer of olive oil. About 300,000 tons (272,155 metric tons) are exported yearly.

- Spain, under the terms of the Treaty of Utrecht of 1713, gave Gibraltar to Britain in perpetuity.

France and Monaco

Monaco Harbor is often filled with the yachts of the extremely wea

France is a feast for the senses. The sights, scents, and flavors of Western Europe's largest country have been celebrated for hundreds of years. The French are proud of their nation's history and culture. They treasure their artistic and architectural accomplishments and savor their country's fine cuisine and flair for fashion.

Paris, the City of Light, is France's capital and cultural center. The city sits on the banks of the Seine River, and is a magnet for writers and artists. It is considered to be one of the world's most romantic cities and an ideal place to people-watch at a sidewalk cafe.

Most of France's 65 million residents live in cities or towns, but much of the country is fertile farmland. Grapes of all varieties are among the country's main products. France is one of the world's leading wine producers.

In southern France, the resort towns of Nice and Cannes grace the French Riviera. Monaco, the world's second smallest country, hugs the border with Italy. Monaco is known for its casinos.

Data Bank

FRANCE
AREA: 248,429 sq mi (643,428 sq km)
POPULATION: 65,312,249
CAPITAL: Paris
LANGUAGE: French

MONACO
AREA: .75 sq mi (1.94 sq km)
POPULATION: 30,539
CAPITAL: Monaco
LANGUAGES: French (official), English, Italian, Monégasque

France is one of the top cheese exporters in the world. About 400 different types of cheese are made in France.

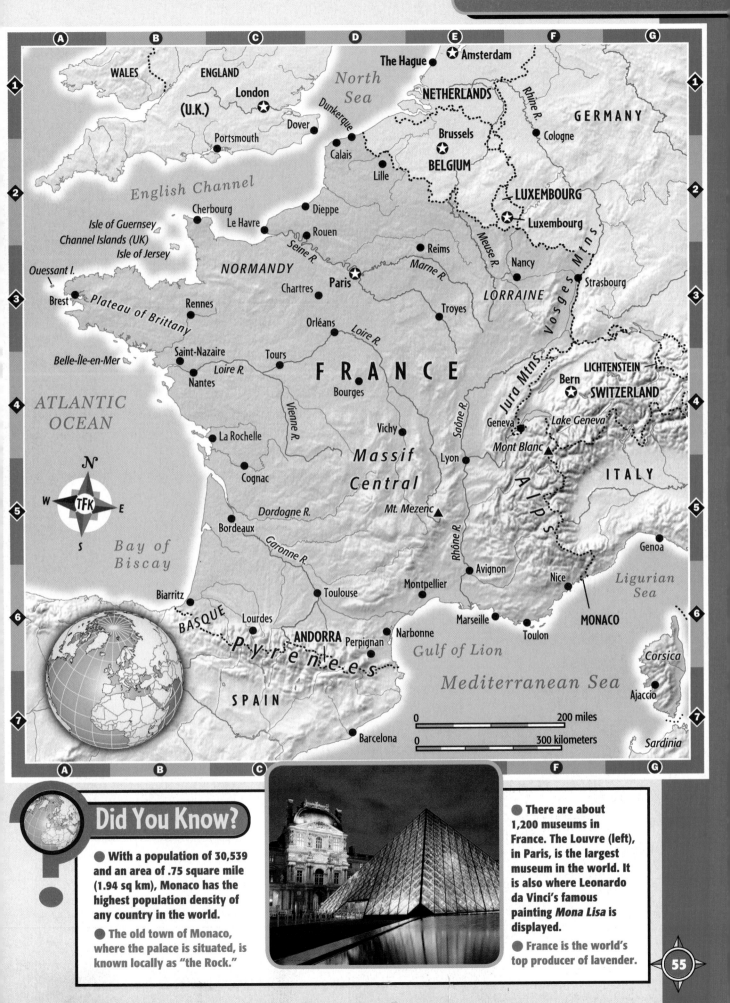

A B C D E F G

WALES ENGLAND

London

(U.K.)

Dover

Portsmouth

English Channel

North Sea

The Hague ★ Amsterdam

NETHERLANDS

GERMANY

Rhine R.

Cologne

Dunkerque

Calais

Lille

Brussels

★ BELGIUM

LUXEMBOURG

Luxembourg ★

Meuse R.

Cherbourg Dieppe

Isle of Guernsey

Channel Islands (UK)

Isle of Jersey

Le Havre Rouen

Seine R.

NORMANDY

Reims

Marne R.

Nancy

Vosges Mtns.

Strasbourg

LORRAINE

Ouessant I.

Brest

Plateau of Brittany

Rennes

Chartres Paris ★

Troyes

Orléans

Loire R.

Saint-Nazaire

Belle-Île-en-Mer

Nantes

Loire R.

Tours

F R A N C E

Bourges

Jura Mtns

Bern ★

LICHTENSTEIN

SWITZERLAND

Vienne R.

ATLANTIC OCEAN

La Rochelle

Vichy

Saône R.

Geneva

Lake Geneva

Mont Blanc ▲

ITALY

Cognac

Massif Central

Lyon

A l p s

N

W E

S

TFK

Dordogne R.

Mt. Mezenc ▲

Rhône R.

Genoa

Bordeaux

Garonne R.

Avignon

Nice

Ligurian Sea

Bay of Biscay

Biarritz

Toulouse

Montpellier

Marseille

Toulon

MONACO

BASQUE

Lourdes

ANDORRA

P y r e n e e s

Perpignan

Narbonne

Gulf of Lion

Corsica

SPAIN

Barcelona

Mediterranean Sea

Ajaccio

Sardinia

0 200 miles

0 300 kilometers

1 2 3 4 5 6 7

Did You Know?

● With a population of 30,539 and an area of .75 square mile (1.94 sq km), Monaco has the highest population density of any country in the world.

● The old town of Monaco, where the palace is situated, is known locally as "the Rock."

● There are about 1,200 museums in France. The Louvre (left), in Paris, is the largest museum in the world. It is also where Leonardo da Vinci's famous painting *Mona Lisa* is displayed.

● France is the world's top producer of lavender.

The Low Countries

The Netherlands exports billions of tulip bulbs each year.

Belgium, Luxembourg, and the Netherlands are often called the Low Countries. It is a fitting name for this densely populated region, as much of its land lies either below, or just slightly above, sea level. The terrain seems endlessly flat, which is perfect for bicycling, a favorite activity. Travel by boat is also essential. Thousands of rivers and canals connect gabled cities, quaint villages, and bountiful farmland throughout the region.

Cycling is a popular mode of transportation in the Netherlands.

The Low Countries produce some of the world's finest flowers, cheeses, and chocolates. The Netherlands (commonly called Holland) is the world's flower hub. It is host to flower festivals and auctions, and exports more blossoms than any other nation. Belgium's capital, Brussels, is called the capital of Europe. A uniquely multicultural city, it houses the headquarters of the European Union (E.U.) as well as NATO (the North Atlantic Treaty Organization).

Luxembourg, one of the world's smallest countries, is tucked just below Belgium. Despite its size—998 square miles (2,585 sq km)—it is an important worldwide banking center. Luxembourg also houses the E.U.'s financial headquarters.

Some of the world's most famous painters came from the Low Countries. Hieronymus Bosch, Rembrandt van Rijn, Johannes Vermeer, and Vincent van Gogh were from the Netherlands; Jan van Eyck, Pieter Brueghel the Elder, and Peter Paul Rubens were from Belgium.

Delft, in the Netherlands, is famous for its hand-painted blue and white ceramic tiles and pottery.

Data Bank

BELGIUM
AREA: 11,787 sq mi (30,528 sq km)
POPULATION: 10,431,477
CAPITAL: Brussels
LANGUAGES: Dutch, French, German (all official)

LUXEMBOURG
AREA: 998 sq mi (2,585 sq km)
POPULATION: 503,302
CAPITAL: Luxembourg
LANGUAGES: Luxembourgish, German, French

NETHERLANDS
AREA: 16,040 sq mi (41,543 sq km)
POPULATION: 16,847,007
CAPITAL: Amsterdam
LANGUAGES: Dutch, Frisian (both official)

A B C D E F G

1

ENGLAND

North
Sea

Terschelling I.
Ameland I.
West Frisian Islands
East Frisian Islands

Vlieland I.
Waddenzee
Dike
Leeuwarden
Groningen
Bremen

Texel I.
IJsselmeer Dam

IJsselmeer

NORTHEAST
POLDER

EASTERN
FLEVOLAND

GERMANY

Haarlem
★ Amsterdam
NETHERLANDS

The Hague
Leiden
Utrecht
Arnhem

Goeree
Delft
Rotterdam
Rhine R.

Brouwers Dam
Schouwen
Oosterschelde Dam
Walcheren

Maas R.
's-Hertogenbosch
Tilburg
Eindhoven

Maas R.

Teutoburg Forest

Ruhr Valley

Essen

Ruhr R.

Düsseldorf

Ostend
Antwerp
Bruges
Ghent
Scheldt R.
Lys R.

FLANDERS
BELGIUM

Cologne

Maastricht
Vaalser Hill ▲
Bonn

Dover
Strait of Dover
Dunkerque
Calais
Boulogne
Lille

★ Brussels

Waterloo
Mons
Namur
Charleroi

Liège
Meuse R.
Spa
▲ Botrange

Koblenz

Frankfurt
am Main

Eifel

Hunsrück

Ardennes
▲ Buurgplaatz
LUXEMBOURG
Weisbaden

Moselle R.

Somme R.
Oise R.

FRANCE

Aisne R.
LORRAINE

Luxembourg ★

Esch-sur-Alzette

Rhine R.

Seine R.

N
W — E
S
TFK

80 miles
120 kilometers

A B C D E F G

Did You Know?

● Belgian chocolates (right) are considered to be the finest chocolates in the world. These gourmet delights are still mostly handmade. Visitors to Belgium flock to the small shops for tours, tastings, and chocolaty souvenirs.

● Antwerp, Belgium, is known for its expert diamond cutting and polishing.

● Residents of Luxembourg are known as Luxembourgian or Luxembourgish. People from the Netherlands are Dutch.

● The name *Netherlands* comes from the Dutch word *nederland*, which means "low land."

Germany

Although Germany is mainly urban, the country has a wide range of natural landscapes. Mountains covered by lush forests dominate the south. Along the edges of the North Sea and the Baltic Sea, low-lying coastal land gives way to a central region of hills and river valleys. Germany is blessed with a temperate climate and fertile soil.

The Bavarian Alps stretch 70 miles (113 km) along the border between Germany and Austria.

Because of the numerous rivers and canals that stretch across the country, Germany developed into a major transportation hub. Centrally located in Europe, it has historically been a crossroads for ideas, cultures—and armies. The country's long history includes the devastating rule of Adolf Hitler, whose actions sparked World War II. The war tore the country apart—Germany was divided into east and west zones—and the economy was destroyed. West Germany rebounded to become a major industrial power, while East Germany allied itself with the Soviet Union. In 1989, the fall of the Berlin Wall, which had separated East and West Germany, helped bring about reunification. In 1991, Germany's capital was moved from Bonn to Berlin.

Europe's most populous nation is divided into 16 states. Bavaria is the largest state, its landscape graced by numerous castles. The elaborate Neuschwanstein Castle, in the Bavarian Alps, was built for King Ludwig II, called "Mad Ludwig."

Germany is well-known for its sausages and sauerkraut.

The Berlin Wall was 96 miles (155 km) long and almost 13 feet (4 m) high.

Data Bank

GERMANY
AREA: 137,846 sq mi (357,020 sq km)
POPULATION: 81,471,834
CAPITAL: Berlin
LANGUAGE: German

Baltic Sea

DENMARK

✪ Copenhagen

Kiel Bay

North Frisian Is.

Nord Ostsee Canal

Fehmarn I.

Rügen

Mecklenburg Bay

Pomeranian Bay

East Frisian Is.

● Kiel

● Rostock

West Frisian Is.

● Hamburg

Lake Müritz

Oder R.

North Sea

Weser R.

● Bremen

Elbe R.

N o r t h   G e r m a n   p l a i n

N
W T F K E
S

✪ Amsterdam

NETHERLANDS

Rhine R.

Teutoburg Forest

● Hannover

Mittelland Canal

● Berlin ✪

POLAND

Oder R.

● Münster

● Magdeburg

▲ Brocken Peak

Harz Mtns.

Ruhr Valley

Rhine R.

● Dortmund

● Essen

● Düsseldorf

● Cologne

G E R M A N Y

● Leipzig

● Dresden

BELGIUM

✪ Brussels

● Bonn

● Erfurt

Erzegebirge

● Liège

Eifel

Moselle R.

● Wiesbaden

▲ Fichtelberg

✪ Prague

● Frankfurt am Main

Main R.

CZECH REPUBLIC

Luxembourg ✪

Hunsrück

Haardt Mtns.

● Würzberg

● Nürnberg

Bohemian Forest

LUXEMBOURG

● Heidelberg

Danube R.

Rhine R.

● Stuttgart

Swabian Jura

● Augsburg

Isar R.

Danube R.

FRANCE

Black Forest

● Ulm

B A V A R I A

✪ Vienna

Lake Constance

● Munich

● Salzburg

AUSTRIA

0   100 miles

0   150 kilometers

LIECHTENSTEIN

SWITZERLAND

B a v a r i a n   A l p s

▲ Zugspitze

Watzmann ▲

Did You Know?

● Many world-renowned classical composers hailed from Germany, including Johann Sebastian Bach and Ludwig van Beethoven.

● The autobahn in Germany is a highway with few speed limits.

● German physicist Daniel Gabriel

Fahrenheit invented the alcohol thermometer in 1709, the mercury thermometer in 1714, and the Fahrenheit scale in 1724.

● On April 12, 1990, Germany inched into the *Guinness Book of World Records* for a traffic jam of 18 million cars on the East German–West German border.

● Germany is known for its cuckoo clocks (left), which were invented in the Black Forest region of southwestern Germany in the 1730s.

Austria, Liechtenstein, and Switzerland

The Alps are a huge chain of mountains that stretches across 750 miles (1,207 km), from the Austrian capital of Vienna to southern Italy. The mountains form a barrier between northern and southern Europe. But for centuries, passes cut through the Alps have provided Europeans with trade routes.

Switzerland, which contains more of the Alps than any other nation, is renowned for its magnificent landscapes. It is a politically neutral nation, and many international organizations, including the United Nations and the Red Cross, have offices there. There is no official Swiss language; instead, the Swiss speak the languages of the countries that surround them: German, French, and Italian.

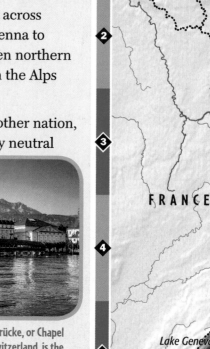

Built in 1333, Kapellbrücke, or Chapel Bridge, in Lucerne, Switzerland, is the oldest wooden bridge in Europe.

Between Switzerland and Austria lies the tiny nation of Liechtenstein. After World War I, Liechtenstein allied itself with Switzerland. That close connection is still strong, and Switzerland represents Liechtenstein diplomatically. Liechtenstein is a constitutional monarchy. It is governed by a prince, but the people are represented by an elected parliament.

Just east of Switzerland and Liechtenstein is Austria. The Danube, Europe's second longest river, passes through Austria's capital city, Vienna. More than 40% of Austria is covered in forests.

Data Bank

AUSTRIA
AREA: 32,383 sq mi (83,872 sq km)
POPULATION: 8,217,280
CAPITAL: Vienna
LANGUAGES: German, Turkish, Serbian, Croatian

LIECHTENSTEIN
AREA: 62 sq mi (161 sq km)
POPULATION: 35,236
CAPITAL: Vaduz
LANGUAGES: German (official), Alemannic dialect

SWITZERLAND
AREA: 15,937 sq mi (41,277 sq km)
POPULATION: 7,639,961
CAPITAL: Bern
LANGUAGES: German, French, Italian, Romansch (all official)

Three men blow alpenhorns in the Swiss Alps. Made from spruce wood, alpenhorns range from 10 to 13 feet (3 to 4 m) long.

BELGIUM

LUXEMBOURG

Luxembou

Nancy

FRANCE

Vosg

Jura M

Lake Geneva   Lausanne

Rhône R.

Geneva

Mont Blanc

Great St. Bernard Pass

Alps

GERMANY

Frankfurt am Main

Main R.

Mannheim

Haardt Mtns.

Swabian Jura

Danube R.

Augsburg

Munich

Lake Constance

ourg

Erzegebirge

Bohemian Forest

Bavarian Forest

Sumava Mtns.

Prague

Elbe R.

CZECH REPUBLIC

Brno

Braunau

Linz

Danube R.

Krems

SLOVAKIA

Bratislava

Vienna

Lake Neusiedler

ST. Gall

Lake Zürich

Zug

Vaduz

LIECHTENSTEIN

Bavarian Alps

Salzburg

AUSTRIA

Enns R.

Salzach R.

Innsbruck

Inn R.

Ötztal Alps

Brenner Pass

Niedere Tauern

Grossglockner

Mur R.

Graz

Rába R.

HUNGARY

Lake Balaton

ITZERLAND

jfrau

Rhaetian Alps

Piz Bernina

Dolomites

Carnic Alps

Dráu R.

Klagenfurt

Maribor

Julian Alps

Ljubljana

SLOVENIA

Zagreb

Alps

plon

nel

Lake Como

Como

Milan

Adige R.

Lake Garda

Padua

Venice

Trieste

CROATIA

Banja Luka

ITALY

Po R.

Ferrara

Adriatic Sea

Pula

BOSNIA AND HERZEGOVINA

Genoa

Ravenna

0   100 miles

0   150 kilometers

W — E (compass with N/S and TFK)

Did You Know?

- **During the late 1800s, Austria was the center of the powerful Austro-Hungarian Empire.**

- Salzburg, Austria, is the birthplace of composer Wolfgang Amadeus Mozart.

- **Edelweiss (right) is a flower native to the Alps.**

- Switzerland and Liechtenstein remained neutral during World War II.

- **Liechtenstein is smaller than Washington, D.C.**

- In 218 B.C., Hannibal, a Carthaginian general, used elephants to carry his troops over the Alps. Many of his men and elephants died from the cold.

- **Bern, Switzerland's capital, is named for the generations of bears that have lived there in a bear pit. The pit was built in 1513.**

- Innsbruck, Austria, has hosted the Winter Olympics twice, in 1964 and 1976.

61

Central Europe

The great plains of Poland, the magnificent rivers of Hungary, and the mountains of Slovakia and the Czech Republic are some of the highlights of this region's landscape. Architectural masterpieces are common throughout each country. Castles decorate the Czech Republic's landscape, illustrating the nation's grand heritage. Prague Castle, in the Czech Republic's capital, is one of the largest castles in the world. Museums in Budapest, Hungary, are decorated with ornate details that are symbolic of the country's love of art and design. Slovakia has its share of impressive monuments, as well as an array of modern buildings that demonstrate its stature as a growing, vibrant country.

Prague Castle, in the Czech Republic, was constructed in the 9th century.

Once a part of the Communist bloc of nations, much of central Europe has adopted a more progressive, enterprising economy in recent years. But some of the advances in manufacturing have led to problems. For example, in the 1980s, Poland struggled with high levels of air and water pollution. Its government has been working to reduce the harm done to the environment.

Each year, more and more tourists visit the region. Some travelers come to hear the captivating folk music of Hungary, others to taste the delicious foods of Warsaw, Poland. As the countries grow more cosmopolitan, each strives to become an integral part of a new, unified Europe while maintaining its own unique character and flavor.

Data Bank

CZECH REPUBLIC
AREA: 30,450 sq mi (78,865 sq km)
POPULATION: 10,190,213
CAPITAL: Prague
LANGUAGES: Czech, Slovak

HUNGARY
AREA: 35,919 sq mi (93,030 sq km)
POPULATION: 9,976,062
CAPITAL: Budapest
LANGUAGE: Hungarian

POLAND
AREA: 120,727 sq mi (312,682 sq km)
POPULATION: 38,441,588
CAPITAL: Warsaw
LANGUAGE: Polish

SLOVAKIA
AREA: 18,933 sq mi (49,036 sq km)
POPULATION: 5,477,038
CAPITAL: Bratislava
LANGUAGES: Slovak (official), Hungarian

Old Town Market Square, in Warsaw, Poland, has been around since the 13th century. It's a popular place to sample Polish cuisine.

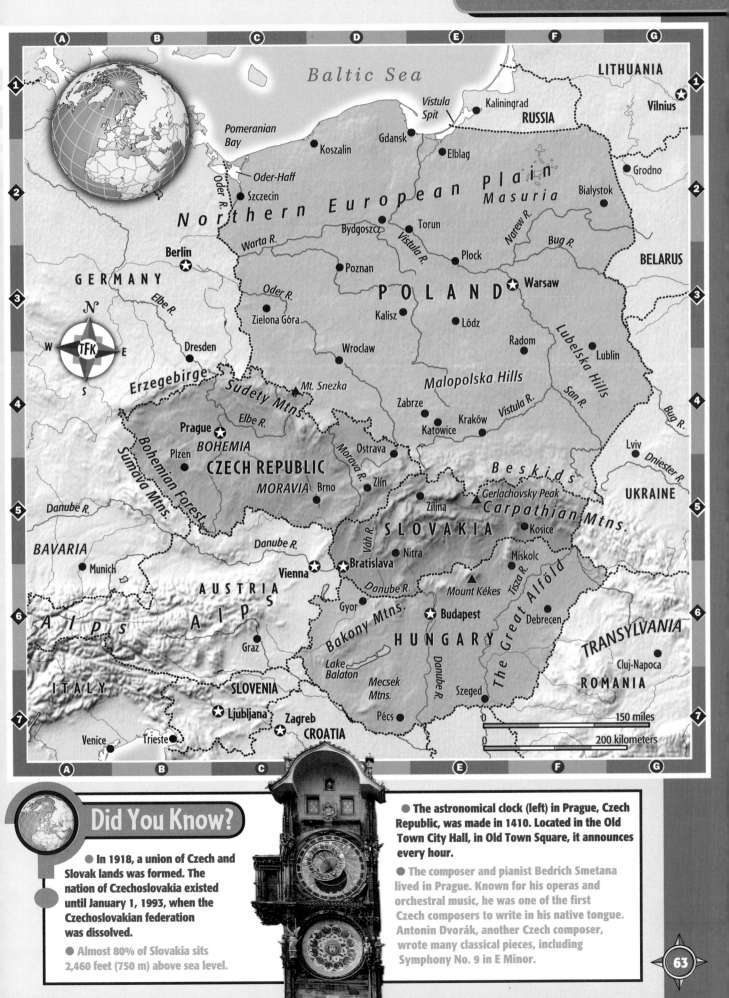

Baltic Sea

LITHUANIA

Vilnius

RUSSIA

Vistula Spit

Kaliningrad

Grodno

Pomeranian Bay

Koszalin

Gdansk

Elblag

Bialystok

BELARUS

Oder-Haff

Szczecin

Northern European plain

Masuria

Narew R.

Bug R.

Berlin

Warta R.

Bydgoszcz

Torun

Vistula R.

Plock

Warsaw

GERMANY

Oder R.

POLAND

Zielona Góra

Kalisz

Poznan

Lódz

Radom

Lublin

Dresden

Wroclaw

Lubelska Hills

San R.

Bug R.

Erzegebirge

Sudety Mtns.

Mt. Snezka

Malopolska Hills

Zabrze

Vistula R.

Lviv

Elbe R.

Kraków

Dniester R.

Prague

BOHEMIA

Katowice

UKRAINE

Plzen

CZECH REPUBLIC

Ostrava

Beskids

Bohemian Forest

MORAVIA

Brno

Morava R.

Zlín

Gerlachovsky Peak

Carpathian Mtns.

Šumava Mtns.

Danube R.

Zilina

SLOVAKIA

Kosice

BAVARIA

Danube R.

Váh R.

Nitra

Miskolc

Tisza R.

Munich

AUSTRIA

Vienna

Bratislava

Mount Kékes

ALPS

ALPS

Gyor

Danube R.

Budapest

Debrecen

TRANSYLVANIA

Graz

Bakony Mtns.

HUNGARY

The Great Alföld

Cluj-Napoca

ITALY

Lake Balaton

Danube R.

ROMANIA

SLOVENIA

Mecsek Mtns.

Szeged

Ljubljana

Zagreb

Pécs

150 miles

Venice

Trieste

CROATIA

200 kilometers

N W S E TFK

Did You Know?

● In 1918, a union of Czech and Slovak lands was formed. The nation of Czechoslovakia existed until January 1, 1993, when the Czechoslovakian federation was dissolved.

● Almost 80% of Slovakia sits 2,460 feet (750 m) above sea level.

● The astronomical clock (left) in Prague, Czech Republic, was made in 1410. Located in the Old Town City Hall, in Old Town Square, it announces every hour.

● The composer and pianist Bedrich Smetana lived in Prague. Known for his operas and orchestral music, he was one of the first Czech composers to write in his native tongue. Antonin Dvorák, another Czech composer, wrote many classical pieces, including Symphony No. 9 in E Minor.

Italy, Malta, San Marino, and Vatican City

Although Italy did not become a unified nation until 1861, Italians are understandably proud of their region's ancient history. The city of Rome, which was founded in 625 B.C., was the center of the Roman Empire. At the height of its power, the empire extended across much of Europe and northern Africa and portions of Asia. Roman monuments, aqueducts, and amphitheaters can still be found throughout Italy.

Italy is as magnificent now as it was in the past. The country is divided into 20 regions, each with its own unique flavor, big cities, and attractions. Rome, Italy's capital and largest city, is located in Lazio. Milan, in Lombardy, is a world-famous fashion center. Florence, in Tuscany, is known for its museums and galleries, and as the birthplace of the Renaissance, which was a time of great artistic and scientific growth. Many people consider Venice, in the Veneto region, the world's most enchanting city.

Construction was stopped at the third floor of the Leaning Tower of Pisa, in Italy, for 94 years after workers noticed the building was leaning.

Italy is a long, boot-shaped peninsula. At the top of the boot, the Alps form a border that separates Italy from France, Switzerland, Austria, and Slovenia. The rest of Italy is surrounded by seas—the Ligurian, Tyrrhenian, Mediterranean, Ionian, and Adriatic. The Apennine Mountains form a backbone that extends down the peninsula. Italy includes two large islands, Sardinia and Sicily, and several small islands. Lying between Sicily and Africa is the tiny island nation of Malta. Sharing the Italian peninsula are San Marino and Vatican City. The Vatican, or Holy See (*see* means "cathedral town"), is the home of the pope, the head of the Roman Catholic Church.

In 1508, Pope Julius II asked Michelangelo to paint the ceiling of the Vatican's Sistine Chapel. It took him four years to complete the project.

Data Bank

ITALY
AREA: 116,348 sq mi (301,340 sq km)
POPULATION: 61,016,804
CAPITAL: Rome
LANGUAGES: Italian (official), German, French, Slovene

MALTA
AREA: 122 sq mi (316 sq km)
POPULATION: 408,333
CAPITAL: Valletta
LANGUAGES: Maltese, English (both official)

SAN MARINO
AREA: 24 sq mi (62 sq km)
POPULATION: 31,817
CAPITAL: San Marino
LANGUAGE: Italian

VATICAN CITY (HOLY SEE)
AREA: .17 sq mi (.44 sq km)
POPULATION: 832
CAPITAL: None
LANGUAGES: Latin, Italian, French, others

A B C D E F G

1
LIECHTENSTEIN
SWITZERLAND
Brenner Pass
A L P S
AUSTRIA
HUNGARY
Danube R.
N
TFK
W E
S

Geneva
Lake Como
A L P S
Dolomites
Piave R.
Ljubljana
SLOVENIA
Zagreb
CROATIA
Belgrade

Mt. Dufour
Piz Bernina
Mont Blanc
FRANCE

2
Milan
Po R.
Lake Garda
Ticino R.
Po R.
Verona
Venice
Padua
Trieste
Gulf of Venice
Rijeka (Fiume)
BOSNIA AND HERZEGOVINA
Turin
Tanaro R.
ITALY
Reno R.

Genoa
Ligurian Sea
Pisa
Florence
Arno R.
Bologna
Ravenna
SAN MARINO
Ancona
Split
Sarajevo
SERBIA

3
Marseille
Nice
MONACO
A p e n n i n e s
Adriatic Sea
MONTENEGRO
Dubrovnik

Capri
Elba I.
TUSCANY
Lake Trasimeno
Tiber R.
Mt. Corno
Pescara

Corsica (France)
Bastia
Tuscan Archipelago

4
Ajaccio
Strait of Bonifacio
VATICAN CITY (Holy See)
Rome
Ofanto R.
Bari
Tirana
ALBANIA

Naples
Mt. Vesuvius (volcano)
Ischia
Salerno
PUGLIA
Brindisi
Strait of Otranto

5
Sardinia
Mount Marmora
Tyrrhenian Sea
CALABRIA
Taranto
Gulf of Taranto
Corfu (Greece)

Cagliari
Stromboli I.
Lipari Islands
Catanzaro
Ionian Sea

6
Palermo
Messina
Strait of Messina
Mt. Etna (volcano)

Strait of Sicily
Sicily
Catania
Ragusa
Syracuse
Mediterranean Sea

7
Tunis
Pantelleria I. (Italy)
0   200 miles
0   300 kilometers

TUNISIA
MALTA
Valletta

ALGERIA

A B C D E F G

Did You Know?

- Mainland Europe has only one active volcano, which is Mount Vesuvius near Naples, Italy.

- The Swiss Guard of Vatican City is the world's smallest army. It consists of 100 men who have sworn allegiance to the pope. The guards' colorful uniform has changed very little since the 16th century.

- The capital of San Marino, also called San Marino, sits on top of Mount Titano.

- The Vatican Museums make up one of the world's largest museum complexes. The museums' 1,400 rooms are filled with antiquities and works of art.

- Each year before Easter, Italians celebrate *Carnevale*, or Mardi Gras, with parades, masquerade balls, parties, and music. Participants often wear elaborate masks, or *maschere*, made in Venice.

The Balkans

The ruins of Butrint is a mountainous area in Eastern Europe. Located between Western Europe and Asia are the nations known as the Balkan states. The western Balkan states include Albania, Bosnia and Herzegovina, Croatia, Macedonia, Serbia, Montenegro, Slovenia, and Kosovo.

Destroyed during the civil war in the 1990s, the Old Bridge in the city of Mostar, in Bosnia and Herzegovina, was rebuilt in 2004.

Albanians are descendants of the Illyrians, whose civilization came before that of the Greeks. Split, Croatia, is the site of ancient Roman ruins, as is Butrint, Albania. Slovenia, a nation of mountains and lakes, has close ties to Germany, Austria, and other Western European countries.

The ruins in Butrint, Albania, date to the 4th century B.C.

Because the Balkan peninsula acts as a land bridge between the East and West, it has great strategic value. As a result, it has been the site of frequent wars. Over many centuries, different portions of the Balkans were conquered by the Roman Empire, the Byzantine Empire, and the Ottoman Empire. But the people of the region have always been fiercely independent. They are proud of their cultures and languages. During the 19th century, ethnic groups in the Balkans began to declare their independence and fight over territory. In 1912, the Balkan Wars began, and two years later, World War I engulfed the area. In the 1990s, much of the Balkans was again caught up in ethnic strife. Today, a fragile peace exists.

Data Bank

ALBANIA
AREA: 11,010 sq mi (28,748 sq km)
POPULATION: 2,994,667
CAPITAL: Tirana
LANGUAGES: Albanian (Tosk is the official dialect), Greek, Vlach, Romany Slavic

BOSNIA AND HERZEGOVINA
AREA: 19,767 sq mi (51,196 sq km)
POPULATION: 4,622,163
CAPITAL: Sarajevo
LANGUAGES: Croatian, Serbian, Bosnian

CROATIA
AREA: 21,851 sq mi (56,594 sq km)
POPULATION: 4,483,804
CAPITAL: Zagreb
LANGUAGE: Croatian

KOSOVO
AREA: 4,203 sq mi (10,886 sq km)
POPULATION: 1,825,632
CAPITAL: Pristina
LANGUAGES: Albanian, Serbian (both official), Bosnian, Turkish, Roma

MACEDONIA
AREA: 9,928 sq mi (25,713 sq km)
POPULATION: 2,077,328
CAPITAL: Skopje
LANGUAGES: Macedonian, Albanian, Turkish, Serbian, Roma

MONTENEGRO
AREA: 5,333 sq mi (13,812 sq km)
POPULATION: 661,807
CAPITAL: Podgorica
LANGUAGES: Serbian, Bosniak, Albanian, Montenegrin

SERBIA
AREA: 29,913 sq mi (77,474 sq km)
POPULATION: 7,310,555
CAPITAL: Belgrade
LANGUAGES: Serbian (official), Romanian, Hungarian, Slovak, Ukrainian, Croatian, Albanian

SLOVENIA
AREA: 7,827 sq mi (20,272 sq km)
POPULATION: 2,000,092
CAPITAL: Ljubljana
LANGUAGES: Slovenian, Serbo-Croatian

In 2006, Montenegro voted in favor of independence from Serbia, and became a separate country.

The newest country to gain independence is Kosovo. It was under Serbian control until 1991, when Kosovo Albanian leaders declared independence. Because of resistance from Serbians, Kosovo did not officially gain its independence until 2008.

The Julian Alps were named for Julius Caesar, a Roman emperor.

Did You Know?

● *Balkan* means "mountain" in Turkish.

● There are more than 115 beaches in Montenegro along the coast of the Adriatic Sea.

● Bosnia and Herzegovina, Croatia, Macedonia, Serbia, Montenegro, and Slovenia were all part of the larger nation of Yugoslavia, which broke into separate countries in 1991.

● Folk dancing and folk music are popular throughout the Balkan region. Turkish music has had a strong influence on the music of Bosnia and Herzegovina.

● The rugged Dinaric and Julian Alps, in the Balkans, are popular with skiers.

Southeastern Europe

The Acropolis in Athens, Greece, is home to the Parthenon, an Athenian ten

Surrounded on three sides by water, Greece is a land of sparkling beauty. Magnificent ruins are framed by deep blue skies and turquoise water. At the center of Greek life is the sea. Much of the country's early power and wealth came from shipping, trading, and fishing. The sea is still important to Greece's economy. Millions of people visit the country's sunny beaches and historic sites each year, making tourism Greece's top industry. Visitors especially love to cruise around the country's nearly 2,000 islands, most of which are uninhabited. Athens is the country's capital and largest city. Its most notable structure is the Parthenon, which was built almost 2,500 years ago.

Tourism also is important for Greece's northeastern neighbors, Bulgaria and Romania. Black Sea resorts boast beautiful sandy beaches, and draw many visitors from neighboring countries.

Impressive limestone rock formations loom above the tiny town of Melnik, Bulgaria.

Data Bank

BULGARIA
AREA: 42,811 sq mi (110,880 sq km)
POPULATION: 7,093,635
CAPITAL: Sofia
LANGUAGES: Bulgarian, Turkish, Roma

GREECE
AREA: 50,942 sq mi (131,939 sq km)
POPULATION: 10,760,136
CAPITAL: Athens
LANGUAGES: Greek (official), English, French

ROMANIA
AREA: 92,043 sq mi (238,390 sq km)
POPULATION: 21,904,551
CAPITAL: Bucharest
LANGUAGES: Romanian, Hungarian, Romany

Did You Know?

● Transylvania, in Romania, is home to Count Dracula, the fictional character in Bram Stoker's classic tale. The Dracula legend is based on Vlad the Impaler, a Romanian leader known for his cruelty.

Bran Castle, in Bucharest, Romania, was a home to Vlad the Impaler. Many people refer to it as Dracula's Castle.

● Bulgarian rose oil, used in fine perfumes around the world, is produced in the Kazanlak region of Bulgaria.

● The word *bucharest* means "city of joy."

● Alexander the Great lived from 356 B.C. to 323 B.C. He made Greece a world power by conquering much of the known world.

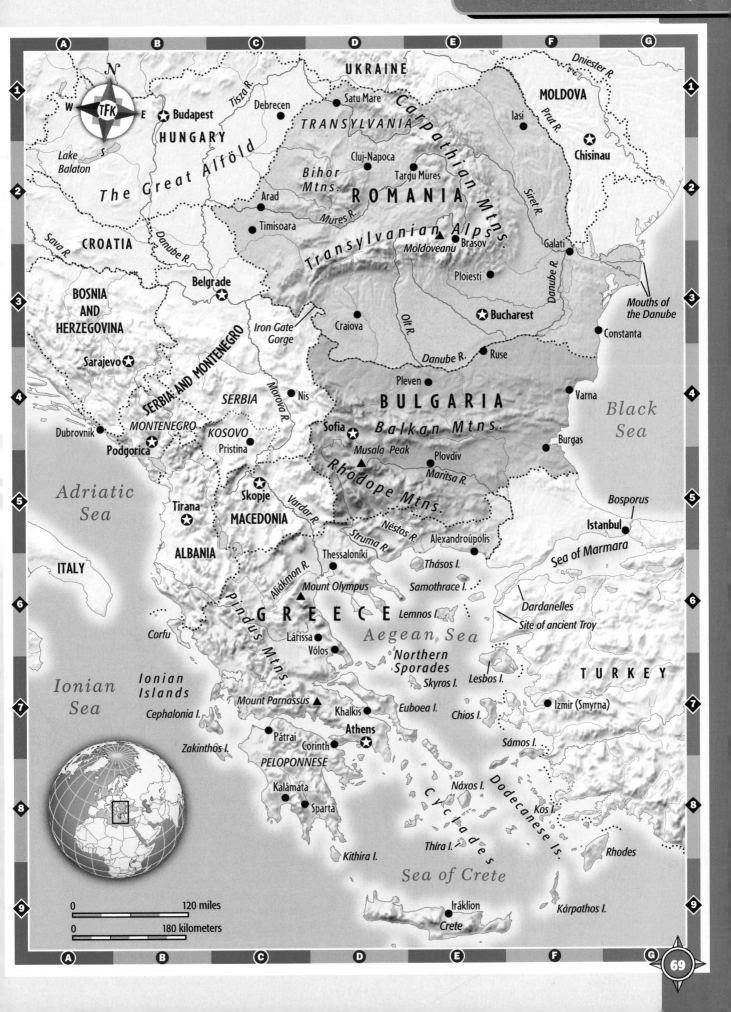

The Baltic States and Belarus

The tower of St. Peter's Church in Riga, Latvia, has been rebuilt several times. It collapsed in 1666, was destroyed by fire in 1677, was struck by lightning in 1721, and then burned to the ground during World War II. The current tower was completed in 1984.

D uring the early 1940s, the Soviet Union expanded its borders by invading the surrounding small nations. Estonia, Latvia, Lithuania, and Belarus all fell to the armies of dictator Joseph Stalin. These ancient independent states became republics of the Soviet Union. Not until the early 1990s did they regain their independence. Today, each of these states is a sovereign nation with its own government, economy, language, and history.

There are nine meteorite craters on the Estonian island of Saaremaa. A lake has formed in the main Kaalijarv crater.

Estonia, Lithuania, and Latvia are known as the Baltic states because they are located on the coast of the Baltic Sea. The Baltic Sea connects these nations to Scandinavia and northern Europe. Tallinn, Estonia's capital, is only 40 miles (64 km) from Helsinki, Finland. Since gaining their independence from the Soviet Union, the Baltic states have proudly reclaimed their historic languages and cultures. They have a rich legacy of music, dance, folklore, and literature. The region is heavily forested, and has a wide range of wildlife, including elk, deer, and wild boar.

Belarus, just east of Lithuania, shares the Baltic states' flat landscape and cool climate. Unlike the Baltics, however, Belarus holds its Soviet past in high regard, and much of its culture is connected to that of Russia and the former Soviet Union. Minsk, the capital of Belarus, was largely rebuilt after World War II.

The Baltic states were invited to join NATO and the European Union in 2002. With these alliances, they are becoming important parts of the global economy. Belarus has continued to maintain its close ties with Russia.

Data Bank

BELARUS
AREA: 80,154 sq mi (207,598 sq km)
POPULATION: 9,577,552
CAPITAL: Minsk
LANGUAGES: Belarusian, Russian

ESTONIA
AREA: 17,462 sq mi (45,226 sq km)
POPULATION: 1,282,963
CAPITAL: Tallinn
LANGUAGES: Estonian (official), Russian

LATVIA
AREA: 24,938 sq mi (64,589 sq km)
POPULATION: 2,204,708
CAPITAL: Riga
LANGUAGES: Latvian (official), Lithuanian, Russian

LITHUANIA
AREA: 25,212 sq mi (65,299 sq km)
POPULATION: 3,535,547
CAPITAL: Vilnius
LANGUAGES: Lithuanian (official), Polish, Russian

The *kokle*, a traditional Latvian folk instrument, is generally played by women and girls. The playing of the *kokle* was banned for a while during Stalin's reign, but it regained popularity after the fall of the Soviet Union.

Gulf of Bothnia

FINLAND

SWEDEN

Helsinki

Gulf of Finland

Stockholm

Tallinn

Narva

St. Petersburg

Lake Ladoga

Hiiumaa I.

ESTONIA

Narva Reservoir

Novgorod

Lake Peipus

Volkhov R.

Valdai Hills

Saaremaa I.

Parnu

Tartu

Lake Ilmen

Gulf of Riga

Lake Pskov

RUSSIA

Point Kolka

Pskov

Gotland

LIVONIA

Velikaya R.

Riga

LATVIA

Baltic Sea

Liepaja

Kurzeme Upland

Daugava R.

Mount Gaizins

Western Dvina R.

Volga R.

Jelgava

Smolensk-Moscow Upland

Dnieper R.

Klaipeda

COURLAND

Siauliai

Daugavpils

KALININGRAD OBLAST (RUSSIA)

LITHUANIA

Polatsk Lowland

Polatsk

Vitsyebsk

Smolensk

Gulf of Gdansk

Neman R.

Neris R.

Kaunas

Kaliningrad

Vilnius

Mahilyow

Dnieper R.

Gdansk

Alytus

Dzerzhinskaya Mountain

Berezina R.

MASURIA

Belorussian Ridge

Minsk

Sozh R.

Hrodna

Neman R.

BELARUS

POLAND

Babruysk

Bug R.

Homyel

Warsaw

Brest

Pinsk

Pripyat R.

Polesye Marshes

Pripyat Marshes

UKRAINE

0   150 miles

0   200 kilometers

Ukraine, Moldova, and the Caucasus Republics

Ukraine, located in northern Europe, stretches across the top of the Black Sea. Its gently rolling countryside, called steppes, is rich in minerals, history, and culture. The country has two mountain regions: the Crimean Mountains in the south and the Carpathians in the west. Because of its fertile black soil, Ukraine is sometimes called the Breadbasket of Europe.

Mt. Elbrus, in the northern Caucasus Mountains, is the highest point in Europe at 18,510 feet (5,642 m) high.

The largest country entirely within Europe, Ukraine became part of the Soviet Union in 1922. Under Soviet rule, much of Ukraine's culture disappeared. Its famous painted Easter eggs (*pysanky*), fast-paced folk music, language, and religious art were repressed because they were considered too nationalistic. Since 1991, when Ukraine declared its independence from the Soviet Union, many of its customs and art forms have been revived.

Armenia, Azerbaijan, Georgia, and Moldova also broke away from the Soviet Union. The republic of Moldova lies to the west of Ukraine. The Caucasus republics—Armenia, Azerbaijan, and Georgia—are considered part of Asia. Nearly half of Azerbaijan is covered by mountains. Georgia, which sits on the Black Sea, enjoys a nice climate.

Data Bank

ARMENIA
AREA: 11,484 sq mi (29,743 sq km)
POPULATION: 2,967,975
CAPITAL: Yerevan
LANGUAGES: Armenian, Russian, Yezidi

AZERBAIJAN
AREA: 33,436 sq mi (86,599 sq km)
POPULATION: 8,372,373
CAPITAL: Baku
LANGUAGES: Azerbaijani (Azeri), Russian, Armenian, Lezgi

GEORGIA
AREA: 26,911 sq mi (69,699 sq km)
POPULATION: 4,585,874
CAPITAL: Tbilisi
LANGUAGES: Georgian (official), Russian, Armenian, Azeri

MOLDOVA
AREA: 13,067 sq mi (33,843 sq km)
POPULATION: 4,314,377
CAPITAL: Chisinau
LANGUAGES: Moldovan (official), Russian, Gagauz

UKRAINE
AREA: 233,032 sq mi (603,550 sq km)
POPULATION: 45,134,707
CAPITAL: Kiev
LANGUAGES: Ukrainian, Russian

The Swallow's Nest Castle, in southern Ukraine, sits atop a cliff 130 feet (40 m) above the Black Sea.

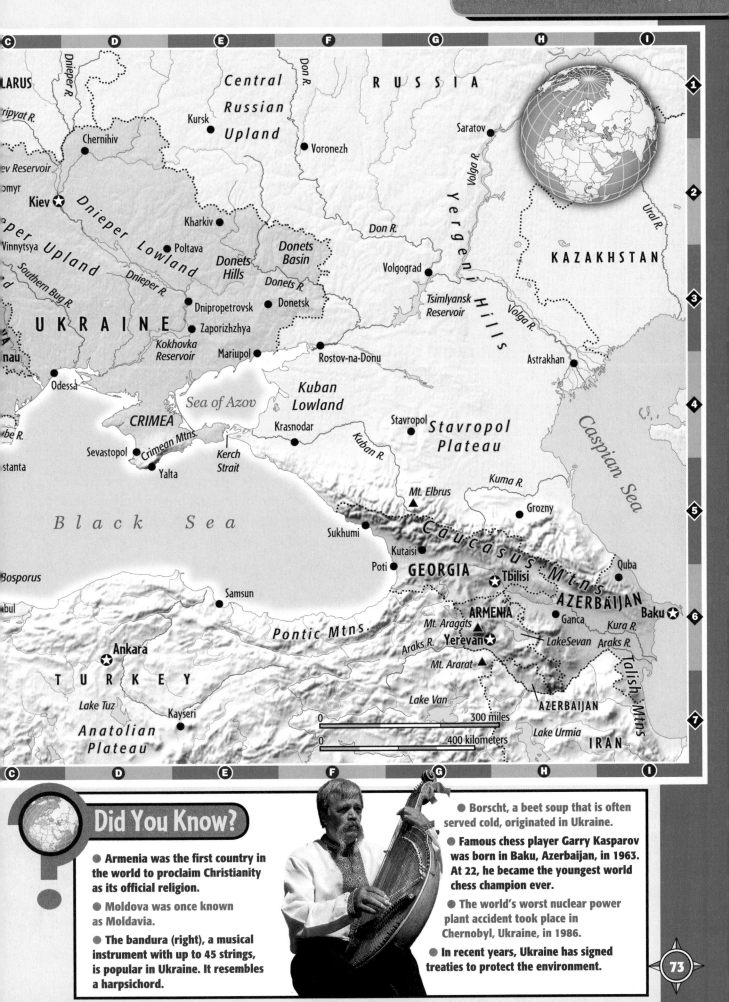

Map labels:

BELARUS · Dnieper R. · Pripyat R. · Chernihiv · Kiev Reservoir · Zhytomyr · Kiev · Vinnytsya Upland · Southern Bug R. · UKRAINE · Dnieper Lowland · Dnieper R. · Poltava · Kharkiv · Donets Hills · Donets Basin · Donets R. · Dnipropetrovsk · Donetsk · Zaporizhzhya · Kokhovka Reservoir · Mariupol · Danube R. · Odessa · CRIMEA · Crimean Mtns. · Sevastopol · Yalta · Kerch Strait · Sea of Azov · Constanta · Bosporus · Istanbul

Central Russian Upland · Kursk · Don R. · Voronezh · RUSSIA · Saratov · Don R. · Volgograd · Tsimlyansk Reservoir · Rostov-na-Donu · Kuban Lowland · Krasnodar · Kuban R. · Stavropol · Stavropol Plateau · Kuma R. · Mt. Elbrus · Grozny

Volga R. · Yergeni Hills · Volga R. · Astrakhan · KAZAKHSTAN · Ural R. · Caspian Sea

Black Sea · Sukhumi · Kutaisi · Poti · GEORGIA · Caucasus Mtns. · Tbilisi · Quba · AZERBAIJAN · Baku · Samsun · Pontic Mtns. · ARMENIA · Mt. Aragats · Ganca · Kura R. · Araks R. · Yerevan · Lake Sevan · Araks R. · Ankara · TURKEY · Mt. Ararat · AZERBAIJAN · Talish Mtns. · Lake Tuz · Kayseri · Anatolian Plateau · Lake Van · Lake Urmia · IRAN

Grid: C D E F G H I · 1 2 3 4 5 6 7

0 — 300 miles · 0 — 400 kilometers

Did You Know?

- Armenia was the first country in the world to proclaim Christianity as its official religion.

- Moldova was once known as Moldavia.

- The bandura (right), a musical instrument with up to 45 strings, is popular in Ukraine. It resembles a harpsichord.

- Borscht, a beet soup that is often served cold, originated in Ukraine.

- Famous chess player Garry Kasparov was born in Baku, Azerbaijan, in 1963. At 22, he became the youngest world chess champion ever.

- The world's worst nuclear power plant accident took place in Chernobyl, Ukraine, in 1986.

- In recent years, Ukraine has signed treaties to protect the environment.

Western Russia

Moscow's State Historical Museum, in Red Square, opened in 1894. It houses a huge collection of artifacts from the Paleolithic period to the present.

R ussia is the world's largest country. It spans two continents—Europe in the west and Asia in the east—and 11 time zones! Stretching across 6.6 million square miles (17 million sq km), it reaches from the Baltic Sea in the west to the Pacific Ocean in the east. Between Russia's coasts lie historic cities, rugged mountain ranges, and, in Siberia, some of the coldest places on Earth.

At the heart of Russia is Moscow, the nation's capital and largest city. More than 850 years old, the city centers around the imposing Kremlin, a walled fortress that encloses elaborate cathedrals, onion-domed churches, and government buildings.

Saint Petersburg is Russia's second largest—and perhaps most European—city. It has been called the Venice of the North for its elegant boulevards, lyrical bridges, and palace-lined waterways. Saint Petersburg was the Russian capital until 1918. Today, it is still a major cultural and intellectual center.

Since 1993, the Moscow Ballet has been touring the United States each year to perform its best known ballet, the *Great Russian Nutcracker*.

Did You Know?

● Moscow's Red Square—the site of Saint Basil's Cathedral and the Lenin Mausoleum—was not named for Communism or the red bricks of the Kremlin. The word for red also means "beautiful" in Russian.

● The opulent Hermitage (right), located in Saint Petersburg, is one of the world's largest museums. The collection includes about 3 million works of art.

● The Trans-Siberian Railroad is the longest in the world, chugging 5,785 miles (9,310 km) from Moscow to Vladivostok, a distance equal to a quarter of the way around the globe.

● Sochi, in southern Russia, will host the 2014 Winter Olympics.

Data Bank

RUSSIA
AREA: 6,601,668 sq mi
(17,098,241 sq km)
POPULATION: 138,739,892
CAPITAL: Moscow
LANGUAGES: Russian, others

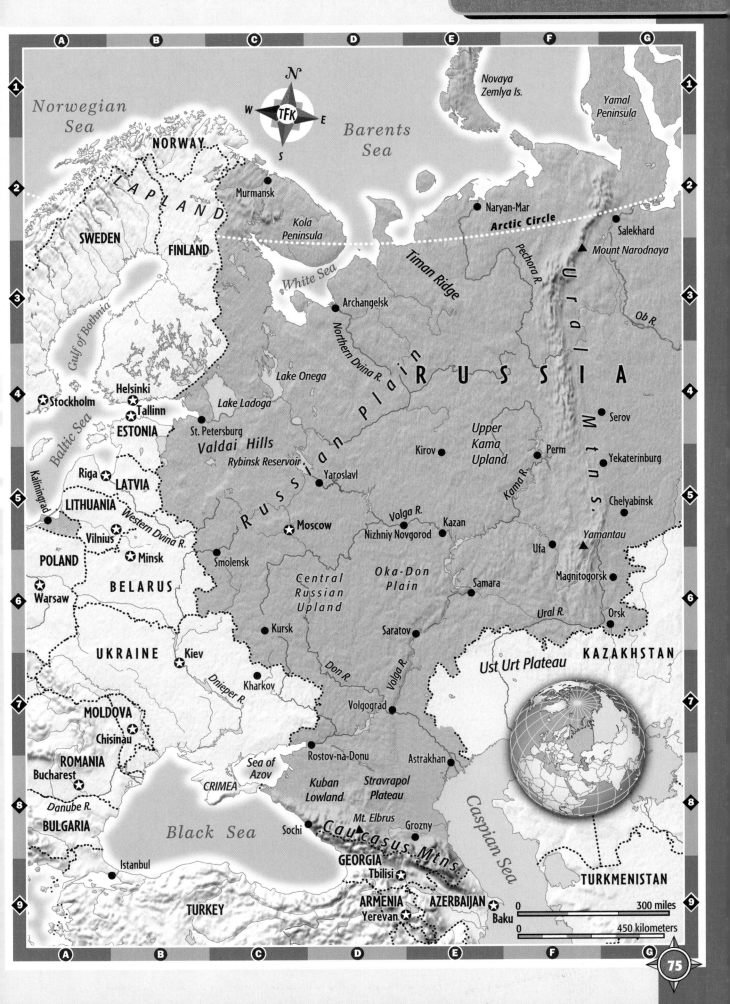

Norwegian Sea

Barents Sea

Novaya Zemlya Is.

Yamal Peninsula

N
W   TFK   E
S

NORWAY

L A P L A N D

Murmansk

Kola Peninsula

Naryan-Mar

Arctic Circle

Salekhard

Mount Narodnaya

SWEDEN

FINLAND

White Sea

Timan Ridge

Pechora R.

U r a l

Ob R.

Archangelsk

Northern Dvina R.

R U S S I A

Gulf of Bothnia

Lake Onega

Lake Ladoga

Stockholm

Helsinki

Tallinn

ESTONIA

St. Petersburg

Valdai Hills

Rybinsk Reservoir

Yaroslavl

Baltic Sea

Upper Kama Upland

Serov

Perm

Yekaterinburg

Kirov

Kama R.

M t n s.

Chelyabinsk

Riga

LATVIA

Kaliningrad

LITHUANIA

Western Dvina R.

Moscow

Volga R.

Nizhniy Novgorod

Kazan

Yamantau

Ufa

Vilnius

Minsk

POLAND

Smolensk

BELARUS

Central Russian Upland

Oka-Don Plain

Samara

Magnitogorsk

Warsaw

Ural R.

Orsk

UKRAINE

Kursk

Kiev

Saratov

KAZAKHSTAN

Volga R.

Ust Urt Plateau

Dnieper R.

Kharkov

Don R.

MOLDOVA

Chisinau

Volgograd

ROMANIA

Bucharest

Rostov-na-Donu

Astrakhan

Sea of Azov

CRIMEA

Kuban Lowland

Stravrapol Plateau

Caspian Sea

Danube R.

BULGARIA

Black Sea

Sochi

Mt. Elbrus

Caucasus Mtns.

Grozny

TURKMENISTAN

Istanbul

GEORGIA

Tbilisi

TURKEY

ARMENIA

Yerevan

AZERBAIJAN

Baku

0   300 miles

0   450 kilometers

Asia

Matsumoto Castle's donjon—a tower in the middle of a medieval castle—is the oldest one in Japan

Asia is the world's largest continent. It includes one-third of the land on Earth. Asia stretches all the way from the Arctic Circle in the north to the Indian Ocean in the southern hemisphere. To the east are the Mediterranean Sea and Red Sea, and to the west are the Ural Mountains. Because the continents of Asia and Europe meet at the Ural Mountains, many geographers consider Asia and Europe to be one enormous landmass called Eurasia.

Asia's terrain is vast and varied. It includes lakes and deserts; rain forests and glaciers; wide, flat plateaus; and the highest mountain range on Earth. The Middle East, which lies just east of Europe and north of Africa, is the home of one of the world's oldest civilizations. Most of the Middle East is flat and dry, though some areas are green and lush. Central Asia includes nations such as Uzbekistan and Turkmenistan, which were part of a large country called the Soviet Union until 1991. East Asia includes China, the most populous nation in the world. Southeast Asia is home to dense rain forests and jungles in countries such as Singapore, Vietnam, and Thailand. Southern Asia, including Nepal, India, and Pakistan, is the location of Mount Everest, the world's tallest mountain.

Asia is home to about 4.1 billion people. Most of these people live clustered in southern and Southeast Asia. Other parts of the continent, such as Mongolia and Siberia, are sparsely inhabited. Some Asian nations, including Cambodia and Afghanistan, are among the poorest in the world. Others, such as Brunei, Japan, and Singapore, are among the wealthiest and most modern.

Continent Facts

NUMBER OF COUNTRIES: 49 countries—Afghanistan, Armenia, Azerbaijan, Bahrain, Bangladesh, Bhutan, Brunei, Cambodia, China, Cyprus, East Timor, Georgia, India, Indonesia, Iran, Iraq, Israel, Japan, Jordan, Kazakhstan, Kuwait, Kyrgyzstan, Laos, Lebanon, Malaysia, Maldives, Mongolia, Myanmar (Burma), Nepal, North Korea, Oman, Pakistan, Philippines, Qatar, Russia, Saudi Arabia, Singapore, South Korea, Sri Lanka, Syria, Taiwan (not recognized internationally as a free and independent nation; it is instead considered to be part of China), Tajikistan, Thailand, Turkey, Turkmenistan, United Arab Emirates, Uzbekistan, Vietnam, Yemen

AREA: 7,212,000 sq mi (44,579,000 sq km)

LONGEST RIVER: The Yangtze, in China, is the longest river in Asia and the third longest river in the world. It flows for 3,915 miles (6,301 km).

LONGEST MOUNTAIN RANGE: The Himalayas are more than 1,550 miles (2,495 km) long.

HIGHEST PEAK: The world's tallest mountain is Mount Everest between Nepal and Tibet, at 29,035 feet (8,850 m).

Asian elephants have smaller, rounder ears than their African cousins. Their ears radiate heat, which helps the elephants to stay cool.

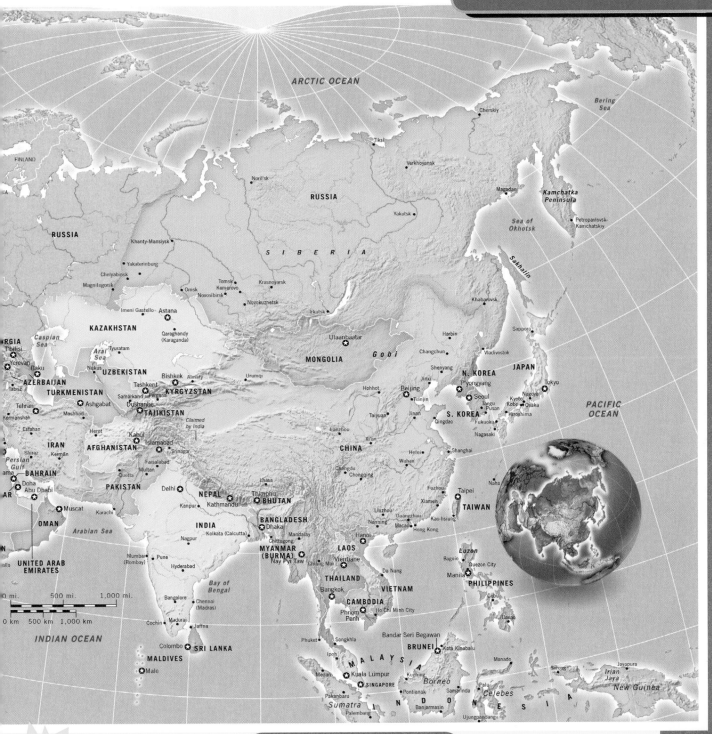

ARCTIC OCEAN

Bering Sea

Cherskiy

Tiksi

Verkhoyansk

RUSSIA

Noril'sk

Magadan

Kamchatka Peninsula

Petropavlovsk-Kamchatskiy

FINLAND

Yakutsk

Sea of Okhotsk

RUSSIA

Khanty-Mansiysk

S I B E R I A

Yakaterinburg

Chelyabinsk

Imeni Gastello

Astana

Magnitogorsk

Tomsk

Krasnoyarsk

Omsk

Kemerovo

Novosibirsk

Novokuznetsk

Irkutsk

Khabarovsk

Sakhalin

KAZAKHSTAN

Qaraghandy (Karaganda)

Ulaanbaatar

Harbin

Sapporo

Caspian Sea

Tyuratam

MONGOLIA

Gobi

Changchun

Vladivostok

RGIA

Tbilisi

Aral Sea

Nukus

Yerevan

Baku

UZBEKISTAN

Bishkek

Almaty

Urumqi

Hohhot

Shenyang

N. KOREA

Pyongyang

JAPAN

Tokyo

AZERBAIJAN

Tabriz

TURKMENISTAN

Tashkent

Fergana

KYRGYZSTAN

Beijing

Jinxi

Seoul

Jiagu

Nagoya

Kyoto

Tehran

Ashgabat

Samarkand

Dushanbe

Tianjin

S. KOREA

Pusan

Kobe

Osaka

Hiroshima

PACIFIC OCEAN

Kermanshah

Mashhad

TAJIKISTAN

Taiyuan

Jinan

Qingdao

Fukuoka

Nagasaki

Esfahan

Herat

Claimed by India

Lanzhou

Xi'an

IRAN

Kerman

Kabul

Islamabad

Srinagar

CHINA

Hefei

Shanghai

Shiraz

AFGHANISTAN

Faisalabad

Wuhan

Persian Gulf

Multan

Chengdu

Chongqing

ama

BAHRAIN

Quetta

PAKISTAN

Lhasa

NEPAL

Thimphu

Fuzhou

Taipei

AR

Doha

Abu Dhabi

Delhi

Kanpur

Kathmandu

BHUTAN

Xiamen

Kao-hsiung

TAIWAN

Muscat

Karachi

BANGLADESH

Liuzhou

Guangzhou

Nanning

Macao

Hong Kong

OMAN

Arabian Sea

INDIA

Kolkata (Calcutta)

Dhaka

Chittagong

Mandalay

Hanoi

Luzon

Baguio

Quezon City

Nagpur

MYANMAR (BURMA)

LAOS

Manila

N

UNITED ARAB EMIRATES

Mumbai (Bombay)

Pune

Hyderabad

Nay Pyi Taw

Chiang Mai

Vientiane

Da Nang

PHILIPPINES

0 mi.

500 mi.

1,000 mi.

THAILAND

VIETNAM

Cebu

Bangalore

Chennai (Madras)

Bangkok

CAMBODIA

Phnom Penh

Ho Chi Minh City

Davao

0 km

500 km

1,000 km

Cochin

Madurai

Jaffna

INDIAN OCEAN

Colombo

SRI LANKA

Phuket

Songkhla

Bandar Seri Begawan

BRUNEI

Kota Kinabalu

Manado

Jayapura

MALDIVES

Male

Ipoh

Kuching

Serong

Irian Jaya

New Guinea

Medan

Kuala Lumpur

MALAYSIA

Borneo

Samarinda

Palu

Celebes

SINGAPORE

Pontianak

INDONESIA

Pakanbaru

Sumatra

Palembang

Banjarmasin

Ujungpandang

Wow Zone!

● **The Dead Sea, which lies between Israel and Jordan, is the lowest point on Earth. Its water is 5 to 10 times saltier than average seawater.**

● The Gobi Desert's terrain is mostly rocky, not sandy. The word *gobi* means "waterless place" in Mongolian.

● **Turkey, Azerbaijan, and Russia are located in both Asia and in Europe.**

The Great Wall of China is 4,160 miles (6,695 km) long and stands roughly 26 feet (8 m) high.

● China and India are the world's most populous countries.

● **Indonesia, which includes more than 17,000 islands, is the largest archipelago, or string of islands, in the world. It covers almost 742,000 square miles (2 million sq km).**

● Beginning in the 5th century B.C., Chinese groups built walls for protection against attacks. Joined together, these fortifications are known as the Great Wall of China. The Great Wall was not completed until the 16th century.

Eastern Russia

East of the Ural Mountains lies Eastern Russia, an enormous territory that stretches more than 5 million square miles (13 million sq km). Commonly called Siberia, the region covers the entire northern part of Asia. It takes up 75% of Russia, the largest country in the world, although fewer than 25% of Russia's people live there. Siberia alone is bigger than all of Canada.

Parts of Siberia can be forbiddingly cold. Two-thirds of the region is covered by permafrost, ground that is frozen year-round. The town of Verkhoyansk, in northeastern Russia, sits in the coldest part of the northern hemisphere. Though the average January temperature there is –58°F (–50°C), the temperature has dropped as low as –90°F (–68°C)! Most of Eastern Russia's population lives in the southern and western parts of the region, where the temperatures are milder. Novosibirsk, a chief city in Siberia and the third largest city in Russia, has an average temperature of 3°F (–16°C) in winter and about 68°F (20°C) in summer.

Though Siberia has few people, it has tremendous natural resources and abundant wildlife. Siberia is Russia's leading producer of gold and diamonds, and is rich in coal, oil, and gas. It is also the home of the only viable population of wild Siberian tigers.

The Trans-Siberian railroad links Moscow in western Russia and Vladivostok in the southeast of the country. A trip from end to end takes eight days!

Mir Mine, in Eastern Sibera, Russia, is one of the largest open-pit diamond mines in the world. Abandoned since 2004, it is 1,722 feet (525 m) deep and 3,900 feet (1,200 m) wide.

Lake Baykal, near the Mongolian border, is the deepest lake in the world. It is about the size of Belgium, and contains one-fifth of the world's freshwater.

Map labels:
A B
Novaya Zemlya Is.
Ka
Naryan Mar
Salekhard
Ural Mtns.
West
Siberian
Plain
3
Khanty-Mansiysk
Surgut
Ob R.
Nizhnevartovsk
Vasyugan Swamp
Kurgan
Irtysh R.
4
Omsk
Tom's
Astana
Novosibirsk
The Steppes
KAZAKHSTAN
5
Kazakh Uplands
Irtysh R.
Lake Balkhash
Almaty
6
Tian Mtns.
Urumqi
Taklimakan Desert
7
CHINA

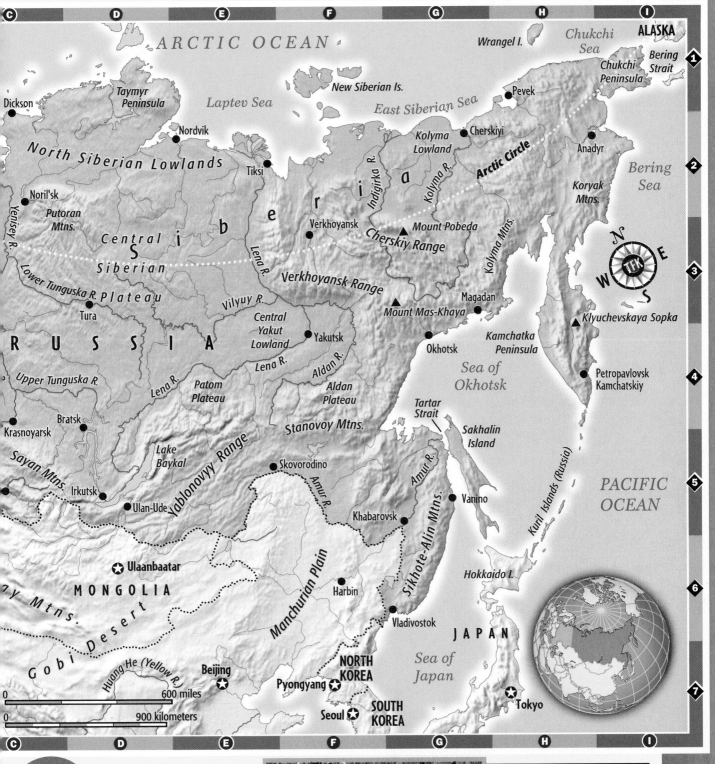

ARCTIC OCEAN

Wrangel I.
Chukchi Sea
ALASKA

Taymyr Peninsula
Laptev Sea
New Siberian Is.
East Siberian Sea
Pevek
Chukchi Peninsula
Bering Strait

Dickson
Nordvik

North Siberian Lowlands
Tiksi

Kolyma Lowland
Cherskiyi
Anadyr

Noril'sk
Putoran Mtns.
Yenisey R.

Siberia

Indigirka R.
Kolyma R.
Arctic Circle

Koryak Mtns.

Bering Sea

Central
Siberian
Plateau

Verkhoyansk
Mount Pobeda
Cherskiy Range

Kolyma Mtns.

Lower Tunguska R.

Tura

Vilyuy R.
Verkhoyansk Range

Mount Mas-Khaya
Magadan
Klyuchevskaya Sopka

Lena R.

Central Yakut Lowland
Yakutsk

Okhotsk
Kamchatka Peninsula

Petropavlovsk Kamchatskiy

Upper Tunguska R.
Lena R.
Aldan R.

Lena R.
Patom Plateau
Aldan Plateau

Sea of Okhotsk

R U S S I A

Bratsk
Krasnoyarsk

Stanovoy Mtns.

Tartar Strait

Sakhalin Island

Sayan Mtns.
Lake Baykal

Yablonovyy Range

Skovorodino

Amur R.

Kuril Islands (Russia)

PACIFIC OCEAN

Irkutsk
Ulan-Ude

Khabarovsk
Amur R.

Vanino

Sikhote-Alin Mtns.

Ulaanbaatar

Hokkaido I.

MONGOLIA

Manchurian Plain

Harbin

Vladivostok

J A P A N

Gobi Desert

Huang He (Yellow R.)
Beijing

NORTH KOREA

Pyongyang

Sea of Japan

Tokyo

0 600 miles
0 900 kilometers

Seoul
SOUTH KOREA

79

Did You Know?

- The Nenets people live in the polar region of northwestern Siberia, and are known for their traditional way of herding and breeding reindeer.

- In some parts of Eastern Russia, the permafrost is almost 1 mile (1.6 km) deep!

A Nenets woman shows off her decorated reindeer at an annual festival in Siberia, Russia.

- The word *siberia* comes from a Tartar word that means "sleeping land."

- Siberia is sometimes called Russia's Cupboard because of its vast natural resources.

- The tip of northeastern Russia is just 50 miles (80.5 km) from Alaska. The Bering Strait separates Russia from Alaska.

Turkey and Cyprus

The Grand Bazaar in Istanbul is Turkey's largest covered market. It houses around 5,000 shops.

Turkey, a nation about the size of the state of Texas, straddles the border between Europe and Asia. On its western border sit Greece and Bulgaria; to the south are Syria and Iraq; and to the east are Iran, Azerbaijan, Armenia, and Georgia. Turkey's unique location means that it is both European and Asian. For more than 4,000 years, it has served as a bridge between the two continents and many different civilizations. Its art, architecture, and customs reflect its complicated past.

Until 1923, Turkey was a Muslim territory under the Ottoman Empire. It was a preindustrial region, with few ties to the modern world. Then Kemal Atatürk, a Turkish soldier who had led a revolution to overthrow the Ottomans, became the leader of the Turkish nation. Atatürk changed many aspects of Turkish culture, including its alphabet, clothing styles, calendar, and relationship to the West.

Cyprus, an island off the coast of Turkey and Greece, has been fought over for centuries. In 1960, it became an independent nation whose government included both Turks and Greeks. Tension between the two nationalities grew until 1974, when conflict split the island into two parts. The Greek-led nation of Cyprus, not the Turkish Republic of Northern Cyprus, is considered to be the official government.

Turkey and Cyprus have a warm, dry climate and rely on farming for income, although both countries are becoming more industrialized.

Data Bank

CYPRUS
AREA: 3,572 sq mi (9,251 sq km)
POPULATION: 1,120,489
CAPITAL: Nicosia
LANGUAGES: Greek, Turkish, English

TURKEY
AREA: 302,535 sq mi (783,562 sq km)
POPULATION: 78,785,548
CAPITAL: Ankara
LANGUAGES: Turkish (official), Kurdish

From its first construction in 360 A.D., the Hagia Sophia, in Istanbul, Turkey, was the center for Orthodox Christianity. Once the Ottoman Empire took over in 1453, it served as the country's grand mosque. By 1935, it had been converted into a museum.

ROMANIA
Danube R.
Constanta
BULGARIA
Varna
Edirne
Bosp
Istanbul
Gallipoli
Sea of Marmara
Dardanelles
Burs
Bergama
Khios I.
Gediz R.
Izmir
Kucukmenderes R.
Deniz
GREECE
Kizla Peak
Rhodes (Greece)

UKRAINE

Sea of Azov

CRIMEA

Krasnodar

Black Sea

RUSSIA

N
W TFK E
S

Mt. Elbrus ▲

Grozny

Caucasus Mtns.

Gagra

Poti

Kutaisi

GEORGIA   Tbilisi ✪

Caspian Sea

Sinop

Samsun

Mount Kackar

Trabzon

Amasya

Koroglu Mtns.

Pontic Mtns.

Kumayri

ARMENIA

Mt. Aragats ▲

Gyandzhe

AZERBAIJAN

Kura R.

Kizil R.

Coruh R.

Yerevan ✪

Lake Sevan

Araks R.

Ankara ✪

TURKEY

Kelkit R.

Aras R.

Sivas

Erzurum

Mt. Ararat ▲

Dagi ▲

Anatolian Plateau

AZERBAIJAN

Mount Erciyas ▲

Kayseri

Seyhan R.

Murat R.

Lake Van

Egridir

Tuz Lake

Malatya

Eastern Taurus Mtns.

Tabriz

Beysehir Lake

Ceyhan R.

Diyarbakir

Batman

Uludoruk Peak ▲

Lake Urmia

Konya

Tigris R.

IRAN

Adana

Gaziantep

Taurus Mtns.

a

Aleppo

Antakya

Euphrates R.

Mosul

TURKISH SECTOR

Nicosia ✪

CYPRUS

Latakia

Hamah

SYRIA

IRAQ

Zagros Mtns.

Larnaca

GREEK SECTOR

Limassol

LEBANON

Beirut ✪

Syrian Desert

Baghdad ✪

Mediterranean Sea

Damascus ✪

Tigris R.

ISRAEL

JORDAN

| 0 | | 200 miles |
| 0 | | 300 kilometers |

Did You Know?

● Istanbul, the largest city in Turkey, is the only city in the world to straddle two continents. Istanbul has been called Byzantium and Constantinople, and was at one time the capital of the Ottoman Empire.

● In Greek mythology, the town of Paphos, in southwest Cyprus, is named as the birthplace of Aphrodite, the goddess of love.

● Cyprus has been inhabited for about 9,000 years. No wonder it's a favorite spot for archaeologists!

● Cappodocia (right) is a district of Turkey famous for its strange and beautiful rock formations. Created by volcanic activity and erosion, they were decorated with frescoes and other works of art.

● Turkish coffee is dark, thick, and sweet, and is served at almost every meal. A common Turkish dish is shish kebab—meat or seafood and vegetables cut into small chunks, threaded onto a skewer, and grilled.

Israel, Lebanon, Jordan, and Syria

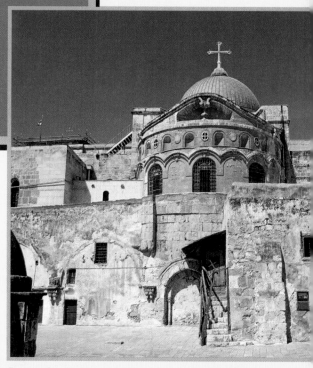

Israel, Lebanon, Jordan, and Syria are Middle Eastern lands of ancient cultures and archaeological treasures. Stretching from the banks of the Tigris River to the Gulf of Aqaba, the region has long been a crossroads of conquerors and Crusaders. Because the land is sacred to Judaism, Christianity, and Islam, it has also been at the center of centuries-old religious conflicts and political disputes.

Emperor Constantine commissioned the building of the Church of the Holy Sepulchre in Jerusalem, Israel, in the 4th century.

Many of the world's holiest sites are found in Israel. Jews pray at the 2,000-year-old Western Wall, in Jerusalem. Muslims pray at the golden Dome of the Rock mosque. Christians pray at the Church of the Holy Sepulchre, site of the tomb of Jesus.

The kingdom of Jordan is also known for its religious and archaeological sites. Petra, the best known of them, is an ancient city of elaborate temples and tombs carved completely from sandstone. Two thousand years ago, the city was a crossroads for the spice trade. Syria, which is to the north of Jordan, has one of the oldest recorded histories in the world. The country's capital, Damascus, has been inhabited since prehistoric times!

The Nabataean people settled Petra, hand chiseling almost 3,000 tombs, homes, banquet halls, and altars into the sandstone cliffs.

Lebanon lies between Israel and Syria. From 1975 to 1990, a civil war raged in Lebanon. Antigovernment protests took place in many cities in Lebanon, Syria, and Jordan, beginning in early 2011.

At the north end of the Old City, the Damascus Gate is one of seven entrances into the ancient walled city of Jerusalem, which is divided into quarters: Jewish, Christian, Muslim, and Armenian

Data Bank

ISRAEL
AREA: 8,522 sq mi (22,072 sq km)
POPULATION: 7,473,052
CAPITAL: Jerusalem
LANGUAGES: Hebrew, Arabic (both official), English

JORDAN
AREA: 34,495 sq mi (89,342 sq km)
POPULATION: 6,508,271
CAPITAL: Amman
LANGUAGES: Arabic (official), English

LEBANON
AREA: 4,015 sq mi (10,399 sq km)
POPULATION: 4,143,101
CAPITAL: Beirut
LANGUAGES: Arabic (official), French, English, Armenian

SYRIA
AREA: 71,498 sq mi (185,179 sq km)
POPULATION: 22,517,750
CAPITAL: Damascus
LANGUAGES: Arabic (official), Kurdish, Armenian, Aramaic, Circassian

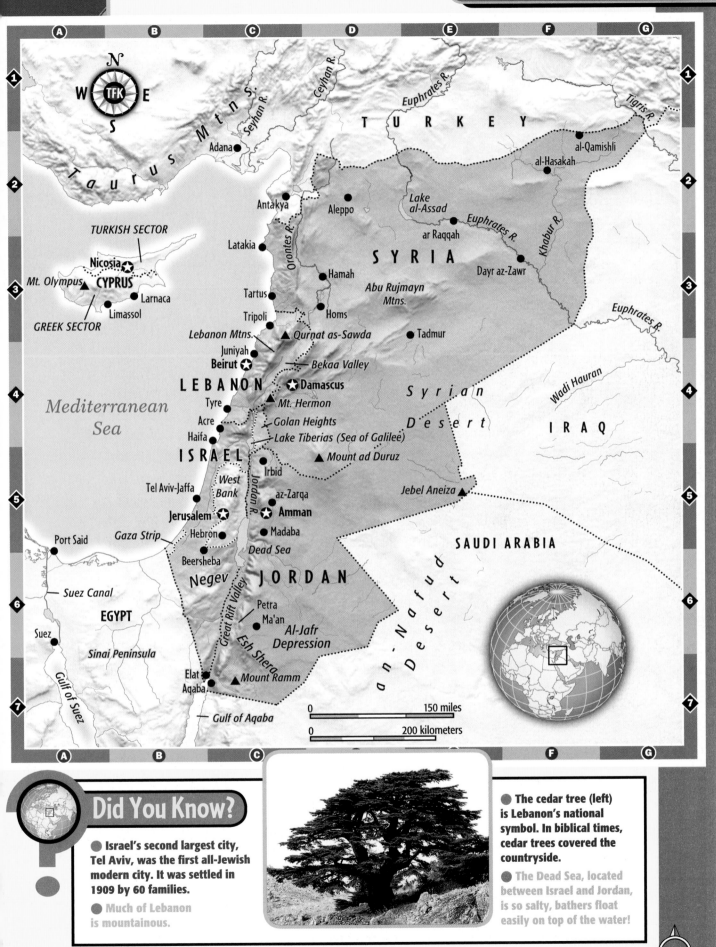

N
W TFK E
S

Taurus Mtns.

Seyhan R.
Ceyhan R.
Euphrates R.
Tigris R.

TURKEY

Adana

al-Qamishli

al-Hasakah

Antakya

Aleppo
Lake
al-Assad
Euphrates R.
Khabur R.

Latakia

SYRIA

ar Raqqah

Orontes R.

Dayr az-Zawr

Tartus

Hamah

Tripoli

Homs

Abu Rujmayn
Mtns.

Lebanon Mtns.
Qurnat as-Sawda

Tadmur

Juniyah
Beirut

Bekaa Valley

LEBANON

Damascus

Syrian

Tyre

Mt. Hermon

Acre
Golan Heights

Desert

IRAQ

Haifa
Lake Tiberias (Sea of Galilee)

ISRAEL
Mount ad Duruz

Wadi Hauran

Euphrates R.

Irbid

Tel Aviv-Jaffa
West
Bank
az-Zarqa
Jebel Aneiza

Jordan R.

Jerusalem
Amman

Gaza Strip
Madaba

Port Said
Hebron

SAUDI ARABIA

Beersheba

Dead Sea

Mediterranean
Sea

Negev

JORDAN

an-Nafud

Suez Canal

EGYPT

Great Rift Valley

Petra
Ma'an
Al-Jafr
Depression

Desert

Suez

Esh Shera

Sinai Peninsula

Gulf of Suez

Elat
Aqaba

Mount Ramm

Gulf of Aqaba

TURKISH SECTOR

Nicosia
CYPRUS

Mt. Olympus
Larnaca
Limassol
GREEK SECTOR

0   150 miles
0   200 kilometers

A B C D E F G
1 1
2 2
3 3
4 4
5 5
6 6
7 7

Did You Know?

● Israel's second largest city,
Tel Aviv, was the first all-Jewish
modern city. It was settled in
1909 by 60 families.

● Much of Lebanon
is mountainous.

● The cedar tree (left)
is Lebanon's national
symbol. In biblical times,
cedar trees covered the
countryside.

● The Dead Sea, located
between Israel and Jordan,
is so salty, bathers float
easily on top of the water!

The Arabian Peninsula

Medina, in Saudi Arabia, is one of Islam's holiest cities. Mecca is the other.

Windblown desert sands cover much of the Arabian Peninsula. The area's climate is generally hot and dry, and the vegetation is sparse. The Arabian Desert, which takes up a large part of Saudi Arabia, Kuwait, Qatar, the United Arab Emirates, and Oman, is the largest subtropical desert in the world. Only the Sahara is larger.

Beneath the desert sands lies a treasure—oil. The countries in this region are highly dependent on the petroleum industry. It has made many of them rich. However, oil has been both a blessing and a curse for Kuwait. In 1990, in a bid to gain control of Kuwait's lucrative oil fields, Iraq invaded its tiny neighbor. The United States and its allies intervened, and in January 1991, they used bombs and ground forces to set Kuwait free. In 2003, the United States went to war against Iraq again. Iraq's leader, Saddam Hussein, was executed for crimes against humanity in 2006.

At the tip of the Arabian Peninsula are Yemen and Oman. Although Yemen does not have the oil riches of its neighbors, its location—at the southern entrance to the Red Sea—is strategic. Qatar, Bahrain, and the United Arab Emirates lie on the Persian Gulf, along the west coast of Saudi Arabia. Bahrain is made up of small islands, and the United Arab Emirates is a union of seven kingdoms.

The Burj Khalifa, in Dubai, United Arab Emirates, is the tallest building in the world, standing 2,716.5 feet (828 m) high.

Data Bank

BAHRAIN
AREA: 286 sq mi (741 sq km)
POPULATION: 1,214,705
CAPITAL: Manama
LANGUAGES: Arabic, English, Farsi, Urdu

IRAQ
AREA: 169,235 sq mi (438,317 sq km)
POPULATION: 30,399,572
CAPITAL: Baghdad
LANGUAGES: Arabic, Kurdish, Assyrian, Armenian

KUWAIT
AREA: 6,880 sq mi (17,819 sq km)
POPULATION: 2,595,628
CAPITAL: Kuwait City
LANGUAGES: Arabic (official), English

OMAN
AREA: 119,499 sq mi (309,501 sq km)
POPULATION: 3,027,959
CAPITAL: Muscat
LANGUAGES: Arabic (official), English, Indian languages

QATAR
AREA: 4,473 sq mi (11,585 sq km)
POPULATION: 848,016
CAPITAL: Doha
LANGUAGES: Arabic (official), English

SAUDI ARABIA
AREA: 830,000 sq mi (2,149,690 sq km)
POPULATION: 26,131,703
CAPITAL: Riyadh
LANGUAGE: Arabic

UNITED ARAB EMIRATES
AREA: 32,278 sq mi (83,600 sq km)
POPULATION: 5,148,664
CAPITAL: Abu Dhabi
LANGUAGES: Arabic (official), Persian, English, Hindi, Urdu

YEMEN
AREA: 203,848 sq mi (527,964 sq km)
POPULATION: 24,133,492
CAPITAL: Sanaa
LANGUAGE: Arabic

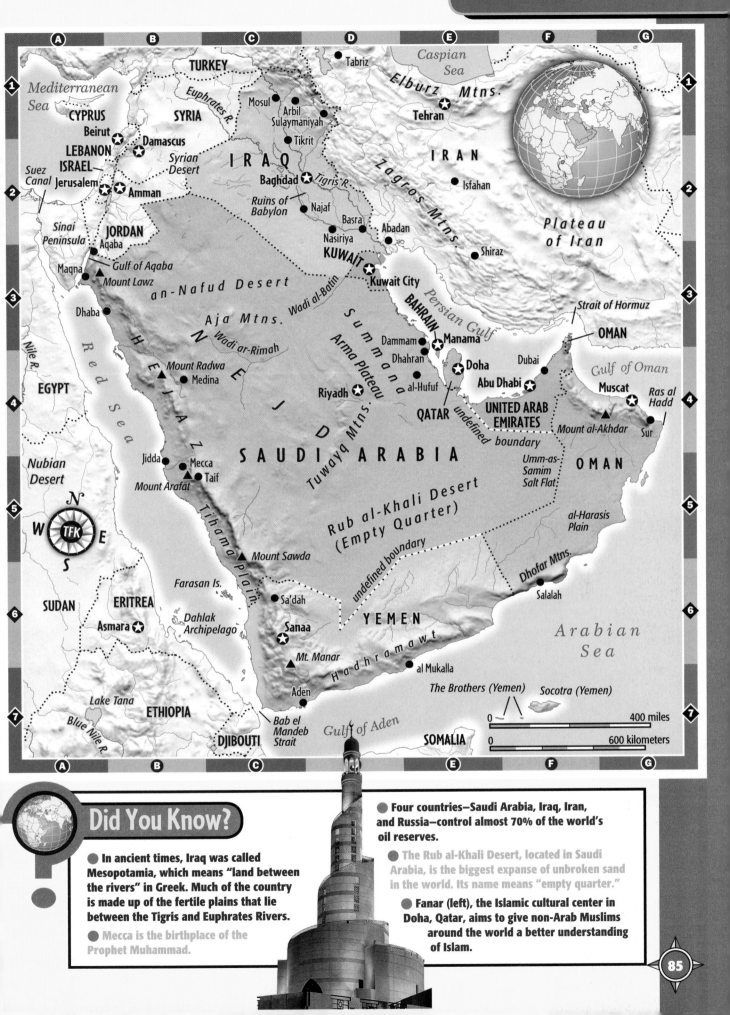

The Arabian Peninsula map

- Mediterranean Sea
- Caspian Sea
- TURKEY
- Elburz Mtns.
- Euphrates R.
- Mosul
- Arbil
- Sulaymaniyah
- Tabriz
- CYPRUS
- SYRIA
- Tehran
- IRAN
- Beirut
- Damascus
- LEBANON
- Tikrit
- IRAQ
- Syrian Desert
- ISRAEL
- Jerusalem
- Amman
- Baghdad
- Tigris R.
- Isfahan
- Zagros Mtns.
- Plateau of Iran
- Sinai Peninsula
- JORDAN
- Ruins of Babylon
- Najaf
- Basra
- Abadan
- Aqaba
- Nasiriya
- Shiraz
- Suez Canal
- Maqna
- Gulf of Aqaba
- Mount Lawz
- KUWAIT
- an-Nafud Desert
- Wadi al-Batin
- Kuwait City
- Persian Gulf
- Strait of Hormuz
- Dhaba
- Aja Mtns.
- Wadi ar-Rimah
- Summan
- BAHRAIN
- Dammam
- Manama
- OMAN
- Nile R.
- Red Sea
- H E J A Z
- N E J D
- Arma Plateau
- Dhahran
- Doha
- Dubai
- Gulf of Oman
- Mount Radwa
- Medina
- Riyadh
- al-Hufuf
- QATAR
- Abu Dhabi
- Muscat
- Ras al Hadd
- EGYPT
- Tuwayq Mtns.
- UNITED ARAB EMIRATES
- Mount al-Akhdar
- Sur
- Nubian Desert
- SAUDI ARABIA
- undefined boundary
- Jidda
- Mecca
- Mount Arafat
- Taif
- OMAN
- Umm-as-Samim Salt Flat
- Tihama Plain
- Rub al-Khali Desert (Empty Quarter)
- al-Harasis Plain
- Mount Sawda
- undefined boundary
- Farasan Is.
- Dhofar Mtns.
- SUDAN
- ERITREA
- Sa'dah
- Salalah
- Asmara
- Dahlak Archipelago
- Sanaa
- YEMEN
- Arabian Sea
- Mt. Manar
- Hadhramawt
- al Mukalla
- Lake Tana
- Blue Nile R.
- ETHIOPIA
- Aden
- The Brothers (Yemen)
- Socotra (Yemen)
- Bab el Mandeb Strait
- Gulf of Aden
- SOMALIA
- DJIBOUTI

N W E S — TFK (compass)

0 — 400 miles
0 — 600 kilometers

Did You Know?

● In ancient times, Iraq was called Mesopotamia, which means "land between the rivers" in Greek. Much of the country is made up of the fertile plains that lie between the Tigris and Euphrates Rivers.

● Mecca is the birthplace of the Prophet Muhammad.

● Four countries—Saudi Arabia, Iraq, Iran, and Russia—control almost 70% of the world's oil reserves.

● The Rub al-Khali Desert, located in Saudi Arabia, is the biggest expanse of unbroken sand in the world. Its name means "empty quarter."

● Fanar (left), the Islamic cultural center in Doha, Qatar, aims to give non-Arab Muslims around the world a better understanding of Islam.

85

Central Asia

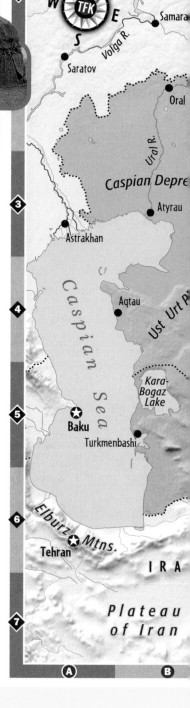

Central Asia, which includes the nations of Kazakhstan, Kyrgyzstan, Tajikistan, Turkmenistan, and Uzbekistan, stretches from Russia and the Ural Mountains all the way to China. To the south, Central Asia borders Iran, Afghanistan, Pakistan, and China. All the nations of Central Asia were once part of the Soviet Union. While the people here are very different from one another, many share a belief in Buddhism or Islam. Many are also nomads, traveling from place to place. The yurt, which is similar to a tent, is the traditional dwelling of these nomadic people.

A traditional yurt is made of latticed, or crisscrossed, pieces of wood. It is secured with belts.

Kazakhstan is the largest Central Asian nation. To the west are the Ural Mountains and their foothills. The remainder of the country includes deserts and vast plains called steppes. Kazakhstan is the most modernized of the Central Asian nations. Turkmenistan, the second largest nation in the region, is almost entirely covered by dry, grassy steppes and the huge Kara-Kum desert. Uzbekistan, like neighboring Turkmenistan, is largely desert and steppes.

The Pamir Mountains, in Tajikistan, are among the highest in the world. Two Central Asian mountain systems, the Tian Shan and the Pamirs, meet in Kyrgyzstan. As a result, it is a nation of peaks and valleys. Since Kyrgyzstan gained its independence in 1991, its economy has grown. Today, it is a major exporter of energy to other Central Asian nations.

Data Bank

KAZAKHSTAN
AREA: 1,052,090 sq mi
(2,724,900 sq km)
POPULATION: 15,522,373
CAPITAL: Astana
LANGUAGES: Russian (official), Kazakh

KYRGYZSTAN
AREA: 77,202 sq mi (199,952 sq km)
POPULATION: 5,587,443
CAPITAL: Bishkek
LANGUAGES: Kyrgyz, Russian (both official), Uzbek

TAJIKISTAN
AREA: 55,251 sq mi (143,099 sq km)
POPULATION: 7,627,200
CAPITAL: Dushanbe
LANGUAGES: Tajik (official), Russian

TURKMENISTAN
AREA: 188,455 sq mi (488,096 sq km)
POPULATION: 4,997,503
CAPITAL: Ashgabat
LANGUAGES: Turkmen, Russian, Uzbek, others

UZBEKISTAN
AREA: 172,740 sq mi
(447,395 sq km)
POPULATION: 28,128,600
CAPITAL: Tashkent
LANGUAGES: Uzbek, Russian, Tajik

Many peaks of the Pamir Mountains, in Tajikistan, reach higher than 20,000 feet (6,100 m).

C **D** **E** **F** **G** **H** **I**

RUSSIA

Ural Mountains

Magnitogorsk

Omsk

Novosibirsk

Tobol R.

Petropavl

Qostanay

Rudnyy

Ishim R.

tobe

Astana

Pavlodar

Irtysh R.

The Steppes

Lake Tengiz

Semey

Oskemen

MONGOLIA

KAZAKHSTAN

Qaraghandy

Kazakh Uplands

Zaysan Lake

Altay Mtns.

Balkhash

Aral

Sarysu R.

Betpaqdala Desert

Lake Balkhash

Taldyqorghan

Urumqi

Aral Sea

Lowlands

Syr Darya R.

Qyzylorda

Qaratau Mtns.

Chu R.

Muyun Kum Desert

Ili R.

Almaty

Pobeda Peak

Tarim R.

Nukus

ran

Amu Darya R.

Kyzyl Kum Desert

Shymkent

Zhambyl

Bishkek

Issyk-Kul

Tian Mountains

CHINA

Dashhowuz

Tashkent

KYRGYZSTAN

Andizhan

Taklimakan Desert

RKMENISTAN

Samarkand

Osh

ra-Kum Desert

Bukhara

Alay Range

Ismail Samani Peak (Communism Peak)

TAJIKISTAN

Pamirs

Ashgabat

Chardzhou

Dushanbe

Border claimed by China

TIBET

Kerki

Khorugh

Karakoram Range

Mazar-e Sharif

Border claimed by India

lashhad

PAKISTAN

Indus R.

JAMMU AND KASHMIR

Border claimed by India

AFGHANISTAN

Border claimed by India

Kabul

Khyber Pass

INDIA

Helmand R.

0   300 miles

0   400 kilometers

C **D** **E** **F** **G** **H** **I**

Did You Know?

● The Aral Sea was once the fourth largest lake in the world. As a result of devastating Soviet environmental policies, the lake has almost completely dried up, destroying the area's fishing industry and damaging its natural environment.

The hull of a ship rusts on dry land that used to be covered by the Aral Sea.

● Uzbekistan is one of the world's top producers of cotton.

● Kazakhstan is the largest landlocked country in the world.

● The Silk Road, an ancient trade route that once connected China to the Mediterranean, ran through Central Asia. Along the Silk Road, people traded wares, including gold, precious stones, ivory, and, of course, silk.

Afghanistan, Iran, and Pakistan

Pakistanis often customize their trucks and buses.

More than 2,000 years ago, the region now called Iran was the center of the Persian Empire. In 518 B.C., Darius I built an immense palace complex called Persepolis. Today, its ruins are an important archaeological site.

Rugged landscapes mark this part of the world. Much of Iran, Afghanistan, and Pakistan is covered by deserts or mountains, although Pakistan also has rich wetlands. An 800-mile (1,287 km) desert covers a large portion of Iran. The Hindu Kush, the world's third highest mountain range, reaches across landlocked Afghanistan into Pakistan. Iran, which lies west of Afghanistan and Pakistan, has a coast on the Caspian Sea to the north and on the Persian Gulf and Arabian Sea to the south. Pakistan, too, has a coast on the Arabian Sea.

All three countries are home to diverse ethnic and religious groups. The different cultures and beliefs have often been a source of tension. The region has struggled with civil unrest and acts of violence. In 2001, the United States went to war with Afghanistan's Taliban government in an effort to combat terrorism. Despite the ongoing conflict, the Afghan people have made some strides toward a democratic, more inclusive system of government. The new government lifted a ban on education for girls age 10 and older.

Data Bank

AFGHANISTAN
AREA: 251,827 sq mi (652,229 sq km)
POPULATION: 29,835,392
CAPITAL: Kabul
LANGUAGES: Afghan Persian (Dari), Pashto

IRAN
AREA: 636,372 sq mi (1,648,196 sq km)
POPULATION: 77,891,220
CAPITAL: Tehran
LANGUAGES: Persian, Turkic, Kurdish

PAKISTAN
AREA: 307,374 sq mi (796,095 sq km)
POPULATION: 187,342,721
CAPITAL: Islamabad
LANGUAGES: Urdu (official), Punjabi, Sindhi, Siraiki, Pashtu, others

Alexander the Great conquered Persepolis in 330 B.C. He carried away the palace's treasures using 20,000 mules and 5,000 camels.

KAZAKHSTAN

UZBEKISTAN

KAZAKHSTAN

Bishkek ✪

KYRGYZSTAN

Dashhowuz

Amu Darya R.

N W E S TFK

Tashkent ✪

CHINA

Caspian Sea

TURKMENISTAN

Kara-Kum Desert

Samarkand

Bukhara

Dushanbe ✪

Ismail Samani Peak ▲

Boundary claimed by India

Damavand (volcano)

Ashgabat ✪

Atrek R.

Kerki

Mazar-e Sharif

Baghlan

TAJIKISTAN

Karakoram Range

K2

Elburz Mtns.

Mashhad

Kunduz R.

Tirich Mir ▲

Nanga Parbat

Indus R.

ehran

Paropamisus Range

Hindu Kush Mtns.

Kabul ✪

Khyber Pass

JAMMU ▲

AND

Himalayas

Great Salt Desert

Hari R.

Mt. Fuladi ▲

Islamabad ✪

Srinagar ✪

KASHMIR

han

Herat

AFGHANISTAN

Peshawar

Rawalpindi

I R A N

Mt. Sangan ▲

Boundary claimed by Pakistan

lateau of Iran

Farah R.

Helmand R.

Chenab R.

Yazd

Margow Desert

Kandahar

Faisalabad

Lahore

s.

RIGESTAN

Multan

Amritsar

Kerman

Dasht-e-Lut

Quetta

Shiraz

Kuh-e Laleh Zar ▲

Zahedan

Sutlej R.

Bam

BALUCHISTAN

P A K I S T A N

I N D I A

Kuh-e Taftan (volcano) ▲

Baluchistan Plateau

Brahui Range

Indus R.

Thar Desert

Mehran R.

Bandar Abbas

Nal R.

Dadu

Strait of Hormuz

OMAN

Turbat

Great Indian Desert

Abu Dhabi ✪

Hyderabad

ITED ARAB EMIRATES

Gulf of Oman

Karachi

Muscat ✪

Ahmadabad

OMAN

Arabian Sea

0 — 400 miles

0 — 600 kilometers

Did You Know?

Indian Subcontinent

The Lotus Temple, in New Delhi, completed in 1986, is one of the most-visited monuments in India.

Chattering monkeys, brightly painted elephants, high-tech computer whizzes, and glamorous movie stars are all found in India. The world's seventh largest country is a vast and diverse land. From snowcapped mountains to leafy jungles and bustling cities, India offers a wealth of sights, smells, and sounds. India, which is predominantly Hindu, has on its northeast border the small, Muslim country of Bangladesh.

The Himalayas, the world's tallest mountains, form India's northern border. Nestled at the foot of the mammoth mountains are the tiny Buddhist kingdoms of Nepal and Bhutan. Despite their rugged setting, the two countries have much to offer. More than 9,500 species of birds can be found in Nepal. The majority of the people in Nepal and Bhutan work in the fields, raising crops or tending livestock. Tourism is an important industry. Nepal's Sherpas are famous for guiding mountain climbers up the steep slopes of Mount Everest and other forbidding peaks.

To India's south, in the Indian Ocean, sits the teardrop-shaped island nation of Sri Lanka. Although ethnic conflict has troubled the country for years, Sri Lanka's natural beauty beckons visitors. Sri Lanka is known for its lovely beaches, exotic wildlife, and large tea plantations.

The official flower of India is the lotus. It represents long life, fortune, and honor.

A Sherpa guides the way along Mount Everest in Nepal.

Data Bank

BANGLADESH
AREA: 55,598 sq mi (143,998 sq km)
POPULATION: 158,570,535
CAPITAL: Dhaka
LANGUAGES: Bangla (official), English

BHUTAN
AREA: 14,824 sq mi (38,394 sq km)
POPULATION: 708,427
CAPITAL: Thimphu
LANGUAGES: Dzongkha (official), others

INDIA
AREA: 1,269,219 sq mi (3,287,262 sq km)
POPULATION: 1,189,172,906
CAPITAL: New Delhi
LANGUAGES: Hindi, Bengali, Telugu, Marathi, others

MALDIVES
AREA: 115 sq mi (298 sq km)
POPULATION: 394,999
CAPITAL: Male
LANGUAGES: Dhivehi (official), English

NEPAL
AREA: 56,827 sq mi (147,181 sq km)
POPULATION: 29,391,883
CAPITAL: Kathmandu
LANGUAGES: Nepali, Maithali, Bhojpuri, others

SRI LANKA
AREA: 25,332 sq mi (65,610 sq km)
POPULATION: 21,283,913
CAPITAL: Colombo
LANGUAGES: Sinhala (official), Tamil, English

A **B** **C** **D** **E** **F** **G**

1 Boundary claimed by India
AFGHANISTAN
Karakoram Range
K2
Kun Lun Mtns.
CHINA
Helmand R.
Kabul
Peshawar
JAMMU
Boundary claimed by India
Yangtze R.
Islamabad
Srinagar
AND
KASHMIR
Boundary claimed by China
Lancang (Mekong) R.
Boundary claimed by Pakistan
Indus R.
Tibetan Plateau
Nu (Salween) R.
2 Lahore
Nanda Devi Peak
Himalayas
TIBET
Boundary claimed by China
PAKISTAN
Yarlung R.
Lhasa
Indus R.
Delhi
NEPAL
Mt. Everest
Thimphu
New Delhi
Annapurna
Kathmandu
BHUTAN
3 Thar Desert
Ganges R.
Indo-
Jumna R.
Jaipur
Lucknow
Gangetic
Brahmaputra R.
Jodhpur
Agra
Kanpur
Ganges R.
Irrawaddy R.
Karachi
Plain
Varanasi
Patna
Dhaka
4 Gulf of Kachchh
Ahmadabad
Vindhya Range
Narmada R.
Kolkata
(Calcutta)
BANGLADESH
MYANMAR
(BURMA)
Kathiawar
Peninsula
INDIA
Mahanadi R.
Deccan Plateau
Nay Pyi Taw
5 Arabian
Sea
Mumbai (Bombay)
Godavari R.
Western Ghats
Bhima R.
Hyderabad
Krishna R.
Eastern Ghats
Vishakhapatnam
Bay of
Bengal
Yangon
6 N
W TFK E
S
Mangalore
Bangalore
Coromandel Coast
Chennai (Madras)
Andaman
Islands
(India)
Laccadive Is.
(India)
Malabar Coast
Cochin
Pondicherry
Palk Strait
Madurai
Jaffna
7 INDIAN
OCEAN
Cape Comorin
Gulf of
Mannar
Kandy
SRI LANKA
Colombo
Dondra Head
MALDIVES
Nicobar
Islands
(India)

0 _____ 500 miles
0 _____ 750 kilometers

A **B** **C** **D** **E** **F** **G**

Did You Know?

● India and Sri Lanka are two of the top coconut-producing countries in the world.

● Bangladesh was known as East Pakistan until 1971, when the country gained its independence.

● One of the most famous monasteries in Bhutan is Taktsang Monastery (left), which sits on a cliff 2,953 feet (900 m) above the Paro valley in western Bhutan.

● India is the world's largest democracy. In the past 10,000 years, it has never invaded another country.

China, Mongolia, and Taiwan

China is a country of giant landmass and giant population. One out of every five people on the planet lives in China. That's more than any other country. The country's varied landscapes include towering mountains, barren deserts, and lush valleys. China is also home to busy cities and gleaming skyscrapers.

Through 2,200 years of recorded history, the Chinese have developed rich traditions in food, festivals, art, and medicine. China has seen the rise and fall of eight great dynasties, or ruling families. In 1949, the country embraced a form of government called Communism. Many nationalists, who resisted the change, fled to the island of Taiwan. China insists that Taiwan is not a separate country but belongs to the mainland. Fewer than 25 countries recognize Taiwan as an independent country.

The Gobi Desert, a huge expanse of rocks and dry grasslands, extends north from China into Mongolia. A landlocked nation, Mongolia has harsh winters and little vegetation. It gained its independence from China in 1921, and is currently one of Asia's most sparsely populated countries.

The third tallest television-and-radio tower in the world is the Oriental Pearl Tower, in Shanghai, China.

Zhangjiajie National Forest Park, in China, is most notable for its 243 quartz sandstone peaks, each standing taller than 3,280 feet (1,000 m).

Data Bank

CHINA
AREA: 3,705,407 sq mi (9,596,960 sq km)
POPULATION: 1,336,718,015
CAPITAL: Beijing
LANGUAGES: Chinese (Mandarin), local dialects

MONGOLIA
AREA: 603,909 sq mi (1,564,117 sq km)
POPULATION: 3,133,318
CAPITAL: Ulaanbaatar
LANGUAGES: Khalkha Mongol, Turkic, Russian

TAIWAN
AREA: 13,892 sq mi (35,980 sq km)
POPULATION: 23,071,779
CAPITAL: Taipei
LANGUAGES: Chinese (Mandarin), Taiwanese, Hakka dialects

A   B

KAZAKHSTAN
Bishkek
KYRGYZSTAN
Victory
Kashi   Tarim R.
Taklimakan De
K2
JAMMU & KASHMIR   Kun
Border claim by China
Indus R.   Tibe
Himalaya
New Delhi
NEPAL
Kathmandu
Ganges R.   Mt. Eve
INDIA

RUSSIA

Lake Baykal

Yenisey R.
Irkutsk
Selenga R.
Amur R.

Lake Uvs
Hangayn Mtns.
Darhan
Kerulen R.
Harbin
Songhua R.

Ulaanbaatar
Choybalsan
MANCHURIA
Lake Khanka

Altay Mtns.
MONGOLIA
Great Hinggan Range
Vladivostok

Urumqi

Shenyang
NORTH KOREA
Sea of Japan

XINJIANG
Gobi Desert
The Great Wall
Yalu R.

Yumen
Hohhot
Huang He
Baotou
Beijing
Pyongyang

ltun Mtns.
Mu Us Desert
Tianjin
Bo Hai
Seoul
SOUTH KOREA

Mtns.
Qinghai Lake
Xining
Huang He (Yellow R.)
Jinan
Qingdao
Yellow Sea
JAPAN

Lanzhou
Wei R.
North China Plain
Hongze Hu

ateau
Yangtze R.
CHINA
Xian
Zhengzhou
East China Sea

BET
Lancang (Mekong) R.
Nanjing
Shanghai

Nu (Salween) R.
Yangtze R.
Wuhan
Tai Hu

Lhasa
Yarlung R.
Chengdu
Hangzhou

Thimphu
Gongga Peak
Chongqing
Yuan R.
Changsha
Gan R.

BHUTAN
Border claimed by China
Dalou Mtns.
Wuyi Mtns.
Fuzhou
Ryukyu Islands (Japan)

aka
Kunming
Guilin
Taipei
PACIFIC OCEAN

ADESH
Hongshui R.
Guangzhou
Taiwan Strait
TAIWAN

MYANMAR (BURMA)
Red R.
Nanning
Hong Kong
Macau
Special Administrative Regions

Nay Pyi Taw
VIETNAM
Hanoi

Bay of Bengal
LAOS
Haikou
South China Sea
0   500 miles
0   750 kilometers

THAILAND
Vientiane
Gulf of Tonkin
Hainan I.

N
W   TFK   E
S

Did You Know?

● The Grand Canal, which runs from Beijing to Hangzhou in China, is the longest and oldest man-made river in the world. Parts of the canal were built almost 2,500 years ago.

● Two-humped camels, or Bactrian camels, originated in Mongolia.

● About 385 species of animals are threatened in China, including the giant panda, the South China tiger, and the crowned crane.

● In 1997, the former British colony of Hong Kong became part of China.

● Peking opera (left) is an art form that combines traditional opera, ballet, acrobatics, theater, martial arts, and mime. It has been performed in China for more than 200 years.

Japan, North Korea, and South Korea

O ff the southeast coast of Asia, in the North Pacific Ocean, lie the islands of Japan. The country is made up of four main islands and 3,900 smaller islands. It is situated in an area known as the Ring of Fire, which is a hot spot known for volcanic eruptions and earthquakes—including a devastating trembler in 2011. Most of the country is made up of volcanic mountains.

Japan has been inhabited for more than 10,000 years, and has a tradition of fine arts. For centuries, artists have painted beautiful portraits and scenes on silks and ceramics. In homes and parks, exquisite gardens feature delicately pruned plants. Japan is also an economic superpower. Tokyo, Japan's capital and largest city, is one of the most important business centers in the world.

Opened in 1980, the N Seoul Tower, in South Korea, is a communications and observation tower that offers visitors a panoramic view of the city.

Not far to Japan's north, the Korean peninsula juts off the mainland of Asia. Through war and peace, Japan and Korea have been closely linked. In 1904, the Japanese invaded Korea and, in 1910, made Korea a Japanese territory. In 1945, following World War II, the Allies separated Japan and Korea and split the Korean peninsula into two separate nations. Today, though sharing a common heritage, North and South Korea remain two distinct and very different countries.

A woman shows off an example of traditonal Japanese dress.

Japan has had a strong influence on the culture of Korea. So, too, has China, which borders North Korea. Yet the peninsula retains its own language, traditions, and cuisine.

Data Bank

JAPAN
AREA: 145,914 sq mi (377,916 sq km)
POPULATION: 126,475,664
CAPITAL: Tokyo
LANGUAGE: Japanese

NORTH KOREA
AREA: 46,540 sq mi (120,538 sq km)
POPULATION: 24,457,492
CAPITAL: Pyongyang
LANGUAGE: Korean

SOUTH KOREA
AREA: 38,502 sq mi (99,720 sq km)
POPULATION: 48,754,657
CAPITAL: Seoul
LANGUAGE: Korean

At 12,388 feet (3,776 m), Mount Fuji is Japan's tallest mountain. It is a volcano that has not erupted since 1707.

Did You Know?

● The people of Korea come from huge clans. Throughout Korea, there are only about a dozen last names.

● According to legend, Japan's islands were formed from the tears of a goddess.

● The Japanese classic *The Tale of Genji*, by Murasaki Shikibu, is considered the world's first novel.

Tokyo has a tightly packed population of 2,293 people per square mile (5,937 per sq km).

● Japan's capital city, Tokyo, has a population of more than 13 million people.

● The world's first cloned dog, Snuppy, an Afghan hound, was created at Seoul National University, in South Korea.

● Chuseok, an important harvest festival in South Korea, is also a time for families to gather to honor their ancestors.

95

Southeast Asia

Southeast Asia is a tropical peninsula covered by thick forests, mighty rivers, fertile plains, and tall mountains. For most of its residents, farming is a way of life. Rice is the region's most important crop. It is grown in flooded rice paddies on the plains and on stair-like green terraces on mountain slopes. Bangkok, Thailand, is a teeming commercial center, a mixture of modern skyscrapers and bicycle taxis, ancient temples, and brightly colored floating markets.

Visitors take elephant taxis to view Thailand's scenery and sights.

A worker plants rice in a paddy in Vietnam.

For many older Americans, Vietnam brings to mind images of war. But the country is also a land of spectacular scenery. From the Red River delta in the north to the Mekong delta in the south, Vietnam is a patchwork of rushing rivers, sandy coastlines, and brilliant green paddy fields.

Vietnam, Cambodia, and Laos have historic ties to France. Myanmar, previously called Burma, was once controlled by Britain. Of the countries in this region, only Thailand was never a European colony. In recent years, Southeast Asia has been plagued by wars and civil unrest. Today, these small countries are slowly rebuilding and attracting more tourists and foreign companies.

Data Bank

CAMBODIA
AREA: 69,900 sq mi (181,040 sq km)
POPULATION: 14,701,717
CAPITAL: Phnom Penh
LANGUAGES: Khmer (official), French, English

LAOS
AREA: 91,429 sq mi (236,800 sq km)
POPULATION: 6,477,211
CAPITAL: Vientiane
LANGUAGES: Lao (official), French, English, ethnic languages

MYANMAR (BURMA)
AREA: 261,228 sq mi (676,577 sq km)
POPULATION: 53,999,804
CAPITAL: Nay Pyi Taw
LANGUAGES: Burmese, minority languages

THAILAND
AREA: 198,117 sq mi (513,121 sq km)
POPULATION: 66,720,153
CAPITAL: Bangkok
LANGUAGES: Thai, English

VIETNAM
AREA: 127,881 sq mi (331,210 sq km)
POPULATION: 90,549,390
CAPITAL: Hanoi
LANGUAGES: Vietnamese (official), English, French, Chinese, Khmer, others

Did You Know?

● Most of Laos is covered by forest. The country's nickname is the Land of One Million Elephants.

● Vietnam produces about 52.8 million gallons (200 million L) of fish sauce a year.

● The world's smallest mammal is the bumblebee bat, found in Thailand.

● Thingyan is a celebration of the New Year in Myanmar. It is a water festival that usually falls in mid-April. There are feasts and performances, and people splash water on one another.

The Wat Rong Khun temple, in Chiang Rai, Thailand, is all white, and decorated with pieces of mirrored glass.

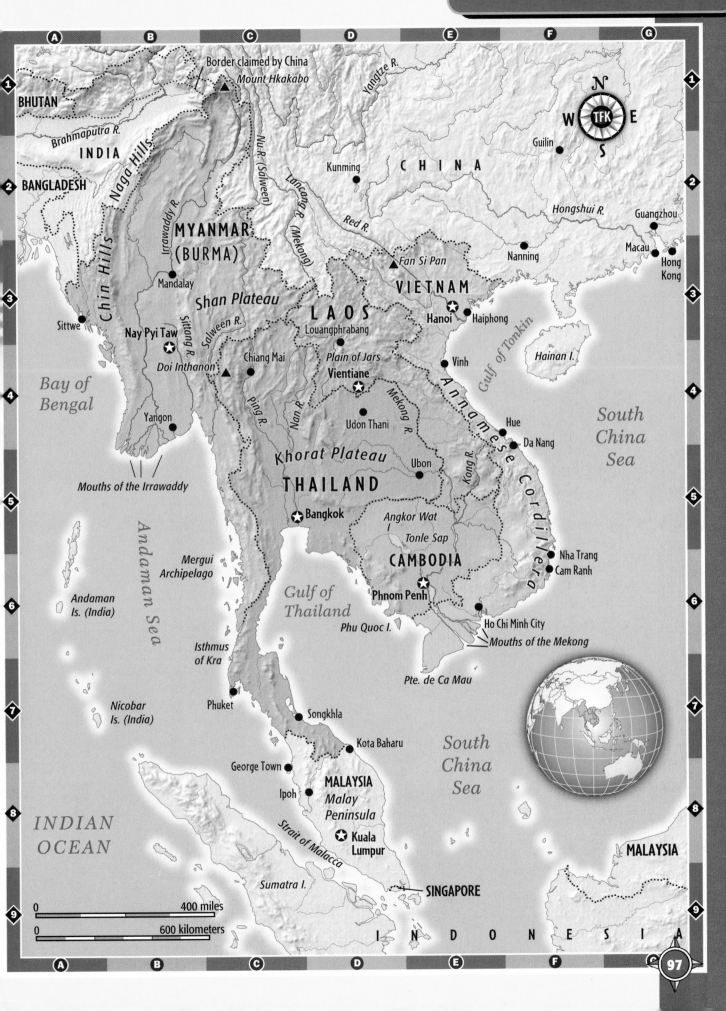

BHUTAN

Border claimed by China
Mount Hkakabo

Brahmaputra R.

INDIA

Yangtze R.

C H I N A

BANGLADESH

Naga Hills

Kunming

Hongshui R.

Guangzhou

Irrawaddy R.

MYANMAR
(BURMA)

Nu R. (Salween)

Lancang R. (Mekong)

Red R.

Nanning

Macau

Hong
Kong

Chin Hills

Mandalay

Fan Si Pan

VIETNAM

Shan Plateau

LAOS

Louangphrabang

Hanoi

Haiphong

Gulf of Tonkin

Hainan I.

Sittwe

Salween R.

Sittang R.

Nay Pyi Taw

Chiang Mai

Doi Inthanon

Plain of Jars

Vientiane

Vinh

Ping R.

Nan R.

Mekong R.

Bay of
Bengal

Udon Thani

Hue

Da Nang

South
China
Sea

Khorat Plateau

Ubon

Kong R.

Annamese Cordillera

Yangon

THAILAND

Mouths of the Irrawaddy

Andaman Sea

Mergui
Archipelago

Bangkok

Angkor Wat

Tonle Sap

Nha Trang

Cam Ranh

Andaman
Is. (India)

Gulf of
Thailand

CAMBODIA

Phu Quoc I.

Phnom Penh

Ho Chi Minh City

Mouths of the Mekong

Nicobar
Is. (India)

Isthmus
of Kra

Pte. de Ca Mau

Phuket

Songkhla

South
China
Sea

Kota Baharu

George Town

Ipoh

MALAYSIA

Malay
Peninsula

MALAYSIA

INDIAN
OCEAN

Strait of Malacca

Kuala
Lumpur

Sumatra I.

SINGAPORE

0   400 miles

0   600 kilometers

I N D O N E S I A

Maritime Southeast Asia

The sea is a major part of this region's geography. Indonesia is the world's largest archipelago, or group of islands. It is made up of about 17,000 islands, with people living on 6,000 of them. The Philippines is made up of more than 7,000 islands. Since the end of World War II, many newly independent nations have emerged in the region. Brunei, Malaysia, and Singapore used to be part of the British Empire. The Philippines was ruled by Spain until 1898, when it became a U.S. possession. The nation gained its independence in 1946. Indonesia was once part of the Netherlands. East Timor did not come into existence until 2002.

Indonesia has more active volcanoes than any other country in the world. One of its most famous active volcanoes is Mount Bromo in East Java.

Much of the region is rain forest, and wildlife is abundant. Malaysia is divided into two areas, one on the Malay Peninsula and the other on the island of Borneo, where elephants, tigers, and orangutans roam. The small nation of Brunei is also located on Borneo. Brunei is made up of two separate areas surrounded by Malaysia and the South China Sea.

Off the tip of the Malay Peninsula lies Singapore. The modern island nation, which gained independence from Malaysia in 1965, boasts one of Asia's best public-transportation systems.

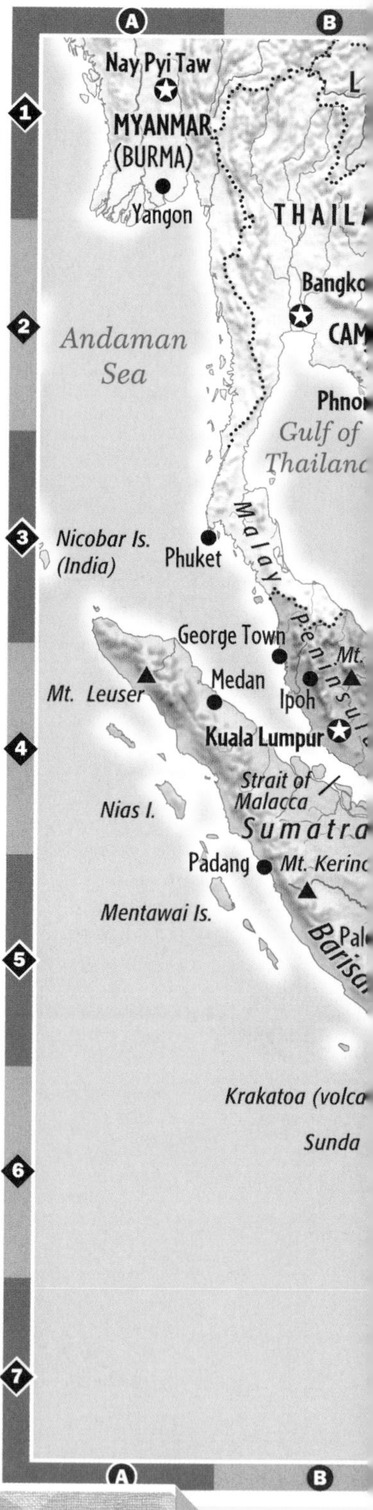

A
B
1
2
3
4
5
6
7
Nay Pyi Taw
MYANMAR (BURMA)
Yangon
THAIL
Bangko
CAM
Andaman Sea
Phno
Gulf of Thailanc
Malay Peninsula
Nicobar Is. (India)
Phuket
George Town
Mt.
Medan
Ipoh
Mt. Leuser
Kuala Lumpur
Strait of Malacca
Nias I.
Sumatra
Padang
Mt. Kerinc
Mentawai Is.
Pal
Barisa
Krakatoa (volca
Sunda

Data Bank

BRUNEI
AREA: 2,228 sq mi (5,770 sq km)
POPULATION: 401,890
CAPITAL: Bandar Seri Begawan
LANGUAGES: Malay (official), English, Chinese

EAST TIMOR
AREA: 5,743 sq mi (14,874 sq km)
POPULATION: 1,177,834
CAPITAL: Dili
LANGUAGES: Tetum, Portuguese (both official), Indonesian, English

INDONESIA
AREA: 735,358 sq mi (1,904,568 sq km)
POPULATION: 245,613,043
CAPITAL: Jakarta
LANGUAGES: Bahasa Indonesian, English, Dutch, local dialects

MALAYSIA
AREA: 127,355 sq mi (329,848 sq km)
POPULATION: 28,728,607
CAPITAL: Kuala Lumpur
LANGUAGES: Bahasa Melaysia (official), English, Chinese, Malayalam, others

PHILIPPINES
AREA: 115,830 sq mi (299,998 sq km)
POPULATION: 101,833,938
CAPITAL: Manila
LANGUAGES: Filipino, English (both official), others

SINGAPORE
AREA: 269 sq mi (697 sq km)
POPULATION: 4,740,737
CAPITAL: Singapore
LANGUAGES: Chinese (Mandarin), English, Malay, Hokkien, others

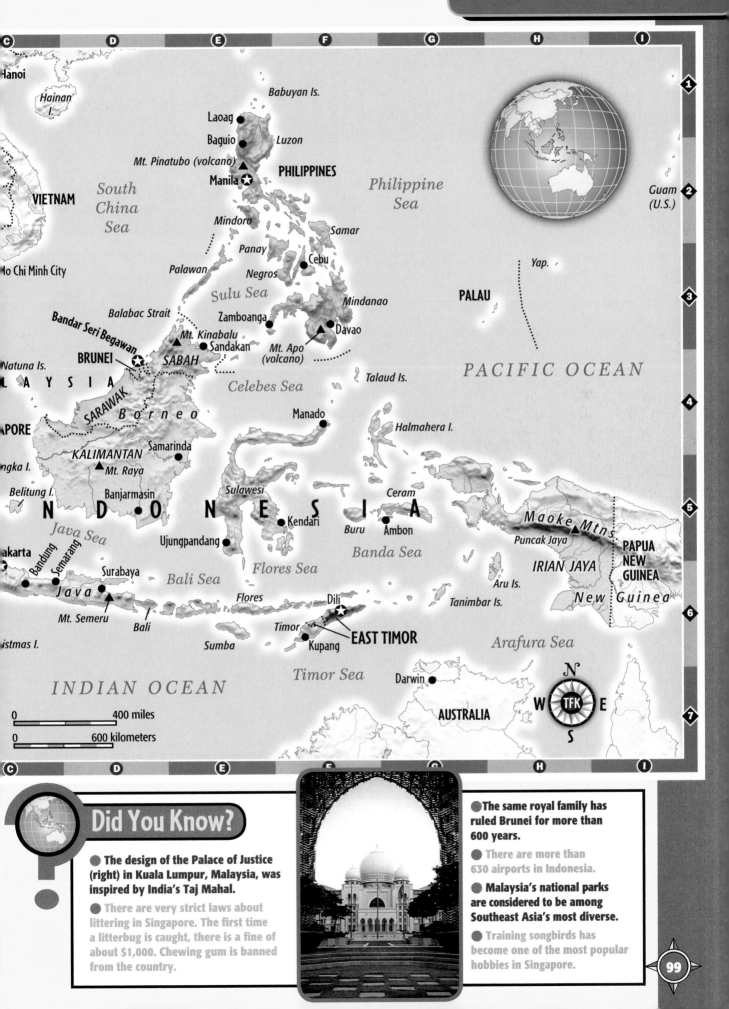

Hanoi

Hainan I.

VIETNAM

South China Sea

Ho Chi Minh City

Babuyan Is.

Laoag

Baguio   Luzon

Mt. Pinatubo (volcano)

Manila   PHILIPPINES

Philippine Sea

Mindoro

Samar

Panay   Cebu

Negros

Palawan

Sulu Sea   Mindanao

Balabac Strait   Zamboanga

Bandar Seri Begawan   Mt. Kinabalu

BRUNEI   Sandakan   Davao

Natuna Is.   SABAH   Mt. Apo (volcano)

LAYSIA   SARAWAK

Celebes Sea   Talaud Is.

PORE   Borneo

KALIMANTAN   Manado   Halmahera I.

Samarinda

ngka I.   Mt. Raya

Belitung I.   Banjarmasin   Sulawesi   Ceram

N D O N E S I A

Kendari   Buru   Ambon

Java Sea   Ujungpandang

akarta   Bandung   Semarang   Banda Sea

Surabaya   Flores Sea

Java   Bali Sea

Mt. Semeru   Bali   Flores   Dili

istmas I.   Sumba   Timor   EAST TIMOR

Kupang

INDIAN OCEAN   Timor Sea

Darwin

AUSTRALIA

PALAU   Yap.

PACIFIC OCEAN

Maoke Mtns.
Puncak Jaya   PAPUA NEW GUINEA

IRIAN JAYA   New Guinea

Aru Is.

Tanimbar Is.

Arafura Sea

Guam (U.S.)

0   400 miles
0   600 kilometers

N
W TFK E
S

C D E F G H I
1 2 3 4 5 6 7

Africa

The world's second largest continent, Africa, is surrounded by water. To the west of Africa lies the Atlantic Ocean; to the east is the Indian Ocean; to the north is the Mediterranean Sea; and to the northeast is the Red Sea. Many islands and island chains, including Madagascar and Seychelles, are part of the African continent.

A pair of giraffes cross an African savanna.

The central part of Africa is one big, flat plain. There, lying across the warm equator, are Africa's rain forests and savannas, or grasslands. On the continent's far north and far south are mountain ranges, deserts, and coastal areas. The vast Sahara desert, in North Africa, separates North Africa from the area known as sub-Saharan Africa.

African elephants are the largest land mammals in the world.

Africa is known for its wide range of amazing wildlife. There are camels in the north, penguins in the south, gorillas in the forests, and lions and giraffes on the savannas. The island of Madagascar, which separated from the African mainland millions of years ago, is home to many unique species of mammals and amphibians.

There are about a billion people in Africa, and they speak more than 2,000 different languages and live in 53 different nations. The African population is growing quickly. Some of the biggest cities in the world are found on the continent, though most people live in rural areas.

Continent Facts

NUMBER OF COUNTRIES: 53 countries–Algeria, Angola, Benin, Botswana, Burkina Faso, Burundi, Cameroon, Cape Verde, Central African Republic, Chad, Comoros, Congo (Democratic Republic of the), Congo (Republic of the), Côte d'Ivoire, Djibouti, Egypt, Equatorial Guinea, Eritrea, Ethiopia, Gabon, Gambia, Ghana, Guinea, Guinea-Bissau, Kenya, Lesotho, Liberia, Libya, Madagascar, Malawi, Mali, Mauritania, Mauritius, Morocco, Mozambique, Namibia, Niger, Nigeria, Rwanda, São Tomé and Príncipe, Senegal, Seychelles, Sierra Leone, Somalia, South Africa, Sudan, Swaziland, Tanzania, Togo, Tunisia, Uganda, Zambia, Zimbabwe

AREA: 11.7 million sq mi (30.3 million sq km)

LONGEST RIVER: The Nile, 4,241 miles (6,825 km)

LONGEST MOUNTAIN RANGE: Atlas Mountain Range in North Africa, about 400 miles (644 km)

HIGHEST PEAK: Mount Kilimanjaro, in Tanzania, 19,340 ft (5,895 m)

LARGEST LAKE: Victoria, 26,828 sq mi (69,484 sq km)

DEEPEST LAKE: Tanganyika, the second deepest lake in the world, has a maximum depth of 4,710 feet (1,436 m).

Wow Zone!

● Victoria Falls (right) on the Zambezi River, in Zimbabwe, is 355 feet (108 m) high and 5,500 feet (1,676 m) wide. It is twice as tall as Niagara Falls.

● The country of Lesotho is surrounded on all sides by South Africa.

● Once populous throughout much of Africa, Asia, and Europe, African lions are now found only in parts of sub-Saharan Africa, except for a small number of Asian lions found only in India's Gir Forests.

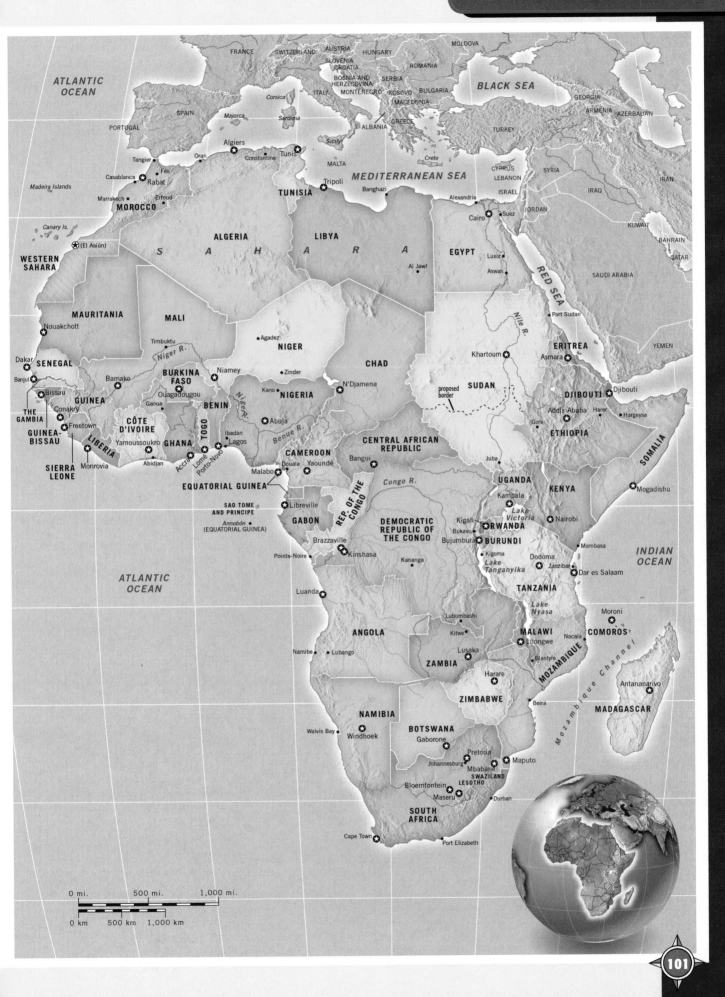

ATLANTIC OCEAN

FRANCE
SWITZERLAND AUSTRIA HUNGARY
SLOVENIA CROATIA ROMANIA
ITALY BOSNIA AND SERBIA
HERZEGOVINA MONTENEGRO KOSOVO BULGARIA
ALBANIA MACEDONIA
GREECE

MOLDOVA

BLACK SEA

GEORGIA
ARMENIA AZERBAIJAN

Corsica
Majorca
Sardinia

SPAIN
PORTUGAL

Crete
MALTA

TURKEY

CYPRUS
LEBANON
ISRAEL
JORDAN

SYRIA

IRAN

IRAQ

Tangier
Casablanca
Rabat
Fes
Erfoud
Marrakech

Algiers
Oran
Constantine
Tunis

Sicily

MEDITERRANEAN SEA

Tripoli
Banghazi

TUNISIA

Alexandria
Cairo
Suez

KUWAIT

BAHRAIN
QATAR

Madeira Islands

MOROCCO

Luxor
Aswan

SAUDI ARABIA

YEMEN

Canary Is.

WESTERN
SAHARA

(El Aaiún)

ALGERIA

LIBYA

EGYPT

Al Jawf

RED SEA

S   A   H   A   R   A

Port Sudan

MAURITANIA

MALI

NIGER

CHAD

Khartoum

ERITREA
Asmara

DJIBOUTI
Djibouti

Nouakchott

Timbuktu

Agadez

proposed
border

SUDAN

Dakar
SENEGAL
Banjul
Bamako
BURKINA
FASO
Niamey
Zinder

Kano
NIGERIA

N'Djamena

Addis Ababa
Gore

Harer
Hargeysa

THE
GAMBIA
Bissau
GUINEA
Conakry
Ouagadougou
Gaoua
BENIN
Ibadan
Abuja
Benue R.

CENTRAL AFRICAN
REPUBLIC

Juba

ETHIOPIA

SOMALIA

GUINEA-
BISSAU
Freetown
CÔTE
D'IVOIRE
Yamoussoukro
GHANA
TOGO
Lagos
Lomé
Porto-Novo

CAMEROON
Douala
Yaoundé

Bangui

Mogadishu

LIBERIA
SIERRA
LEONE
Monrovia
Abidjan
Accra

Malabo

UGANDA
Kampala
KENYA

EQUATORIAL GUINEA

REP. OF THE
CONGO

Congo R.

Lake
Victoria

Nairobi

SAO TOME
AND PRINCIPE

Libreville

GABON

Kigali RWANDA
Bukavu
Bujumbura BURUNDI

Mombasa

Annobón
(EQUATORIAL GUINEA)

DEMOCRATIC
REPUBLIC OF
THE CONGO

Kigoma
Lake
Tanganyika

Dodoma
Zanzibar

INDIAN
OCEAN

Brazzaville
Pointe-Noire
Kinshasa

Kananga

TANZANIA

Dar es Salaam

ATLANTIC
OCEAN

Luanda

Lubumbashi

Lake
Nyasa

Moroni

COMOROS

Kitwe
ANGOLA
MALAWI
Lilongwe
Nacala

Namibe
Lubango
ZAMBIA
Lusaka
Blantyre

MOZAMBIQUE

Mozambique Channel

Harare

Walvis Bay
NAMIBIA
Windhoek

BOTSWANA
Gaborone

ZIMBABWE
Beira

MADAGASCAR
Antananarivo

Pretoria
Johannesburg
Mbabane
SWAZILAND
Maputo

Bloemfontein
LESOTHO
Maseru

Durban

SOUTH
AFRICA

Cape Town
Port Elizabeth

0 mi.   500 mi.   1,000 mi.

0 km   500 km   1,000 km

Northeastern Africa

The Great Sphinx, in Egypt, has a human head and a lion's body. It is 240 feet (73 m) long and 66 feet (20 m) tall. For centuries, the monument was buried under sand.

K hartoum, the capital of Sudan, stands at the crossroads of the Blue Nile and the White Nile. The two rivers converge to form the Nile, the world's longest river. The Nile flows through Sudan and Egypt. The river's waters are precious to the area's people, who live and work near its banks. Nearly 95% of Egypt is desert.

Almost 5,000 years ago, Egypt had already established one of the world's most advanced civilizations. Ancient Egyptians mastered a new writing system, unique art forms, and grand architecture. In neighboring Nubia, which today is part of Sudan, another great civilization flourished. There, archaeologists have found beautiful ceramic figurines and bowls that date from at least 8,000 B.C. That's 3,000 years older than any known Egyptian object!

Most people in northern Sudan are Arab Muslims, and most residents of southern Sudan are black Africans of other faiths. This has led to many conflicts over the last 50 years. In January 2011, citizens in southern Sudan voted to become independent from the North. To the east of Sudan lie Eritrea and Ethiopia, which is sub-Saharan Africa's oldest country. Until recently, both countries were involved in costly and destructive border clashes.

Harsh weather conditions and drought play important roles in the lives of the people of the region. Djibouti, which lies at the edge of the Red Sea, is mostly desert. Many parts of Somalia receive less than 1 quart (about 1 L) of rain a year.

Data Bank

DJIBOUTI
AREA: 8,958 sq mi (23,201 sq km)
POPULATION: 757,074
CAPITAL: Djibouti
LANGUAGES: French, Arabic (both official), Somali, Afar

EGYPT
AREA: 386,660 sq mi (1,001,445 sq km)
POPULATION: 82,079,636
CAPITAL: Cairo
LANGUAGE: Arabic (official)

ERITREA
AREA: 45,406 sq mi (117,601 sq km)
POPULATION: 5,939,484
CAPITAL: Asmara
LANGUAGES: Tigrinya, Arabic, English (all official), Tigre, Kunama, Afar, others

ETHIOPIA
AREA: 426,373 sq mi (1,104,300 sq km)
POPULATION: 90,783,739
CAPITAL: Addis Ababa
LANGUAGES: Amarigna, Oromigna, others

SOMALIA
AREA: 246,199 sq mi (637,652 sq km)
POPULATION: 9,925,640
CAPITAL: Mogadishu
LANGUAGES: Somali (official), Arabic, English, Italian

SUDAN
AREA: 967,503 sq mi (2,505,821 sq km)
POPULATION: 45,047,502
CAPITAL: Khartoum
LANGUAGES: Arabic, English (both official), Nubian, Ta Bedawie

Geladas are found only in the mountain meadows of Ethiopia. They are about the size of baboons, and spend most of the day sitting and eating grass.

Mediterranean Sea

Benghazi

A **B** **C** **D** **E** **F** **G**

ISRAEL
Suez Canal
Alexandria
Cairo
Western Desert
Suez
El Faiyum
Sinai Peninsula

JORDAN

Baghdad
IRAQ

KUWAIT

Persian Gulf

IRAN

Abu Dhabi
Doha
QATAR

N
W T·F·K E
S

EGYPT

LIBYA

Gulf of Suez

Nile R.

Luxor

Red Sea

BAHRAIN
Riyadh

U.A.E.

Libyan Desert

Aswan
Lake Nasser

Mecca

SAUDI ARABIA

OMAN

Kufra Oasis

Uweinat Mtn.

Nubian Desert

Port Sudan

YEMEN

Sahara

Nile R.

Atbara R.

ERITREA

Sanaa

Socotra
(Yemen)

CHAD

Omdurman
Khartoum
Wad Medani

Asmara

Bab el Mandeb Strait

Raas Caseyr

SUDAN

Ras Dashan

Gulf of Aden

Mount Marra
El Obeid   Kosti

Blue Nile R.

Gondar

DJIBOUTI
Djibouti
Berbera

Marra Mtns.

White Nile R.

Lake Tana

Ahmar Mtns.
Karkar Mtns.

proposed border

Choke Mtns.

CENTRAL AFRICAN REPUBLIC

Lol R.

Sudd

Malakal

Addis Ababa

Dire Dawa
Harar

Eyl

Wau

Badigeru Swamp

ETHIOPIA

Goba

Shebele R.

Congo R.

Juba

Ethiopian Highlands

SOMALIA

INDIAN OCEAN

Equator

DEMOCRATIC REPUBLIC OF THE CONGO

UGANDA

Great Rift Valley

Lake Turkana

KENYA

Mogadishu

Kampala

Lake Victoria

Kismaayo

0   400 miles
0   600 kilometers

Did You Know?

● Egypt's Suez Canal, which links the Mediterranean Sea with the Red Sea, was opened in 1869.

● King Tut, Egypt's most famous mummy, was only 9 years old when he became pharoah.

● Sudan has more pyramids than Egypt.

King Tutankhamen's gold mask weighs 24 pounds (11 kg).

● Somalia has been without a national government since the end of its civil war in 1991.

● Ethiopia's royal family claims to be descended from King Solomon and the Queen of Sheba.

● Two-thirds of Djibouti's residents live in the capital city, Djibouti.

Northwestern Africa

In El Jem, in Tunisia, is a Roman colosseum. It is almost as big as the one in Rome, but it is better preserved

High on the northwest shoulder of Africa sit the countries of Morocco, Algeria, Tunisia, and Libya, and the territory of Western Sahara. Since ancient times, conquerors—such as Vandals, Romans, Ottoman Turks, and the French—have been drawn to the sparkling coast along the Atlantic and the southern Mediterranean Sea. In modern times, the area retains Islamic and French influences.

The geography of northwestern Africa is varied and dramatic. Along the fertile coast, crops of wheat, olives, figs, and citrus fruits are grown, and the palm-fringed beaches of Morocco and Tunisia attract many tourists. Just south is a ribbon of mountains, called the Atlas, that stretches 1,200 miles (1,931 km) from Morocco across Algeria to Tunisia. And below this ridge is the great desert of the Sahara.

Tunisia, the small finger of land between Algeria and Libya, freed itself from French rule in 1956. Ruins of two great civilizations, the Phoenician and the Roman, can be viewed in Carthage, on the Tunisian coast. Other popular destinations for visitors to this region are the pink-walled city of Marrakech, in Morocco, and the Leptis Magna, in Libya, the site of impressive Roman ruins. The territory of Western Sahara, once held by Spain but now overseen by Morocco, has been the object of many conflicts.

Angered by the rising cost of food, the high rate of joblessness, and other conditions, crowds of Tunisian protesters took to the streets in December 2010. In response to their demands, President Zine el Abidine Ben Ali stepped down. Demonstrators in Libya also insisted that their country's long-time leader resign, but Muammar Gaddafi refused. Violence erupted, and countries around the world, including the United States, Britain, and France, intervened to help protect Libyan citizens.

The ancient city of Ait Ben Haddou, in southern Morocco, was once an important stop-off point for caravans crossing the Sahara desert to Marrakech, Morocco.

ATLANTIC OCEAN

Madeira Is. (Portugal)

Canary Is. (Spain)
Santa Cruz de Teneri
Tarf

el Aaiun ✪

WESTERN SAHARA (occupied by Morocco)

Sma

Dakhla

Nouakchott ✪

MAURITA

Data Bank

ALGERIA
AREA: 919,595 sq mi (2,381,740 sq km)
POPULATION: 34,994,937
CAPITAL: Algiers
LANGUAGES: Arabic (official), French, Berber dialects

LIBYA
AREA: 679,362 sq mi (1,759,540 sq km)
POPULATION: 6,597,960
CAPITAL: Tripoli
LANGUAGES: Arabic, Italian, English

MOROCCO
AREA: 172,413 sq mi (446,550 sq km)
POPULATION: 31,968,361
CAPITAL: Rabat
LANGUAGES: Arabic (official), Berber dialects, French

TUNISIA
AREA: 63,170 sq mi (163,610 sq km)
POPULATION: 10,629,186
CAPITAL: Tunis
LANGUAGES: Arabic (official), French

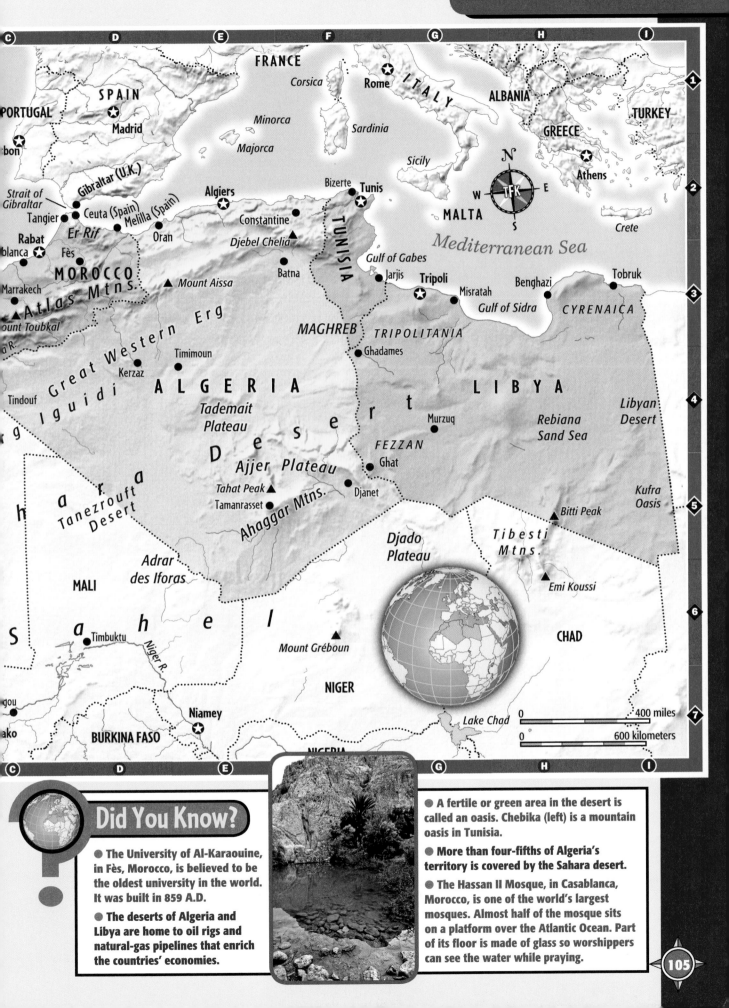

FRANCE

Corsica

Rome ITALY

ALBANIA

GREECE

TURKEY

SPAIN

Madrid

Minorca

Sardinia

PORTUGAL

bon

Gibraltar (U.K.)

Strait of Gibraltar

Tangier

Ceuta (Spain) Melilla (Spain)

Er Rif Oran

Rabat

blanca

Fès

MOROCCO

Marrakech

Atlas Mtns.

ount Toubkal

a R.

Algiers

Constantine

Djebel Chelia

Batna

Mount Aissa

Great Western Erg

Timimoun

Kerzaz

Tindouf

ALGERIA

Iguidi

Tademait Plateau

Ajjer Plateau

Tahat Peak

Tamanrasset

Ahaggar Mtns.

Bizerte Tunis

TUNISIA

Majorca

Sicily

MALTA

Gulf of Gabes

Jarjis

Misratah

Tripoli

MAGHREB TRIPOLITANIA

Ghadames

Mediterranean Sea

Benghazi

Gulf of Sidra

CYRENAICA

Crete

Tobruk

LIBYA

Libyan Desert

Sahara Desert

Murzuq

FEZZAN

Ghat

Djanet

Tanezrouft Desert

h

Adrar des Iforas

MALI

S

a

h

e

Timbuktu

Niger R.

gou

ako

Niamey

BURKINA FASO

Rebiana Sand Sea

Kufra Oasis

Bitti Peak

Tibesti Mtns.

Emi Koussi

Djado Plateau

Mount Gréboun

l

NIGER

Lake Chad

NIGERIA

CHAD

0   400 miles

0   600 kilometers

105

Did You Know?

- The University of Al-Karaouine, in Fès, Morocco, is believed to be the oldest university in the world. It was built in 859 A.D.

- The deserts of Algeria and Libya are home to oil rigs and natural-gas pipelines that enrich the countries' economies.

- A fertile or green area in the desert is called an oasis. Chebika (left) is a mountain oasis in Tunisia.

- More than four-fifths of Algeria's territory is covered by the Sahara desert.

- The Hassan II Mosque, in Casablanca, Morocco, is one of the world's largest mosques. Almost half of the mosque sits on a platform over the Atlantic Ocean. Part of its floor is made of glass so worshippers can see the water while praying.

Western Africa

The western edge of Africa looks like a puzzle piece that would fit snuggly against the eastern side of South America, across the Atlantic. And in fact, the two continents used to be one, until they broke up and drifted apart about 200 million years ago.

West Africa includes the southern stretch of the Sahara desert and, just south of it, a vast swath of grasslands called the Sahel. The Sahel has been over-farmed and plagued by drought. The coastal regions of West Africa—from Senegal to the Niger River delta—have rain forests and crops of coffee, cotton, rubber, and cacao.

The Dogon are an isolated cliff-dwelling people in Mali. They wear masks during traditional funerals and ceremonies.

Canary Islands (Spain)

CAPE VERDE
Santa Antao
Mindela
Sal
São Tiago
Boa Viste
600 miles
Praia
50 mile

Cape Blanc

③ Nouakchott

Saint-Louis
Dakar
Cape Verde ④ SENEGA

Senegal
GAMBIA
Banjul
Gambi
GUINEA-BISSAU Bissau

Conakry
Freetown

Data Bank

BENIN
AREA: 43,483 sq mi (112,620 sq km)
POPULATION: 9,325,032
CAPITAL: Porto-Novo
LANGUAGES: French (official), African languages

BURKINA FASO
AREA: 105,870 sq mi (274,202 sq km)
POPULATION: 16,751,455
CAPITAL: Ouagadougou
LANGUAGES: French (official), African languages

CAPE VERDE
AREA: 1,557 sq mi (4,033 sq km)
POPULATION: 516,100
CAPITAL: Praia
LANGUAGES: Portuguese, Crioulo

COTE D'IVOIRE
AREA: 124,502 sq mi (322,459 sq km)
POPULATION: 21,504,162
CAPITAL: Yamoussoukro
LANGUAGES: French (official), African languages

GAMBIA, THE
AREA: 4,363 sq mi (11,300 sq km)
POPULATION: 1,797,860
CAPITAL: Banjul
LANGUAGES: English (official), native languages

GHANA
AREA: 92,098 sq mi (238,533 sq km)
POPULATION: 24,791,073
CAPITAL: Accra
LANGUAGES: English (official), African languages

GUINEA
AREA: 94,925 sq mi (245,855 sq km)
POPULATION: 10,601,009
CAPITAL: Conakry
LANGUAGES: French (official), native languages

GUINEA-BISSAU
AREA: 13,946 sq mi (36,120 sq km)
POPULATION: 1,596,677
CAPITAL: Bissau
LANGUAGES: Portuguese (official), Crioulo, African languages

LIBERIA
AREA: 43,000 sq mi (111,370 sq km)
POPULATION: 3,786,764
CAPITAL: Monrovia
LANGUAGES: English (official), tribal dialects

MALI
AREA: 478,841 sq mi (1,240,192 sq km)
POPULATION: 14,159,904
CAPITAL: Bamako
LANGUAGES: French (official), Bambara

MAURITANIA
AREA: 397,955 sq mi (1,030,700 sq km)
POPULATION: 3,281,634
CAPITAL: Nouakchott
LANGUAGES: Arabic (official), Pulaar, Soninke, Wolof, French, Hassaniya

NIGER
AREA: 489,189 sq mi (1,266,994 sq km)
POPULATION: 16,468,886
CAPITAL: Niamey
LANGUAGES: French (official), Hausa, Djerma

The *djembe* is a traditional West African drum. Shaped like a goblet, it can produce many different tones.

NIGERIA
AREA: 356,669 sq mi (923,768 sq km)
POPULATION: 155,215,573
CAPITAL: Abuja
LANGUAGES: English (official), Hausa, Yoruba, Igbo, Fulani

SENEGAL
AREA: 75,955 sq mi (196,723 sq km)
POPULATION: 12,643,799
CAPITAL: Dakar
LANGUAGES: French (official), Wolof, Pulaar, Jola, Mandinka

SIERRA LEONE
AREA: 27,699 sq mi (71,740 sq km)
POPULATION: 5,363,669
CAPITAL: Freetown
LANGUAGES: English (official), Mende, Temne, Krio

TOGO
AREA: 21,925 sq mi (56,785 sq km)
POPULATION: 6,771,993
CAPITAL: Lomé
LANGUAGES: French (official), Éwé, Mina, Kabyé, Dagomba

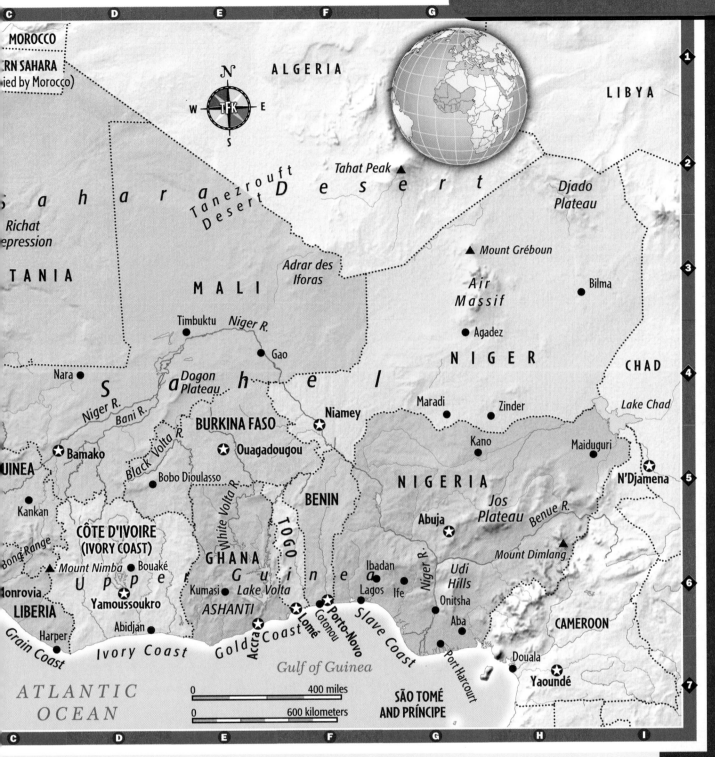

C D E F G

MOROCCO

RN SAHARA
ied by Morocco)

ALGERIA

LIBYA

Tahat Peak ▲

*Tanezrouft
Desert*

D e s e r t

*Djado
Plateau*

Sahara

*Richat
epression*

TANIA

▲ Mount Gréboun

*Air
Massif*

Bilma

MALI

*Adrar des
Iforas*

Timbuktu

Niger R.

Gao

NIGER

CHAD

Nara

S

*Dogon
Plateau*

Agadez

Sahel

Maradi

Zinder

Lake Chad

Niger R.

Bani R.

BURKINA FASO

Niamey

Kano

Maiduguri

UINEA

Bamako

Ouagadougou

Black Volta R.

N'Djamena

Kankan

Bobo Dioulasso

White Volta R.

BENIN

NIGERIA

*Jos
Plateau*

Benue R.

CÔTE D'IVOIRE
(IVORY COAST)

GHANA

Abuja

Bong Range

▲ Mount Nimba

Bouaké

Guinea

Ibadan

Niger R.

Mount Dimlang ▲

UPPER

Kumasi

Lake Volta

Lagos

Ife

*Udi
Hills*

Monrovia

Yamoussoukro

ASHANTI

Onitsha

LIBERIA

Abidjan

Accra

Lomé

Cotonou

Porto-Novo

Slave Coast

Aba

CAMEROON

Harper

Gold Coast

Douala

Ivory Coast

Grain Coast

Gulf of Guinea

Port Harcourt

Yaoundé

ATLANTIC
OCEAN

0 ——— 400 miles
0 ——— 600 kilometers

SÃO TOMÉ
AND PRÍNCIPE

C D E F G H I

Did You Know?

● The Niger River flows northeast from Guinea through Mali, then southeast through Niger and Nigeria. At 2,600 miles (4,184 km) long, it is West Africa's most vital river.

● In 2001, Ghanaian Kofi Annan won a joint Nobel Peace Prize with the U.N. for establishing the Global Fund to Fight AIDS, Tuberculosis and Malaria, supporting the health of people from needy countries.

● Ghana is famous for its kente cloth (left). Its name comes from the Ashanti word *kenten*, which means "basket," because its design resembles a woven basket. Traditionally, clothing made from kente cloth is worn by African royalty during ceremonial events.

● In the 1820s, freed U.S. slaves and free African Americans established Liberia, which means "land of the free."

● Because of its position near the Niger River, the ancient city of Timbuktu, in Mali, was an important trading port between North and West Africa.

107

Central Africa

African forest elephants are smaller than the elephants that live in the savanna. Their tusks are slimmer and straighter, and their skin is smoother. These characteristics help forest elephants move through thick forests more easily.

River towns bustling with markets, untouched wilderness areas where lowland gorillas and forest elephants roam, barren deserts and dry grasslands are all found in Central Africa. The Congo River and its tributaries form a lifeline for the people of the Republic of the Congo and the Democratic Republic of the Congo. Riverboats navigate the waters, bringing people, food, and trade.

Much of northern Chad is desert land. In recent years, long periods of drought have taken a heavy toll on the country and its people. The Sahara is growing and moving southward. The Sahel, a semi-arid grassland that stretches across south central Chad, is expanding into neighboring savannas. To the south of Chad lies the Central African Republic, which forms a transitional area between the sub-Saharan zone in Chad and the equatorial zone to the south.

Dense forests cover large parts of Central African Republic, Democratic Republic of the Congo, Republic of the Congo, Equatorial Guinea, and Gabon. These countries lie near the equator, and their climate is hot and humid. Monkeys, baboons, gorillas, lions, leopards, and a vast array of birds make their home in the jungle. Although natural resources are abundant in some of these lands, poverty, disease, government corruption, and warfare are sad facts of daily life for the people.

Data Bank

CAMEROON
AREA: 183,567 sq mi (475,436 sq km)
POPULATION: 19,711,291
CAPITAL: Yaoundé
LANGUAGES: English, French (both official), African languages

CENTRAL AFRICAN REPUBLIC
AREA: 240,535 sq mi (622,983 sq km)
POPULATION: 4,950,027
CAPITAL: Bangui
LANGUAGES: French (official), Sangho, tribal languages

CHAD
AREA: 495,755 sq mi (1,284,000 sq km)
POPULATION: 10,758,945
CAPITAL: N'Djamena
LANGUAGES: French, Arabic (both official), Sara, African languages

CONGO (DEMOCRATIC REPUBLIC OF THE)
AREA: 905,355 sq mi (2,344,859 sq km)
POPULATION: 71,712,867
CAPITAL: Kinshasa
LANGUAGES: French (official), Lingala, Kingwana, Kikongo, others

CONGO (REPUBLIC OF THE)
AREA: 132,046 sq mi (342,000 sq km)
POPULATION: 4,243,929
CAPITAL: Brazzaville
LANGUAGES: French (official), Lingala, Monokutuba, other African languages

EQUATORIAL GUINEA
AREA: 10,830 sq mi (28,050 sq km)
POPULATION: 668,225
CAPITAL: Malabo
LANGUAGES: Spanish, French (both official), Fang, Bubi

GABON
AREA: 103,347 sq mi (267,668 sq km)
POPULATION: 1,576,665
CAPITAL: Libreville
LANGUAGES: French (official), Fang, Myene, Nzebi, Bapounou/Eschira, Bandjabi

SAO TOME AND PRINCIPE
AREA: 349 sq mi (904 sq km)
POPULATION: 179,506
CAPITAL: São Tomé
LANGUAGE: Portuguese

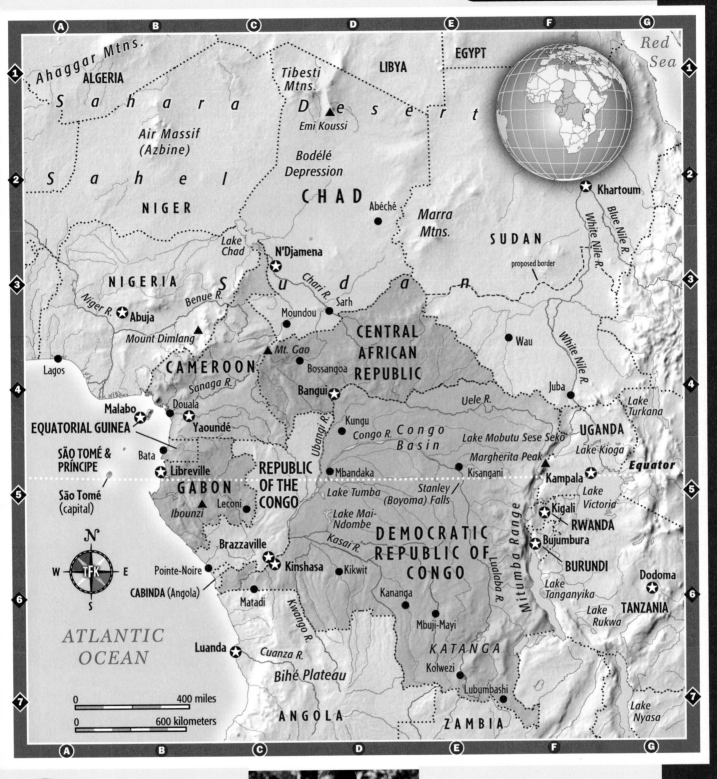

A **B** **C** **D** **E** **F** **G**

Red Sea

Ahaggar Mtns.
ALGERIA
Sahara
Air Massif (Azbine)
Sahel
Desert
Tibesti Mtns.
Emi Koussi
Bodélé Depression
LIBYA
EGYPT
Khartoum
NIGER
CHAD
Abéché
Marra Mtns.
SUDAN
proposed border
White Nile R.
Blue Nile R.
Lake Chad
N'Djamena
Chari R.
Sahel
Sudan
Moundou
Sarh
Wau
White Nile R.
NIGERIA
Niger R.
Abuja
Benue R.
Mount Dimlang
Mt. Gao
Bossangoa
CENTRAL AFRICAN REPUBLIC
Juba
Lake Turkana
Lagos
CAMEROON
Sanaga R.
Bangui
Ubangi R.
Kungu
Congo R.
Uele R.
Lake Mobutu Sese Seko
Margherita Peak
UGANDA
Lake Kioga
Equator
Malabo
Douala
EQUATORIAL GUINEA
Yaoundé
Bata
SÃO TOMÉ & PRÍNCIPE
Libreville
GABON
REPUBLIC OF THE CONGO
Congo Basin
Mbandaka
Kisangani
Stanley / (Boyoma) Falls
Lake Tumba
Kampala
Lake Victoria
Kigali
RWANDA
Bujumbura
Mitumba Range
São Tomé (capital)
Ibounzi
Leconi
Lake Mai-Ndombe
DEMOCRATIC REPUBLIC OF CONGO
Kasai R.
Lake Tanganyika
BURUNDI
Dodoma
Brazzaville
Kinshasa
Kikwit
Kwango R.
Lualaba R.
Lake Rukwa
TANZANIA
Pointe-Noire
CABINDA (Angola)
Matadi
Kananga
Mbuji-Mayi
KATANGA
ATLANTIC OCEAN
Luanda
Cuanza R.
Bihé Plateau
Kolwezi
Lubumbashi
Lake Nyasa
N W E S TFK
0 400 miles
0 600 kilometers
ANGOLA
ZAMBIA

Did You Know?

● Pygmies, a group of people found in Central Africa, are an average height of 4 feet (1.2 m).

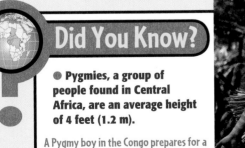

A Pygmy boy in the Congo prepares for a traditional initiation ceremony.

● The Kota people of the Central African Republic believe that their ancestors help them communicate with God.

● The Congo basin spans 1.3 million square miles (3.4 million sq km) across Central Africa. It is home to a variety of wildlife, from rare butterflies and forest elephants to lowland and mountain gorillas. Bonobos are found only in the Congo basin.

109

East Central Africa

An acacia tree flourishes on the Serengeti Plain in Tanzania.

Spectacular highlands, rolling plains dotted with acacia trees, lush grasslands teeming with wildlife, and sparkling freshwater and saltwater lakes are the prominent features of this part of Africa. Clustered around Lake Victoria, which is the continent's largest lake, are Uganda, Kenya, and Tanzania. Africa's deepest lake, Lake Tanganyika, lies at the western edge of Tanzania and Burundi. The small, landlocked country of Rwanda shares borders with Burundi, Tanzania, and Uganda.

East central Africa has many lakes, but water is still considered a precious gift. Kenyans often greet one another by asking, "Does it rain where you live?" For many of the region's people, years of drought, grinding poverty, government corruption, ethnic rivalries, and an AIDS epidemic have combined to make everyday life difficult.

In 1964, Tanganyika joined with the island of Zanzibar to form the country of Tanzania. South of Zanzibar, in the Indian Ocean, are the small island nations of Comoros and Seychelles. Still further south is Madagascar, the fourth largest island in the world.

Africa's second largest lake, Lake Bunyonyi, in Uganda, is believed to have been formed 8,000 years ago when lava caused damming at the Ndego River.

Data Bank

BURUNDI
AREA: 10,745 sq mi (27,829 sq km)
POPULATION: 10,216,190
CAPITAL: Bujumbura
LANGUAGES: Kirundi, French
(both official), Swahili

COMOROS
AREA: 863 sq mi (2,235 sq km)
POPULATION: 794,683
CAPITAL: Moroni
LANGUAGES: Arabic, French
(both official), Shikomoro

KENYA
AREA: 224,081 sq mi (580,367 sq km)
POPULATION: 41,070,934
CAPITAL: Nairobi
LANGUAGES: English, Kiswahili
(both official), native languages

MADAGASCAR
AREA: 226,657 sq mi (587,039 sq km)
POPULATION: 21,926,221
CAPITAL: Antananarivo
LANGUAGES: French, Malagasy
(both official), English

MALAWI
AREA: 45,745 sq mi (118,479 sq km)
POPULATION: 15,879,252
CAPITAL: Lilongwe
LANGUAGES: Chichewa (official),
Chinyanja, Chiyao, Chitumbuka, others

MAURITIUS
AREA: 788 sq mi (2,041 sq km)
POPULATION: 1,303,717
CAPITAL: Port Louis
LANGUAGES: English (official), Creole,
Bhojpuri, French

MOZAMBIQUE
AREA: 308,642 sq mi (799,379 sq km)
POPULATION: 22,948,858
CAPITAL: Maputo
LANGUAGES: Portuguese (official),
Bantu languages

RWANDA
AREA: 10,169 sq mi (26,338 sq km)
POPULATION: 11,370,425
CAPITAL: Kigali
LANGUAGES: Kinyarwanda, French, English
(all official), Bantu, Kiswahili

SEYCHELLES
AREA: 176 sq mi (456 sq km)
POPULATION: 89,188
CAPITAL: Victoria
LANGUAGES: English, Creole (both official)

TANZANIA
AREA: 365,755 sq mi (947,301 sq km)
POPULATION: 42,746,620
CAPITALS: Dar es Salaam (commercial),
Dodoma (political)
LANGUAGES: Kiswahili, English
(both official), Arabic

UGANDA
AREA: 93,065 sq mi (241,037 sq km)
POPULATION: 34,612,250
CAPITAL: Kampala
LANGUAGES: English (official), Ganda,
other native languages

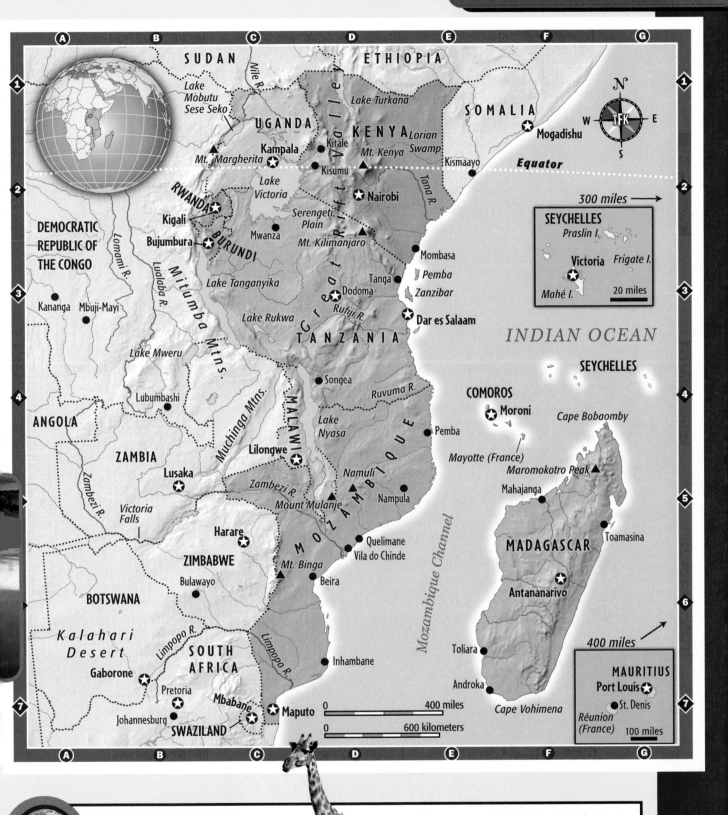

SUDAN **ETHIOPIA**

Lake Mobutu Sese Seko

Nile R.

UGANDA Lake Turkana

KENYA Lorian Swamp

SOMALIA

Mogadishu

Kampala · Kitale

Mt. Margherita ▲ Mt. Kenya ▲

Kisumu

Kismaayo

Equator

N
W — TFK — E
S

300 miles →

RWANDA

Kigali

BURUNDI

Bujumbura ·

Lake Victoria

Serengeti Plain

Mwanza

Mt. Kilimanjaro ▲

Nairobi ☆

Tana R.

SEYCHELLES
Praslin I.

Victoria ☆   Frigate I.

Mahé I.   20 miles

DEMOCRATIC REPUBLIC OF THE CONGO

Lomami R.

Lualaba R.

Mitumba Mtns.

Lake Tanganyika

Mombasa

Pemba

Tanga

Dodoma

Zanzibar

Kananga · Mbuji-Mayi

Lake Rukwa

Rufiji R.

TANZANIA

Dar es Salaam ☆

INDIAN OCEAN

Lake Mweru

Muchinga Mtns.

Songea ·

Ruvuma R.

SEYCHELLES

Lubumbashi ·

MALAWI

Lake Nyasa

COMOROS

Moroni ☆

Cape Bobaomby

ANGOLA

ZAMBIA

Lilongwe ☆

Pemba ·

Mayotte (France)

Maromokotro Peak ▲

Mahajanga ·

Lusaka ☆

Zambezi R.

Zambezi R.

Namuli ▲

MOZAMBIQUE

Nampula ·

Mount Mulanje ▲

MADAGASCAR

Toamasina ·

Victoria Falls

Harare ☆

Quelimane ·

Vila do Chinde

Mozambique Channel

Antananarivo ☆

ZIMBABWE

Bulawayo ·

Mt. Binga ▲

Beira

BOTSWANA

Kalahari Desert

Limpopo R.

SOUTH AFRICA

Inhambane ·

Toliara ·

400 miles →

Gaborone ☆

Limpopo R.

Androka ·

MAURITIUS
Port Louis ☆

Pretoria ☆

Mbabane ☆

Maputo ☆

0   400 miles

0   600 kilometers

Cape Vohimena

St. Denis ·

Réunion (France)   100 miles

Johannesburg ·

SWAZILAND

Did You Know?

● The coelacanth (*see-la-canth*), an ancient type of fish, was believed to be extinct. In 1938, one was found swimming in the Indian Ocean, near Comoros.

● Seychelles was believed to be a popular hide-out for pirates. The name Anse Forbans, a beach on the Seychelles island of Mahé, means "pirate cove."

● There are nine subspecies of giraffes in the giraffe family, which are distinguished by their color and coat patterns. Three subspecies are found in Kenya: the reticulated giraffe, the Masai giraffe (left), and the Rothschild's giraffe.

● Nearly 80% of animal species found in Madagascar cannot be found anywhere else in the world. These animals include several species of lemurs, the narrow-striped mongoose, and the tomato frog.

Southern Africa

Spotted cheetahs, lumbering elephants, magnificent lions, meerkats, and hundreds of bird species—these are the hallmarks of southern Africa. The region's vast savannas, mountains, and plateaus host an astonishing array of plant and animal life. Tourists come from around the world to take safaris, adventures whose name means "journey" in Swahili. The southern part of Africa is rich in natural resources, such as diamonds, gold, and copper, as well as physical beauty. At Zimbabwe's spectacular Victoria Falls, the Zambezi River plunges nearly 355 feet (108 m) into a rain-forested gorge. Thundering over the rocks is some 33,000 cubic feet (935 cubic m) of water per second!

The richest, most modern country on the continent is South Africa. Comprising more than 30 ethnic groups, the country has undergone many political and social changes. For hundreds of years, a small white minority ruled a mostly black population. Following the country's first free election, in 1994, South Africa entered a new era of equality and cooperation.

Meerkats live in large groups. For safety reasons, at least one meerkat is always standing on its hind legs, watching out for predators.

The Bogenfels rock arch is a naturally occurring rock formation in the Namib Desert, one of the oldest deserts in the world.

Data Bank

ANGOLA
AREA: 481,354 sq mi (1,246,701 sq km)
POPULATION: 13,338,541
CAPITAL: Luanda
LANGUAGES: Portuguese (official), Bantu, other African languages

BOTSWANA
AREA: 224,607 sq mi (581,730 sq km)
POPULATION: 2,065,398
CAPITAL: Gaborone
LANGUAGES: English (official), Setswana, Kalanga, Sekgalgadi

LESOTHO
AREA: 11,720 sq mi (30,355 sq km)
POPULATION: 1,924,886
CAPITAL: Maseru
LANGUAGES: English (official), Sesotho (southern Sotho), Zulu, Xhosa

NAMIBIA
AREA: 318,261 sq mi (824,292 sq km)
POPULATION: 2,147,585
CAPITAL: Windhoek
LANGUAGES: English (official), Afrikaans, native languages

SOUTH AFRICA
AREA: 470,693 sq mi (1,219,090 sq km)
POPULATION: 49,004,031
CAPITALS: Pretoria (administrative), Cape Town (legislative), Bloemfontein (judicial)
LANGUAGES: IsiZulu, IsiXhosa, Afrikaans, Sepedi, English, Setswana, others

SWAZILAND
AREA: 6,704 sq mi (17,363 sq km)
POPULATION: 1,370,424
CAPITAL: Mbabane
LANGUAGES: siSwati, English (both official)

ZAMBIA
AREA: 290,586 sq mi (752,614 sq km)
POPULATION: 13,881,336
CAPITAL: Lusaka
LANGUAGES: Bemba, Nyanja, Tonga, Lozi, Lunda, Kaonde, Luvale, English (all official)

ZIMBABWE
AREA: 150,872 sq mi (390,757 sq km)
POPULATION: 12,084,304
CAPITAL: Harare
LANGUAGES: English (official), Shona, Sindebele, native languages

Table Mountain near Cape Town, South Africa, can be seen from almost anywhere in the city. Its highest point reaches 3,563 feet (1,086 m).

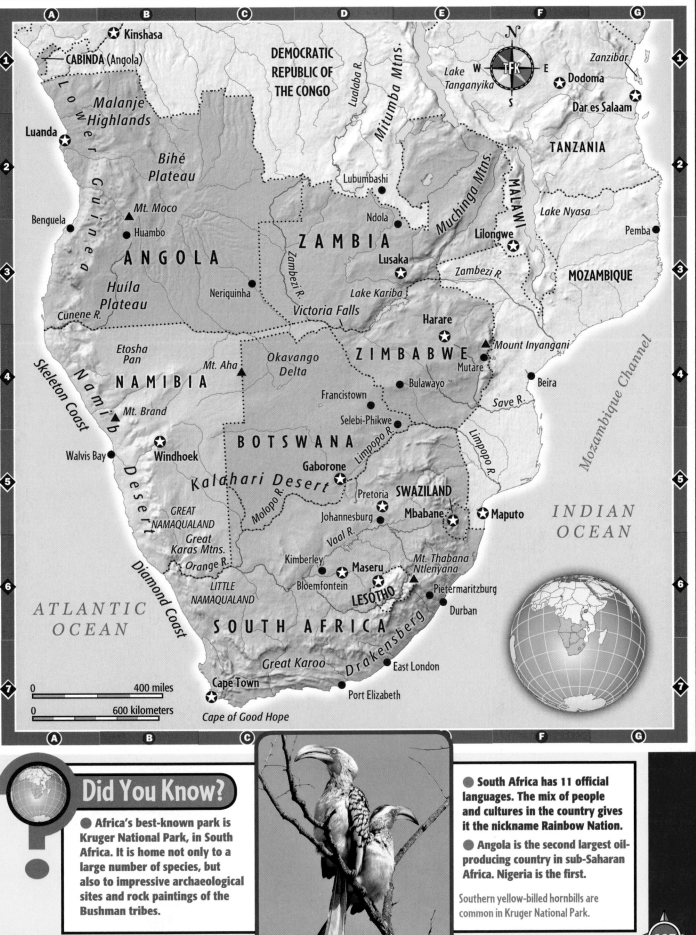

A | B | C | D | E | F | G

1

Kinshasa

CABINDA (Angola)

Lower Guinea

Malanje Highlands

Luanda

Bihé Plateau

Benguela

▲ Mt. Moco

● Huambo

A N G O L A

Huíla Plateau

Cunene R.

DEMOCRATIC REPUBLIC OF THE CONGO

Lualaba R.

Mitumba Mtns.

Lake Tanganyika

N W TFK E S

Zanzibar

Dodoma

Dar es Salaam

TANZANIA

● Lubumbashi

● Ndola

Z A M B I A

Zambezi R.

Lusaka

Lake Kariba

Victoria Falls

Neriquinha

Muchinga Mtns.

MALAWI

Lilongwe

Lake Nyasa

Zambezi R.

MOZAMBIQUE

Pemba

Harare

Z I M B A B W E

▲ Mount Inyangani

Mutare

Beira

Etosha Pan

N A M I B I A

▲ Mt. Aha

Okavango Delta

Save R.

Skeleton Coast

Namib Desert

▲ Mt. Brand

Bulawayo

Francistown

Selebi-Phikwe

Limpopo R.

Limpopo R.

Mozambique Channel

Walvis Bay

Windhoek

B O T S W A N A

Gaborone

Kalahari Desert

Pretoria

SWAZILAND

Mbabane

Maputo

INDIAN OCEAN

GREAT NAMAQUALAND

Great Karas Mtns.

Molopo R.

Johannesburg

Vaal R.

Mt. Thabana Ntlenyana ▲

Orange R.

Kimberley

Maseru

Pietermaritzburg

ATLANTIC OCEAN

Diamond Coast

LITTLE NAMAQUALAND

Bloemfontein

LESOTHO

Durban

S O U T H   A F R I C A

Great Karoo

Drakensberg

East London

0 — 400 miles

0 — 600 kilometers

Cape Town

Port Elizabeth

Cape of Good Hope

Did You Know?

● Africa's best-known park is Kruger National Park, in South Africa. It is home not only to a large number of species, but also to impressive archaeological sites and rock paintings of the Bushman tribes.

● South Africa has 11 official languages. The mix of people and cultures in the country gives it the nickname Rainbow Nation.

● Angola is the second largest oil-producing country in sub-Saharan Africa. Nigeria is the first.

Southern yellow-billed hornbills are common in Kruger National Park.

113

Australia and the Pacific Islands

ustralia is the smallest, flattest, and—with the exception of Antarctica—the driest continent. It is also a region with many different landscapes: parched deserts, vast grasslands, tropical rain forests, and plains dotted with mammoth rocks. Aborigines were the first people to settle in Australia, and are believed to have migrated from Asia 70,000 years ago, bringing with them a culture of storytelling and art.

Aboriginal art once flourished as rock carvings, body painting, and ground designs. These art forms date back more than 30,000 years.

Located between the Indian and Pacific Oceans, Australia is relatively isolated from other continents. It is home to unusual plant and animal life, including (with New Guinea) the only egg-laying mammals on Earth, the platypus and the echidna. Off Australia's northeast coast, the Great Barrier Reef contains an unparalleled treasure of brilliant corals and marine life.

To the east of Australia lie the Pacific Islands, a collection of more than 10,000 islands, atolls, and islets. The largest of this group are New Zealand and New Guinea. New Guinea is the world's second largest island, after Greenland. Half the island is part of Indonesia; the other half is the independent country Papua New Guinea.

The Pacific Islands are known for their awe-inspiring scenery. In New Zealand alone, the terrain ranges from snowy glaciers and sparkling fjords to active volcanoes, temperate rain forests, and sandy beaches.

Regional Facts

NUMBER OF COUNTRIES: 14 countries—Australia, Fiji, Kiribati, Marshall Islands, Micronesia, Nauru, New Zealand, Palau, Papua New Guinea, Samoa, Solomon Islands, Tonga, Tuvalu, Vanuatu

AREA, AUSTRALIA: 2,988,902 sq mi (7,741,221 sq km)

LAND AREA, PACIFIC ISLANDS: 317,700 sq mi (822,839 sq km)

HIGHEST POINT: Mount Wilhelm, Papua New Guinea, 14,793 feet (4,509 m)

LOWEST POINT: Lake Eyre, Australia, 49 feet (15 m) below sea level

The roof of Australia's Sydney Opera House was designed to look like boat sails in the Sydney Harbor.

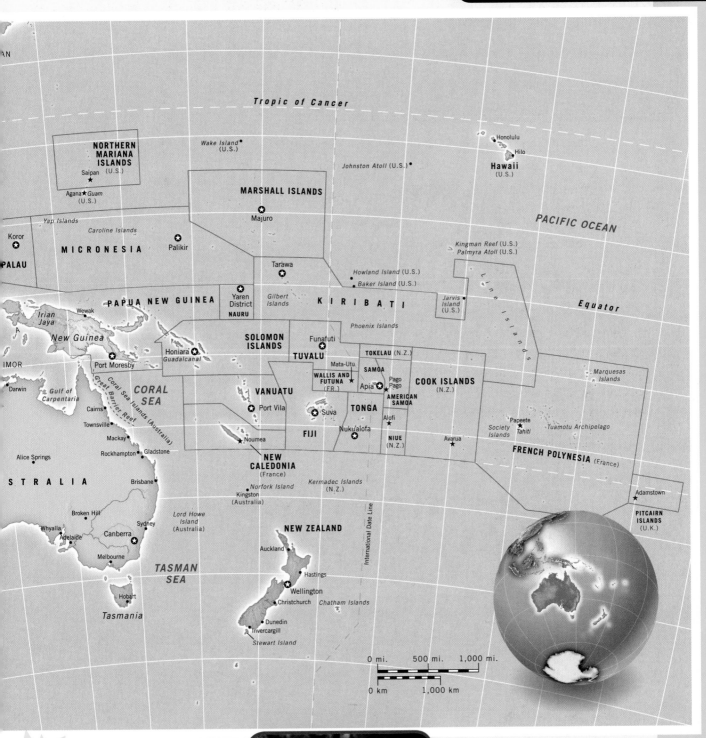

Tropic of Cancer

PACIFIC OCEAN

NORTHERN MARIANA ISLANDS
Saipan ★ (U.S.)
Agana ★ Guam (U.S.)

Wake Island ● (U.S.)

Johnston Atoll (U.S.) ●

Honolulu ●
Hilo ●
Hawaii (U.S.)

MARSHALL ISLANDS
Majuro ●

Yap Islands
Koror
Caroline Islands
MICRONESIA
Palikir ●

PALAU

Kingman Reef (U.S.)
Palmyra Atoll (U.S.)

Tarawa ●

Howland Island (U.S.) ●
Baker Island (U.S.) ●

Jarvis Island (U.S.) ●

Equator

Line Islands

PAPUA NEW GUINEA
Wewak
Irian Jaya
New Guinea
Port Moresby
IMOR
Darwin
Gulf of Carpentaria

Yaren District
NAURU

Gilbert Islands

K I R I B A T I

Phoenix Islands

Marquesas Islands

SOLOMON ISLANDS
Honiara ★ Guadalcanal

Funafuti ●
TUVALU

TOKELAU (N.Z.)

Mata-Utu ●
WALLIS AND FUTUNA (FR.)
SAMOA
Apia ★
Pago Pago
AMERICAN SAMOA

COOK ISLANDS (N.Z.)

CORAL SEA
Coral Sea Islands (Australia)
Great Barrier Reef (Australia)
Cairns
Townsville
Mackay
Rockhampton ● Gladstone

VANUATU
Port Vila ★

Suva ★
FIJI

TONGA
Alofi ★
Nuku'alofa ●
NIUE (N.Z.)

Avarua ★

Society Islands
Papeete ●
Tahiti
Tuamotu Archipelago

FRENCH POLYNESIA (France)

STRALIA
Alice Springs
Brisbane ●
Broken Hill
Whyalla
Adelaide ●
Canberra ●
Sydney ●
Melbourne ●

Noumea ★
NEW CALEDONIA (France)
Norfork Island (Australia)
Kingston (Australia)
Kermadec Islands (N.Z.)

Lord Howe Island (Australia)

Adamstown ★
PITCAIRN ISLANDS (U.K.)

TASMAN SEA
Tasmania
Hobart ●

NEW ZEALAND
Auckland ●
Hastings ●
Wellington ●
Christchurch ● Chatham Islands
Dunedin ●
Invercargill ●
Stewart Island

International Date Line

0 mi.   500 mi.   1,000 mi.

0 km   1,000 km

Wow Zone!

● The only land mammals native to New Zealand are bats.

● More than one-third of Australia's land is desert.

● The two main islands of New Zealand are separated by the Cook Strait.

● Koalas are not bears. They are marsupials. They carry their young in a pouch.

● Many of Australia's most stunning beaches are completely deserted because of dangerous animals. The saltwater crocodile, the blue-ringed octopus, and the scorpion fish (left) are a few of Australia's most deadly creatures. On land, there are 36 species of poisonous spiders and 20 kinds of venomous snakes there.

● Fiji contains more than 800 islands and islets spread across 1 million square miles (2.6 million sq km). Only about 100 of Fiji's islands are inhabited.

Australia and Papua New Guinea

The Great Barrier Reef, the world's largest coral reef, lies off Aust[...] northeastern coast, and stretches 1,250 miles (2,011 km). This c[...] habitat contains nearly 3,000 reefs, and as many as 2,000 species [...]

Australia is a hot, dry country of stunning sunsets and vast plains. Known for its unusual animals and colorful birds, the Land Down Under is home to kangaroos, koalas, lorikeets, and rosellas. Australia stretches across almost 3 million square miles (8 million sq km), making it the world's sixth largest country. It is almost as big as the United States, but its population is less than 10% the size of the United States' population. Most of Australia's interior, which is called the outback, has so little water that hardly anyone can live there. Most Australians—about 70% of the population— live in the country's large coastal cities. Sydney has 4.5 million residents, and is Australia's largest urban center. The island of Tasmania is located off Australia's southern coast. It is the only place on Earth where you will find the fierce little mammal aptly named Tasmanian devil.

Off the northern coast of Australia lies Papua New Guinea. This rugged country occupies the eastern half of the island of New Guinea (the other half of the island belongs to Indonesia). Papua New Guinea was an Australian territory until it gained independence in 1975.

Koalas spend most of their lives sleeping—as much as 18 hours each day!

Data Bank

AUSTRALIA
AREA: 2,988,902 sq mi (7,741,221 sq km)
POPULATION: 21,766,711
CAPITAL: Canberra
LANGUAGES: English, native languages

PAPUA NEW GUINEA
AREA: 178,703 sq mi (462,839 sq km)
POPULATION: 6,187,591
CAPITAL: Port Moresby
LANGUAGES: Tok Pisin, English, Hiri Motu (all official), native languages

Tasmania's Cradle Mountain region is home to diverse plants and wildlife, including Tasmanian devils, platypuses, and ancient celery-top pine trees.

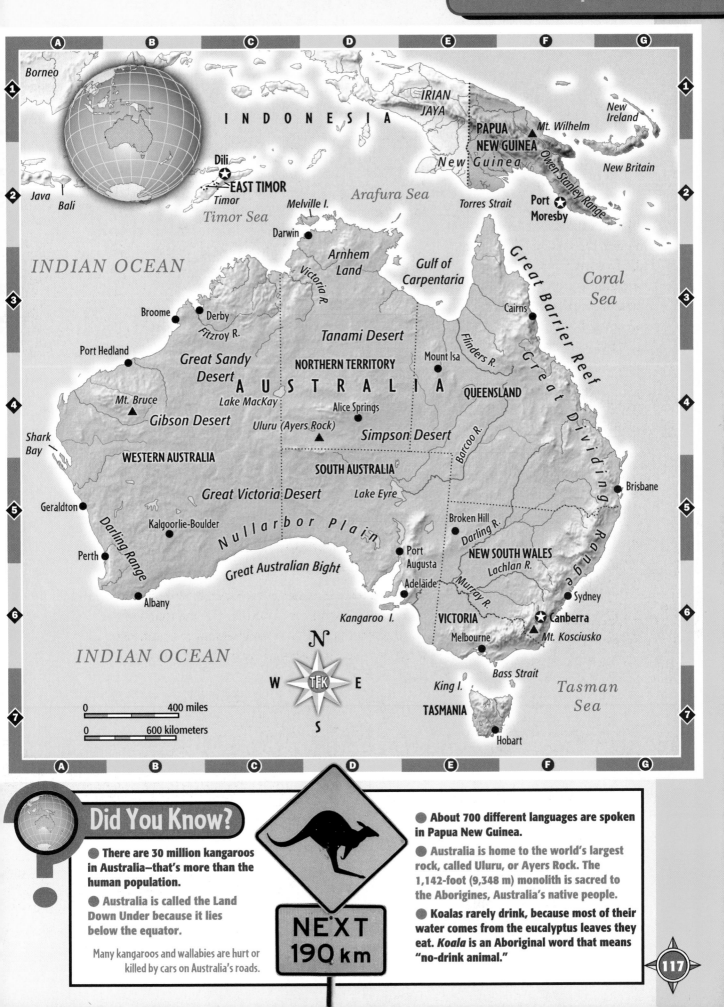

INDONESIA

IRIAN JAYA

PAPUA NEW GUINEA

Mt. Wilhelm

New Guinea

New Ireland

New Britain

Borneo

Java

Bali

Dili

EAST TIMOR

Timor

Timor Sea

Melville I.

Arafura Sea

Torres Strait

Port Moresby

Owen Stanley Range

Coral Sea

INDIAN OCEAN

Darwin

Arnhem Land

Victoria R.

Gulf of Carpentaria

Great Barrier Reef

Broome

Derby

Fitzroy R.

Cairns

Port Hedland

Great Sandy Desert

Tanami Desert

Mount Isa

Flinders R.

NORTHERN TERRITORY

A U S T R A L I A

QUEENSLAND

Great Dividing Range

Mt. Bruce

Lake MacKay

Alice Springs

Gibson Desert

Uluru (Ayers Rock)

Simpson Desert

Barcoo R.

Shark Bay

WESTERN AUSTRALIA

SOUTH AUSTRALIA

Brisbane

Geraldton

Great Victoria Desert

Lake Eyre

Broken Hill

Darling R.

Darling Range

Kalgoorlie-Boulder

Nullarbor Plain

Port Augusta

NEW SOUTH WALES

Lachlan R.

Perth

Great Australian Bight

Adelaide

Murray R.

Sydney

Albany

Kangaroo I.

VICTORIA

Canberra

Mt. Kosciusko

INDIAN OCEAN

Melbourne

N

W TFK E

S

Bass Strait

King I.

Tasman Sea

0   400 miles

0   600 kilometers

TASMANIA

Hobart

Did You Know?

● There are 30 million kangaroos in Australia—that's more than the human population.

● Australia is called the Land Down Under because it lies below the equator.

Many kangaroos and wallabies are hurt or killed by cars on Australia's roads.

NEXT 190 km

● About 700 different languages are spoken in Papua New Guinea.

● Australia is home to the world's largest rock, called Uluru, or Ayers Rock. The 1,142-foot (9,348 m) monolith is sacred to the Aborigines, Australia's native people.

● Koalas rarely drink, because most of their water comes from the eucalyptus leaves they eat. *Koala* is an Aboriginal word that means "no-drink animal."

New Zealand and the Pacific Islands

More than 10,000 coral and volcanic islands dot the vast central Pacific Ocean. Within the Pacific Islands, also known as Oceania, are three groups: Melanesia, Polynesia, and Micronesia. Oceania—with its coral reefs, blue lagoons, soaring volcanic mountains, and mild climate—is one of the most picturesque places in the world.

Most Pacific Island nations include many small islands—Micronesia has more than 600 islands and islets, Fiji has more than 800—and all share a similar mild climate. The people of Oceania speak dozens of different languages.

New Guinea and the islands of New Zealand make up 90% of the Pacific Islands' land area.

Palau is made up of eight main islands and more than 250 small islets. The country covers an area of about 177 square miles (492 sq km).

Data Bank

FIJI
AREA: 7,054 sq mi (18,270 sq km)
POPULATION: 883,125
CAPITAL: Suva
LANGUAGES: English, Fijian (both official), Hindustani

KIRIBATI
AREA: 313 sq mi (811 sq km)
POPULATION: 100,743
CAPITAL: Tarawa
LANGUAGES: English (official), I-Kiribati

MARSHALL ISLANDS
AREA: 70 sq mi (181 sq km)
POPULATION: 67,182
CAPITAL: Majuro
LANGUAGES: Marshallese, English (both official), Japanese

MICRONESIA
AREA: 271 sq mi (702 sq km)
POPULATION: 106,836
CAPITAL: Palikir
LANGUAGES: English (official), others

NAURU
AREA: 8 sq mi (21 sq km)
POPULATION: 9,322
CAPITAL: Yaren District
LANGUAGES: Nauruan, English

NEW ZEALAND
AREA: 103,363 sq mi (267,709 sq km)
POPULATION: 4,290,347
CAPITAL: Wellington
LANGUAGES: English, Maori, sign language (all official)

PALAU
AREA: 177 sq mi (458 sq km)
POPULATION: 20,956
CAPITAL: Melekeok
LANGUAGES: English, Palauan, Sonsoralese, Tobi, others

SAMOA
AREA: 1,093 sq mi (2,831 sq km)
POPULATION: 193,161
CAPITAL: Apia
LANGUAGES: Samoan (Polynesian), English

SOLOMON ISLANDS
AREA: 11,157 sq mi (28,896 sq km)
POPULATION: 571,890
CAPITAL: Honiara
LANGUAGES: English (official), Melanesian pidgin, native languages

TONGA
AREA: 289 sq mi (749 sq km)
POPULATION: 105,916
CAPITAL: Nuku'alofa
LANGUAGES: Tongan, English

TUVALU
AREA: 10 sq mi (26 sq km)
POPULATION: 10,544
CAPITAL: Funafuti
LANGUAGES: Tuvaluan, English, Samoan, Kiribati

VANUATU
AREA: 4,706 sq mi (12,188 sq km)
POPULATION: 224,564
CAPITAL: Port-Vila
LANGUAGES: English, French, Bislama (all official), others

CHINA
TAIWAN
PHILIPPINES
Iwo (Ja
Okinawa (Japan)
North Mar
Islands (U
Guam
Yap
PALAU
INDONESIA
AUSTRALIA

C D E F G H I

MEXICO

1

POLYNESIA

Midway Is. (U.S.)

Wake I. (U.S.)

Hawaii (U.S.)

Bikini I. MARSHALL ISLANDS

NORTH PACIFIC OCEAN

2

roline nds

MICRONESIA

ATED STATES MICRONESIA

Gilbert Islands

Equator

3

NAURU

KIRIBATI

MA

SOLOMON ISLANDS

TUVALU

EA

Wallis & Futuna (France)

Tokelau (N.Z.)

MELANESIA

American Samoa (U.S.)

French Polynesia (France)

4

VANUATU

FIJI

SAMOA

Tahiti

Pitcairn Is . (U.K.)

New Caledonia (France)

TONGA

Cook Is. (N.Z.)

NEW ZEALAND

Auckland

SOUTH PACIFIC OCEAN

Brisbane

North Island

5

Lord Howe I. (Australia)

Norfolk I. (Australia)

Sydney

North Island

N

W TFK E

Tasman Sea

Mount Ruapehu

Wellington

mania

South Island

Chatham Is. (N.Z.)

S

6

Wellington

South Island

Southern Alps

Christchurch

Mt. Cook

NEW ZEALAND

Bounty Is. (N.Z.)

Auckland I. (N.Z.)

Antipodes Is. (N.Z.)

Dunedin

PACIFIC OCEAN

cquarie I. (Australia)

Campbell I. (N.Z.)

1000 miles

1500 kilometers

SOUTHERN OCEAN

Stewart I.

0   200 miles

0   300 kilometers

7

C D E F G H I

Did You Know?

● There are several extinct volcanoes within the borders of Auckland, New Zealand.

● New Zealand was the first country to give women the vote.

● Fiji was once referred to as the Cannibal Isles because cannibalism was practiced there until the mid-19th century.

● When British explorer Captain James Cook first discovered New Zealand, the native Maori men stuck out their tongues at him. He learned that this was intended to scare him off. Eventually, he and the Maori people became friendly.

● In 1999, two small, uninhabited islands that were part of Kiribati disappeared underwater. Rising sea levels caused by global warming may overtake more islands in the Pacific.

● The Solomon Islands include six main volcanic islands and about 1,000 smaller ones.

A Samoan man performs a traditional dance.

119

Antarctica

Antarctica is the highest, driest, coldest, and windiest place on Earth. It is also the location of the South Pole—the southernmost point on Earth. Almost all of Antarctica is covered by an ice sheet. The rest of the continent is barren rock. During the winter months, from June until August, night lasts for 24 hours, and huge blizzards and windstorms sweep across the frozen plains. Yet with its soaring ice cliffs and amazing views of the aurora australis, or southern lights, Antarctica is one of the most magnificent places in the world. It is also home to an amazing array of animals, including many kinds of whales, birds, fish, insects, and mammals. Penguins are probably Antarctica's most famous residents.

About 500 million years ago, the frozen land of Antarctica was located near the equator. As recently as 65 million years ago—during the age of dinosaurs—it was warm enough in Antarctica for many life forms to thrive. Now scientists are discovering amazingly well-preserved fossils of dinosaurs and other ancient life forms on the continent.

Human beings are not native to Antarctica. Since the first explorers reached the South Pole, in 1911, scientists and adventurers have traveled to the frozen land to learn more about it. Each year, as many as 4,000 people from 27 nations live, work, and study at research centers. An additional 1,000 scientists sail to the Antarctic seas to study marine life and oceanography.

There are 17 known species of penguins, but only six live around the Antarctic Circle: Adélies, chinstraps, emperors, gentoos, kings, and macaronis.

Continent Facts

NUMBER OF COUNTRIES AND TERRITORIES: There are no national governments in Antarctica. Instead, Antarctica is governed by a treaty signed by 45 nations. The treaty states that Antarctica is a free and peaceful territory. The treaty also supports open scientific exchange and protects Antarctica's natural environment.

AREA: 5,405,430 sq mi (14,000,000 sq km)

LONGEST RIVER: There are no true rivers in Antarctica. The Onyx River, a snowmelt area, is only about 18 miles (29 km) long.

LONGEST MOUNTAIN RANGE: The Transantarctic Mountains are 3,000 miles long (4,828 km).

HIGHEST PEAK: Mount Vinson, 16,067 feet (4,897 m)

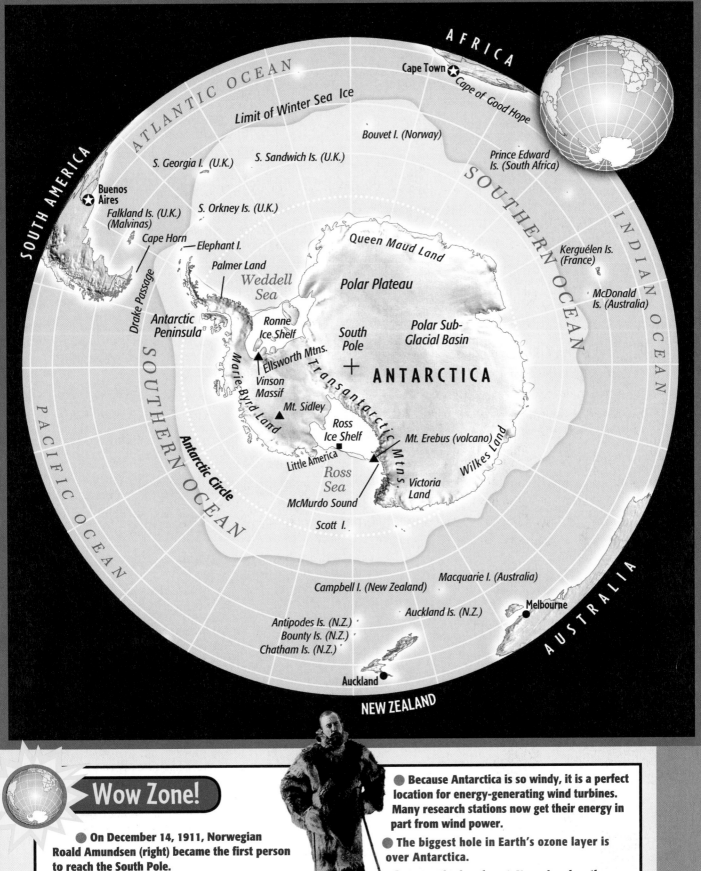

AFRICA

ATLANTIC OCEAN

Cape Town ✪
Cape of Good Hope

Limit of Winter Sea Ice

Bouvet I. (Norway)

S. Georgia I. (U.K.)

S. Sandwich Is. (U.K.)

Prince Edward
Is. (South Africa)

SOUTHERN OCEAN

SOUTH AMERICA

Buenos ✪
Aires

Falkland Is. (U.K.)
(Malvinas)

S. Orkney Is. (U.K.)

INDIAN OCEAN

Kerguélen Is.
(France)

Cape Horn

Elephant I.

Queen Maud Land

McDonald
Is. (Australia)

Drake Passage

Palmer Land

Weddell
Sea

Polar Plateau

Antarctic
Peninsula

Ronne
Ice Shelf

South
Pole

Polar Sub-
Glacial Basin

Ellsworth Mtns.

+ ANTARCTICA

SOUTHERN OCEAN

Marie Byrd Land

Vinson
Massif

Mt. Sidley

Transantarctic Mtns.

Ross
Ice Shelf

Mt. Erebus (volcano)

Wilkes Land

PACIFIC OCEAN

Antarctic Circle

Little America

Ross
Sea

Victoria
Land

McMurdo Sound

Scott I.

Macquarie I. (Australia)

Campbell I. (New Zealand)

Auckland Is. (N.Z.)

Melbourne

Antipodes Is. (N.Z.)
Bounty Is. (N.Z.)
Chatham Is. (N.Z.)

AUSTRALIA

Auckland

NEW ZEALAND

Wow Zone!

● On December 14, 1911, Norwegian Roald Amundsen (right) became the first person to reach the South Pole.

● In 1983, scientists measured the coldest temperature ever recorded on Earth: −128.6°F (−88.0°C). It was in Antarctica!

● Because Antarctica is so windy, it is a perfect location for energy-generating wind turbines. Many research stations now get their energy in part from wind power.

● The biggest hole in Earth's ozone layer is over Antarctica.

● Antarctica is a desert. It receives less than 2 inches (5 cm) of rain a year, about as much as the Sahara desert.

World-at-a-Glance

AFGHANISTAN
AREA: 251,827 sq mi (652,229 sq km)
POPULATION: 29,835,392
CAPITAL: Kabul
LANGUAGES: Afghan Persian (Dari), Pashto
GOVERNMENT: Islamic republic
RELIGIONS: Sunni Muslim, Shia Muslim
LITERACY RATE: 28%
CURRENCY: Afghani
MAIN EXPORTS: Fruit and nuts, carpets, wool, cotton, hides and pelts, precious and semiprecious gems

ALBANIA
AREA: 11,010 sq mi (28,748 sq km)
POPULATION: 2,994,667
CAPITAL: Tirana
LANGUAGES: Albanian (Tosk is the official dialect), Greek, Vlach, Romani, Slavic
GOVERNMENT: Republic
RELIGIONS: Muslim, Albanian Orthodox, Roman Catholic
LITERACY RATE: 99%
CURRENCY: Lek
MAIN EXPORTS: Textiles and footwear, asphalt, metals, crude oil, vegetables, fruit, tobacco

ALGERIA
AREA: 919,595 sq mi (2,381,740 sq km)
POPULATION: 34,994,937
CAPITAL: Algiers
LANGUAGES: Arabic (official), French, Berber dialects
GOVERNMENT: Republic
RELIGION: Sunni Muslim
LITERACY RATE: 70%
CURRENCY: Algerian dinar
MAIN EXPORTS: Petroleum, natural gas, petroleum products

ANDORRA
AREA: 181 sq mi (469 sq km)
POPULATION: 84,825
CAPITAL: Andorra la Vella
LANGUAGES: Catalan (official), French, Castilian, Portuguese
GOVERNMENT: Parliamentary democracy
RELIGION: Roman Catholic
LITERACY RATE: 100%

CURRENCY: Euro
MAIN EXPORTS: Tobacco products, furniture

ANGOLA
AREA: 481,354 sq mi (1,246,701 sq km)
POPULATION: 13,338,541
CAPITAL: Luanda
LANGUAGES: Portuguese (official), Bantu and other African languages
GOVERNMENT: Republic; multiparty presidential regime
RELIGIONS: Native beliefs, Roman Catholic, Protestant
LITERACY RATE: 67%
CURRENCY: Kwanza
MAIN EXPORTS: Crude oil, diamonds, refined petroleum products, coffee, sisal, fish, timber, cotton

ANTIGUA AND BARBUDA
AREA: 171 sq mi (443 sq km)
POPULATION: 87,884
CAPITAL: Saint John's
LANGUAGES: English (official), local dialects
GOVERNMENT: Constitutional monarchy
RELIGIONS: Moravian, Roman Catholic, Protestant
LITERACY RATE: 86%
CURRENCY: East Caribbean dollar
MAIN EXPORTS: Petroleum products, handicrafts, electronic components, transport equipment, food, live animals

ARGENTINA
AREA: 1,068,302 sq mi (2,766,889 sq km)
POPULATION: 41,769,726
CAPITAL: Buenos Aires
LANGUAGES: Spanish (official), English, Italian, German, French
GOVERNMENT: Republic
RELIGIONS: Roman Catholic, Protestant, Jewish
LITERACY RATE: 97%
CURRENCY: Argentine peso
MAIN EXPORTS: Soybeans and derivatives, petroleum and gas, vehicles, corn, wheat

ARMENIA
AREA: 11,484 sq mi (29,743 sq km)
POPULATION: 2,967,975
CAPITAL: Yerevan

LANGUAGES: Armenian, Russian, Yezidi
GOVERNMENT: Republic
RELIGIONS: Armenian Apostolic, other Christian, Yezidi
LITERACY RATE: 99%
CURRENCY: Dram
MAIN EXPORTS: Pig iron, unwrought copper, nonferrous metals, diamonds, mineral products

AUSTRALIA
AREA: 2,988,902 sq mi (7,741,221 sq km)
POPULATION: 21,766,711
CAPITAL: Canberra
LANGUAGES: English, native languages
GOVERNMENT: Federal parliamentary democracy
RELIGIONS: Catholic, Anglican, others
LITERACY RATE: 99%
CURRENCY: Australian dollar
MAIN EXPORTS: Coal, gold, meat, wool, alumina, iron ore, wheat, machinery and transport equipment

AUSTRIA
AREA: 32,383 sq mi (83,872 sq km)
POPULATION: 8,217,280
CAPITAL: Vienna
LANGUAGES: German, Turkish, Serbian, Croatian
GOVERNMENT: Federal republic
RELIGIONS: Roman Catholic, Protestant, Muslim
LITERACY RATE: 98%
CURRENCY: Euro
MAIN EXPORTS: Machinery, motor vehicles and parts, paper, metal goods, chemicals, iron, steel, textiles, foodstuffs

AZERBAIJAN
AREA: 33,436 sq mi (86,599 sq km)
POPULATION: 8,372,373
CAPITAL: Baku
LANGUAGES: Azerbaijani (Azeri), Russian, Armenian, Lezgi
GOVERNMENT: Republic
RELIGIONS: Muslim, Russian Orthodox, Armenian Orthodox
LITERACY RATE: 99%
CURRENCY: Azerbaijani manat
MAIN EXPORTS: Oil and gas, machinery, cotton, foodstuffs

BAHAMAS
AREA: 5,359 sq mi
(13,880 sq km)
POPULATION:
313,312
CAPITAL: Nassau
LANGUAGE: English (official)
GOVERNMENT: Constitutional parliamentary democracy
RELIGIONS: Protestant, Roman Catholic
LITERACY RATE: 96%
CURRENCY: Bahamian dollar
MAIN EXPORTS: Mineral products and salt, animal products, chemicals, fruit and vegetables

BAHRAIN
AREA: 286 sq mi
(741 sq km)
POPULATION:
1,214,705
CAPITAL: Manama
LANGUAGES: Arabic, English, Farsi, Urdu
GOVERNMENT: Constitutional monarchy
RELIGIONS: Shia Muslim, Sunni Muslim, Christian, others
LITERACY RATE: 87%
CURRENCY: Bahraini dinar
MAIN EXPORTS: Petroleum and petroleum products, aluminum, textiles

BANGLADESH
AREA: 55,598 sq mi
(143,998 sq km)
POPULATION:
158,570,535
CAPITAL: Dhaka
LANGUAGES: Bangla (official), English
GOVERNMENT: Parliamentary democracy
RELIGIONS: Muslim, Hindu
LITERACY RATE: 48%
CURRENCY: Taka
MAIN EXPORTS: Clothing, jute, leather, frozen fish and seafood

BARBADOS
AREA: 166 sq mi
(430 sq km)
POPULATION:
286,705
CAPITAL: Bridgetown
LANGUAGE: English
GOVERNMENT: Parliamentary democracy
RELIGIONS: Protestant, Roman Catholic
LITERACY RATE: 100%
CURRENCY: Barbadian dollar
MAIN EXPORTS: Sugar and molasses, rum, foodstuffs, chemicals, electrical components

BELARUS
AREA: 80,154 sq mi
(207,598 sq km)
POPULATION:
9,577,552
CAPITAL: Minsk
LANGUAGES: Belarusian, Russian
GOVERNMENT: Republic

RELIGIONS: Eastern Orthodox, Roman Catholic, Protestant, Jewish, Muslim
LITERACY RATE: 100%
CURRENCY: Belarusian ruble
MAIN EXPORTS: Machinery and equipment, mineral products, chemicals, metals, textiles, foodstuffs

BELGIUM
AREA: 11,787 sq mi
(30,528 sq km)
POPULATION:
10,431,477
CAPITAL: Brussels
LANGUAGES: Dutch, French, German (all official)
GOVERNMENT: Federal parliamentary democracy under a constitutional monarch
RELIGIONS: Roman Catholic, Protestant
LITERACY RATE: 99%
CURRENCY: Euro
MAIN EXPORTS: Machinery and equipment, chemicals, diamonds, metals and metal products, foodstuffs

BELIZE
AREA: 8,867 sq mi
(22,965 sq km)
POPULATION:
321,115
CAPITAL: Belmopan
LANGUAGES: English (official), Spanish, Mayan, Garifuna (Carib)
GOVERNMENT: Parliamentary democracy
RELIGIONS: Roman Catholic, Protestant
LITERACY RATE: 77%
CURRENCY: Belizean dollar
MAIN EXPORTS: Sugar, bananas, citrus, clothing, fish products, molasses, wood, crude oil

BENIN
AREA: 43,483 sq mi
(112,620 sq km)
POPULATION:
9,325,032
CAPITAL: Porto-Novo
LANGUAGES: French (official), African languages
GOVERNMENT: Republic
RELIGIONS: Native beliefs, Christian, Muslim
LITERACY RATE: 35%
CURRENCY: Communauté Financière Africaine franc
MAIN EXPORTS: Cotton, cashews, shea butter, textiles, palm products, seafood

BHUTAN
AREA: 14,824 sq mi
(38,394 sq km)
POPULATION:
708,427
CAPITAL: Thimphu
LANGUAGES: Dzongkha (official), others
GOVERNMENT: Constitutional monarchy
RELIGIONS: Buddhist, Hindu
LITERACY RATE: 47%
CURRENCY: Ngultrum

MAIN EXPORTS: Electricity, ferrosilicon, cement, calcium carbide, copper wire, manganese, vegetable oil

BOLIVIA
AREA: 424,162 sq mi
(1,098,754 sq km)
POPULATION:
10,118,683
CAPITAL: La Paz (seat of government); Sucre (legal capital)
LANGUAGES: Spanish, Quechua, Aymara (all official)
GOVERNMENT: Republic
RELIGIONS: Roman Catholic, Protestant
LITERACY RATE: 87%
CURRENCY: Boliviano
MAIN EXPORTS: Natural gas, soybeans and soy products, crude petroleum, zinc ore, tin

BOSNIA AND HERZEGOVINA
AREA: 19,767 sq mi
(51,196 sq km)
POPULATION: 4,622,163
CAPITAL: Sarajevo
LANGUAGES: Croatian, Serbian, Bosnian
GOVERNMENT: Emerging federal democratic republic
RELIGIONS: Muslim, Orthodox, Roman Catholic
LITERACY RATE: 97%
CURRENCY: Marka
MAIN EXPORTS: Metals, clothing, wood products

BOTSWANA
AREA: 224,607 sq mi
(581,730 sq km)
POPULATION:
2,065,398
CAPITAL: Gaborone
LANGUAGES: English (official), Setswana, Kalanga, Sekgalagadi
GOVERNMENT: Parliamentary republic
RELIGIONS: Native beliefs, Christian
LITERACY RATE: 80%
CURRENCY: Pula
MAIN EXPORTS: Diamonds, copper, nickel, soda ash, meat, textiles

BRAZIL
AREA: 3,286,488 sq mi
(8,511,965 sq km)
POPULATION:
203,429,773
CAPITAL: Brasília
LANGUAGES: Portuguese (official), Spanish, German, Italian, Japanese, English, others
GOVERNMENT: Federal republic
RELIGION: Roman Catholic, Protestant
LITERACY RATE: 89%
CURRENCY: Real
MAIN EXPORTS: Transport equipment, iron ore, soybeans, footwear, coffee, motor vehicles

BRUNEI
AREA: 2,228 sq mi
(5,770 sq km)
POPULATION:
401,890
CAPITAL: Bandar Seri Begawan
LANGUAGES: Malay (official), English, Chinese
GOVERNMENT: Constitutional sultanate
RELIGIONS: Muslim, Buddhist, Christian, others
LITERACY RATE: 93%
CURRENCY: Bruneian dollar
MAIN EXPORTS: Crude oil, natural gas, garments

BULGARIA
AREA: 42,811 sq mi
(110,880 sq km)
POPULATION:
7,093,635
CAPITAL: Sofia
LANGUAGES: Bulgarian, Turkish, Roma
GOVERNMENT: Parliamentary democracy
RELIGIONS: Bulgarian Orthodox, Muslim
LITERACY RATE: 99%
CURRENCY: Lev
MAIN EXPORTS: Clothing, footwear, iron and steel, machinery and equipment, fuels

BURKINA FASO
AREA: 105,870 sq mi
(274,202 sq km)
POPULATION:
16,751,455
CAPITAL: Ouagadougou
LANGUAGES: French (official), African languages
GOVERNMENT: Parliamentary republic
RELIGIONS: Native beliefs, Muslim, Christian
LITERACY RATE: 22%
CURRENCY: Communauté Financière Africaine franc
MAIN EXPORTS: Cotton, livestock, gold

BURUNDI
AREA: 10,745 sq mi
(27,829 sq km)
POPULATION:
10,216,190
CAPITAL: Bujumbura
LANGUAGES: Kirundi, French (both official), Swahili
GOVERNMENT: Republic
RELIGION: Roman Catholic, native beliefs, Muslim, Protestant
LITERACY RATE: 59%
CURRENCY: Burundi franc
MAIN EXPORTS: Coffee, tea, sugar, cotton, hides

CAMBODIA
AREA: 69,900 sq mi
(181,040 sq km)
POPULATION:
14,701,717
CAPITAL: Phnom Penh
LANGUAGES: Khmer (official), French, English

GOVERNMENT: Multiparty democracy under a constitutional monarchy
RELIGIONS: Buddhist, Muslim, others
LITERACY RATE: 74%
CURRENCY: Riel
MAIN EXPORTS: Timber, garments, rubber, rice, fish, tobacco, footwear

CAMEROON
AREA: 183,567 sq mi
(475,436 sq km)
POPULATION:
19,711,291
CAPITAL: Yaoundé
LANGUAGES: English, French (both official), African languages
GOVERNMENT: Republic and multiparty presidential regime
RELIGIONS: Native beliefs, Christian, Muslim
LITERACY RATE: 68%
CURRENCY: Communauté Financière Africaine franc
MAIN EXPORTS: Crude oil and petroleum products, lumber, cocoa beans, aluminum, coffee, cotton

CANADA
AREA:
3,855,085 sq mi
(9,984,624 sq km)
POPULATION: 34,030,589
CAPITAL: Ottawa
LANGUAGES: English, French (both official), others
GOVERNMENT: Parliamentary democracy, federation, and constitutional monarchy
RELIGIONS: Roman Catholic, Protestant, others
LITERACY RATE: 99%
CURRENCY: Canadian dollar
MAIN EXPORTS: Automobiles, industrial machinery, aircraft, telecommunications equipment, chemicals, plastics, fertilizers, wood pulp, timber, crude petroleum

CAPE VERDE
AREA: 1,557 sq mi
(4,033 sq km)
POPULATION:
516,100
CAPITAL: Praia
LANGUAGES: Portuguese, Crioulo
GOVERNMENT: Republic
RELIGIONS: Roman Catholic, Protestant
LITERACY RATE: 77%
CURRENCY: Cape Verdean escudo
MAIN EXPORTS: Foodstuffs, industrial products, transport equipment, fuels

CENTRAL AFRICAN REPUBLIC
AREA: 240,535 sq mi
(622,983 sq km)
POPULATION: 4,950,027
CAPITAL: Bangui
LANGUAGES: French (official), Sangho, tribal languages
GOVERNMENT: Republic

RELIGIONS: Native beliefs, Protestant, Roman Catholic, Muslim
LITERACY RATE: 49%
CURRENCY: Communauté Financière Africaine franc
MAIN EXPORTS: Diamonds, timber, cotton, coffee, tobacco

CHAD
AREA: 495,755 sq mi
(1,284,000 sq km)
POPULATION:
10,758,945
CAPITAL: N'Djamena
LANGUAGES: French, Arabic (both official), Sara, African languages
GOVERNMENT: Republic
RELIGIONS: Muslim, Christian, animist
LITERACY RATE: 26%
CURRENCY: Communauté Financière Africaine franc
MAIN EXPORTS: Cotton, cattle, gum arabic

CHILE
AREA: 291,933 sq mi
(756,103 sq km)
POPULATION:
16,888,760
CAPITAL: Santiago
LANGUAGES: Spanish, Mapudungun, German, English
GOVERNMENT: Republic
RELIGIONS: Roman Catholic, Evangelical
LITERACY RATE: 96%
CURRENCY: Chilean peso
MAIN EXPORTS: Copper, fish, fruit, paper and pulp, chemicals, wine

CHINA
AREA: 3,705,407 sq mi
(9,596,960 sq km)
POPULATION:
1,336,718,015
CAPITAL: Beijing
LANGUAGES: Chinese (Mandarin), local dialects
GOVERNMENT: Communist state
RELIGIONS: Taoist, Buddhist, Muslim, Christian
LITERACY RATE: 91%
CURRENCY: Renminbi yuan
MAIN EXPORTS: Electrical and other machinery, apparel, textiles, iron and steel, optical and medical

COLOMBIA
AREA: 439,733 sq mi
(1,138,903 sq km)
POPULATION:
44,725,543
CAPITAL: Bogotá
LANGUAGE: Spanish
GOVERNMENT: Republic
RELIGION: Roman Catholic
LITERACY RATE: 90%
CURRENCY: Colombian peso
MAIN EXPORTS: Petroleum, coffee, coal, clothing, bananas, flowers, nickel, emeralds

COMOROS

AREA: 863 sq mi (2,235 sq km)
POPULATION: 794,683
CAPITAL: Moroni
LANGUAGES: Arabic, French (both official), Shikomoro
GOVERNMENT: Republic
RELIGIONS: Sunni Muslim, Roman Catholic
LITERACY RATE: 57%
CURRENCY: Comoran franc
MAIN EXPORTS: Vanilla, ylang-ylang, cloves, copra

CONGO, DEMOCRATIC REPUBLIC OF THE

AREA: 905,355 sq mi (2,344,859 sq km)
POPULATION: 71,712,867
CAPITAL: Kinshasa
LANGUAGES: French (official), Lingala, Kingwana, Kikongo, other African languages
GOVERNMENT: Republic
RELIGIONS: Roman Catholic, Protestant, Kimbanguist, Muslim, native beliefs
LITERACY RATE: 66%
CURRENCY: Congolese franc
MAIN EXPORTS: Diamonds, copper, crude oil, coffee, cobalt, gold, wood products

CONGO, REPUBLIC OF THE

AREA: 132,046 sq mi (342,000 sq km)
POPULATION: 4,243,929
CAPITAL: Brazzaville
LANGUAGES: French (official), Lingala, Monokutuba, other African languages
GOVERNMENT: Republic
RELIGIONS: Christian, animist, Muslim
LITERACY RATE: 90%
CURRENCY: Communauté Financière Africaine franc
MAIN EXPORTS: Petroleum, lumber, plywood, sugar, cocoa, coffee, diamonds

COSTA RICA

AREA: 19,730 sq mi (51,100 sq km)
POPULATION: 4,576,562
CAPITAL: San José
LANGUAGE: Spanish (official)
GOVERNMENT: Democratic republic
RELIGIONS: Roman Catholic, Evangelical, others
LITERACY RATE: 96%
CURRENCY: Costa Rican colón
MAIN EXPORTS: Bananas, pineapples, coffee, melons, ornamental plants, sugar, beef, seafood, medical equipment

COTE D'IVOIRE

AREA: 124,502 sq mi (322,459 sq km)
POPULATION: 21,504,162
CAPITAL: Yamoussoukro
LANGUAGES: French (official), African languages
GOVERNMENT: Republic
RELIGION: Muslim, Christian, native beliefs
LITERACY RATE: 49%
CURRENCY: Communauté Financière Africaine franc
MAIN EXPORTS: Cocoa, coffee, timber, petroleum, cotton, bananas, pineapples

CROATIA

AREA: 21,851 sq mi (56,594 sq km)
POPULATION: 4,483,804
CAPITAL: Zagreb
LANGUAGE: Croatian
GOVERNMENT: Presidential/parliamentary democracy
RELIGIONS: Roman Catholic, Orthodox, Muslim
LITERACY RATE: 99%
CURRENCY: Kuna
MAIN EXPORTS: Transport equipment, textiles, chemicals, foodstuffs, fuels

CUBA

AREA: 42,803 sq mi (110,859 sq km)
POPULATION: 11,087,330
CAPITAL: Havana
LANGUAGE: Spanish
GOVERNMENT: Communist state
RELIGION: Roman Catholic, Protestant
LITERACY RATE: 100%
CURRENCY: Cuban peso
MAIN EXPORTS: Sugar, nickel, tobacco, fish, medical products, citrus, coffee

CYPRUS

AREA: 3,572 sq mi (9,251 sq km)
POPULATION: 1,120,489
CAPITAL: Nicosia
LANGUAGES: Greek, Turkish, English
GOVERNMENT: Republic
RELIGIONS: Greek Orthodox, Muslim, Maronite, Armenian Apostolic
LITERACY RATE: 98%
CURRENCY: Euro
MAIN EXPORTS: Citrus, potatoes, pharmaceuticals, cement

CZECH REPUBLIC

AREA: 30,450 sq mi (78,865 sq km)
POPULATION: 10,190,213
CAPITAL: Prague
LANGUAGE: Czech, Slovak
GOVERNMENT: Parliamentary democracy
RELIGIONS: Roman Catholic, Protestant
LITERACY RATE: 99%
CURRENCY: Koruna
MAIN EXPORTS: Machinery and transport equipment, chemicals, raw materials, fuel

DENMARK

AREA: 16,639 sq mi (43,095 sq km)
POPULATION: 5,529,888
CAPITAL: Copenhagen
LANGUAGES: Danish, Faroese, Greenlandic, German
GOVERNMENT: Constitutional monarchy
RELIGION: Evangelical Lutheran
LITERACY RATE: 99%
CURRENCY: Danish kroner
MAIN EXPORTS: Machinery and instruments, meat and meat products, dairy products, fish, pharmaceuticals, furniture, windmills

DJIBOUTI

AREA: 8,958 sq mi (23,201 sq km)
POPULATION: 757,074
CAPITAL: Djibouti
LANGUAGES: French, Arabic (both official), Somali, Afar
GOVERNMENT: Republic
RELIGIONS: Muslim, Christian
LITERACY RATE: 68%
CURRENCY: Djiboutian franc
MAIN EXPORTS: Re-exports, hides and skins, coffee

DOMINICA

AREA: 290 sq mi (751 sq km)
POPULATION: 72,969
CAPITAL: Roseau
LANGUAGES: English (official), French patois
GOVERNMENT: Parliamentary democracy
RELIGIONS: Roman Catholic, Protestant
LITERACY RATE: 94%
CURRENCY: East Caribbean dollar
MAIN EXPORTS: Bananas, soap, bay oil, vegetables, grapefruit, oranges

DOMINICAN REPUBLIC

AREA: 18,792 sq mi (48,671 sq km)
POPULATION: 9,956,648
CAPITAL: Santo Domingo
LANGUAGE: Spanish
GOVERNMENT: Democratic republic
RELIGION: Roman Catholic
LITERACY RATE: 87%
CURRENCY: Dominican peso
MAIN EXPORTS: Ferronickel, sugar, gold, silver, coffee, cocoa, tobacco, meats

EAST TIMOR

AREA: 5,743 sq mi (14,874 sq km)
POPULATION: 1,177,834

CAPITAL: Dili
LANGUAGES: Tetum, Portuguese (both official), Indonesian, English
GOVERNMENT: Republic
RELIGIONS: Roman Catholic, Muslim, Protestant
LITERACY RATE: 59%
CURRENCY: U.S. dollar
MAIN EXPORTS: Coffee, sandalwood, marble

ECUADOR
AREA: 109,483 sq mi (283,560 sq km)
POPULATION: 15,007,343

CAPITAL: Quito
LANGUAGES: Spanish (official), Amerindian languages
GOVERNMENT: Republic
RELIGION: Roman Catholic
LITERACY RATE: 91%
CURRENCY: U.S. dollar
MAIN EXPORTS: Petroleum, bananas, flowers, shrimp, cacao, coffee, hemp, wood, fish

EGYPT
AREA: 386,660 sq mi (1,001,445 sq km)
POPULATION: 82,079,636

CAPITAL: Cairo
LANGUAGE: Arabic (official)
GOVERNMENT: Republic
RELIGIONS: Muslim (mostly Sunni), Coptic Christian
LITERACY RATE: 71%
CURRENCY: Egyptian pound
MAIN EXPORTS: Crude oil and petroleum products, cotton, textiles, metal products

EL SALVADOR
AREA: 8,124 sq mi (21,041 sq km)
POPULATION: 6,071,774

CAPITAL: San Salvador
LANGUAGES: Spanish, Nahuati
GOVERNMENT: Republic
RELIGION: Roman Catholic
LITERACY RATE: 80%
CURRENCY: U.S. dollar
MAIN EXPORTS: Offshore assembly exports, coffee, sugar, shrimp, textiles, chemicals, electricity

EQUATORIAL GUINEA
AREA: 10,830 sq mi (28,050 sq km)
POPULATION: 668,225

CAPITAL: Malabo
LANGUAGES: Spanish, French (both official), Fang, Bubi
GOVERNMENT: Republic
RELIGION: Christian
LITERACY RATE: 86%
CURRENCY: Communauté Financière Africaine franc

MAIN EXPORTS: Petroleum, methanol, timber, cocoa

ERITREA
AREA: 45,406 sq mi (117,601 sq km)
POPULATION: 5,939,484

CAPITAL: Asmara
LANGUAGES: Afar, Arabic, Tigre, Kunama, others
GOVERNMENT: Transitional
RELIGIONS: Muslim, Coptic Christian, Roman Catholic, Protestant
LITERACY RATE: 59%
CURRENCY: Nakfa
MAIN EXPORTS: Livestock, sorghum, textiles, food, small manufactures

ESTONIA
AREA: 17,462 sq mi (45,226 sq km)
POPULATION: 1,282,963

CAPITAL: Tallinn
LANGUAGES: Estonian (official), Russian
GOVERNMENT: Parliamentary republic
RELIGIONS: Evangelical Lutheran, Orthodox, Christian
LITERACY RATE: 100%
CURRENCY: Euro
MAIN EXPORTS: Machinery and equipment, wood and paper, textiles, food products, metals

ETHIOPIA
AREA: 426,373 sq mi (1,104,300 sq km)
POPULATION: 90,783,739

CAPITAL: Addis Ababa
LANGUAGES: Amarigna, Oromigna, others
GOVERNMENT: Federal republic
RELIGIONS: Christian, Muslim
LITERACY RATE: 43%
CURRENCY: Birr
MAIN EXPORTS: Coffee, khat, gold, leather products, live animals, oilseeds

FIJI
AREA: 7,054 sq mi (18,270 sq km)
POPULATION: 883,125

CAPITAL: Suva
LANGUAGES: English, Fijian (both official), Hindustani
GOVERNMENT: Republic
RELIGIONS: Christian, Hindu, Muslim
LITERACY RATE: 94%
CURRENCY: Fijian dollar
MAIN EXPORTS: Sugar, garments, gold, timber, fish, molasses, coconut oil

FINLAND
AREA: 130,559 sq mi (338,146 sq km)
POPULATION: 5,259,250

CAPITAL: Helsinki
LANGUAGES: Finnish, Swedish (both official)
GOVERNMENT: Republic
RELIGIONS: Lutheran, Orthodox
LITERACY RATE: 100%
CURRENCY: Euro
MAIN EXPORTS: Machinery and equipment, chemicals, metals, timber, paper, pulp

FRANCE
AREA: 248,429 sq mi (643,428 sq km)
POPULATION: 65,312,249

CAPITAL: Paris
LANGUAGE: French
GOVERNMENT: Republic
RELIGIONS: Roman Catholic, Protestant, Jewish, Muslim
LITERACY RATE: 99%
CURRENCY: Euro
MAIN EXPORTS: Machinery and transportation equipment, aircraft, plastics, chemicals, pharmaceutical products, iron and steel, beverages

GABON
AREA: 103,347 sq mi (267,668 sq km)
POPULATION: 1,576,665

CAPITAL: Libreville
LANGUAGES: French (official), Fang, Myene, Nzebi, Bapounou/Eschira, Bandjabi
GOVERNMENT: Multiparty presidential regime
RELIGIONS: Christian, animist, Muslim
LITERACY RATE: 63%
CURRENCY: Communauté Financière Africaine franc
MAIN EXPORTS: Crude oil, timber, manganese, uranium

GAMBIA, THE
AREA: 4,363 sq mi (11,300 sq km)
POPULATION: 1,797,860

CAPITAL: Banjul
LANGUAGES: English (official), native languages
GOVERNMENT: Republic
RELIGIONS: Muslim, Christian, indigenous beliefs
LITERACY RATE: 40%
CURRENCY: Dalasi
MAIN EXPORTS: Peanut products, fish, cotton lint, palm kernels, re-exports

GEORGIA
AREA: 26,911 sq mi (69,699 sq km)
POPULATION: 4,585,874

CAPITAL: Tbilisi
LANGUAGES: Georgian (official), Russian, Armenian, Azeri
GOVERNMENT: Republic

RELIGIONS: Orthodox Christian, Muslim, Armenian-Gregorian, Catholic

LITERACY RATE: 100%

CURRENCY: Lari

MAIN EXPORTS: Scrap metal, wine, mineral water, ores, automobiles, fruit and nuts

GERMANY

AREA: 137,846 sq mi (357,020 sq km)

POPULATION: 81,471,834

CAPITAL: Berlin

LANGUAGE: German

GOVERNMENT: Federal republic

RELIGIONS: Protestant, Roman Catholic, Muslim

LITERACY RATE: 99%

CURRENCY: Euro

MAIN EXPORTS: Machinery, vehicles, chemicals, metals and manufactures, foodstuffs, textiles

GHANA

AREA: 92,098 sq mi (238,533 sq km)

POPULATION: 24,791,073

CAPITAL: Accra

LANGUAGES: English (official), African languages

GOVERNMENT: Constitutional democracy

RELIGIONS: Christian, Muslim, native beliefs

LITERACY RATE: 58%

CURRENCY: Cedi

MAIN EXPORTS: Gold, cocoa, timber, tuna, bauxite, aluminum, diamonds, manganese ore

GREECE

AREA: 50,942 sq mi (131,939 sq km)

POPULATION: 10,760,136

CAPITAL: Athens

LANGUAGES: Greek (official), English, French

GOVERNMENT: Parliamentary republic

RELIGIONS: Greek Orthodox, Muslim

LITERACY RATE: 98%

CURRENCY: Euro

MAIN EXPORTS: Food and beverages, petroleum products, chemicals, textiles

GRENADA

AREA: 133 sq mi (344 sq km)

POPULATION: 108,419

CAPITAL: St. George's

LANGUAGES: English (official), French patois

GOVERNMENT: Parliamentary democracy

RELIGIONS: Roman Catholic, Protestant, Anglican

LITERACY RATE: 96%

CURRENCY: East Caribbean dollar

MAIN EXPORTS: Bananas, cocoa, nutmeg, fruit and vegetables, clothing, mace

GUATEMALA

AREA: 42,042 sq mi (108,888 sq km)

POPULATION: 13,824,463

CAPITAL: Guatemala City

LANGUAGES: Spanish, Amerindian languages

GOVERNMENT: Constitutional democratic republic

RELIGIONS: Roman Catholic, Protestant, native Mayan beliefs

LITERACY RATE: 69%

CURRENCY: Quetzal

MAIN EXPORTS: Coffee, sugar, bananas, fruit and vegetables, cardamom, apparel

GUINEA

AREA: 94,925 sq mi (245,855 sq km)

POPULATION: 10,601,009

CAPITAL: Conakry

LANGUAGES: French (official), native languages

GOVERNMENT: Republic

RELIGIONS: Muslim, Christian, native beliefs

LITERACY RATE: 30%

CURRENCY: Guinean franc

MAIN EXPORTS: Bauxite, alumina, gold, diamonds, coffee, fish, agricultural products

GUINEA-BISSAU

AREA: 13,946 sq mi (36,120 sq km)

POPULATION: 1,596,677

CAPITAL: Bissau

LANGUAGES: Portuguese (official), Crioulo, African languages

GOVERNMENT: Republic

RELIGIONS: Native beliefs, Muslim, Christian

LITERACY RATE: 42%

CURRENCY: Communauté Financière Africaine franc

MAIN EXPORTS: Cashew nuts, shrimp, peanuts, palm kernels, sawn lumber

GUYANA

AREA: 83,000 sq mi (214,969 sq km)

POPULATION: 744,768

CAPITAL: Georgetown

LANGUAGES: English, Amerindian dialects, Creole, Hindi, Urdu

GOVERNMENT: Republic

RELIGIONS: Hindu, Pentecostal, Roman Catholic, Anglican, others

LITERACY RATE: 99%

CURRENCY: Guyanese dollar

MAIN EXPORTS: Sugar, gold, rice, shrimp, bauxite, alumina, molasses, rum, timber

HAITI

AREA: 10,714 sq mi (27,749 sq km)

POPULATION: 9,719,932

CAPITAL: Port-au-Prince

LANGUAGES: French, Creole (both official)

GOVERNMENT: Republic

RELIGIONS: Roman Catholic, Protestant, others

LITERACY RATE: 53%

CURRENCY: Gourde

MAIN EXPORTS: Manufactures, coffee, oils, cocoa, mangoes, apparel

HONDURAS

AREA: 43,278 sq mi (112,090 sq km)

POPULATION: 8,143,564

CAPITAL: Tegucigalpa

LANGUAGES: Spanish, Amerindian dialects

GOVERNMENT: Democratic constitutional republic

RELIGIONS: Roman Catholic, Protestant

LITERACY RATE: 80%

CURRENCY: Lempira

MAIN EXPORTS: Apparel, coffee, shrimp, bananas, gold, palm oil, fruit, lobster, lumber

HUNGARY

AREA: 35,919 sq mi (93,030 sq km)

POPULATION: 9,976,062

CAPITAL: Budapest

LANGUAGE: Hungarian

GOVERNMENT: Parliamentary democracy

RELIGIONS: Roman Catholic, Calvinist, Lutheran

LITERACY RATE: 99%

CURRENCY: Forint

MAIN EXPORTS: Machinery and equipment, other manufactures, food products, raw materials, fuels and electricity

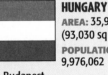

ICELAND

AREA: 39,768 sq mi (102,999 sq km)

POPULATION: 311,058

CAPITAL: Reykjavik

LANGUAGES: Icelandic, English, Nordic languages, German

GOVERNMENT: Constitutional republic

RELIGION: Lutheran, Roman Catholic

LITERACY RATE: 99%

CURRENCY: Icelandic krona

MAIN EXPORTS: Fish and fish products, animal products, aluminum, diatomite, ferrosilicon

INDIA

AREA: 1,269,219 sq mi (3,287,262 sq km)

POPULATION: 1,189,172,906

CAPITAL: New Delhi

LANGUAGES: Hindi, Bengali, Telugu, Marathi, others

GOVERNMENT: Federal republic
RELIGIONS: Hindu, Muslim, Christian, Sikh
LITERACY RATE: 60%
CURRENCY: Indian rupee
MAIN EXPORTS: Petroleum products, precious stones, machinery, iron and steel

INDONESIA
AREA: 735,358 sq mi (1,904,568 sq km)
POPULATION: 245,613,043
CAPITAL: Jakarta
LANGUAGES: Bahasa Indonesian, English, Dutch, local dialects
GOVERNMENT: Republic
RELIGIONS: Muslim, Protestant, Roman Catholic, Hindu
LITERACY RATE: 90%
CURRENCY: Indonesian rupiah
MAIN EXPORTS: Oil and gas, electrical appliances, plywood, textiles, rubber

IRAN
AREA: 636,372 sq mi (1,648,196 sq km)
POPULATION: 77,891,220
CAPITAL: Tehran
LANGUAGES: Persian, Turkic, Kurdish
GOVERNMENT: Theocratic republic
RELIGIONS: Shia Muslim, Sunni Muslim, Zoroastrianist, Jewish, Christian, Baha'i
LITERACY RATE: 77%
CURRENCY: Iranian rial
MAIN EXPORTS: Petroleum, carpets, fruit and nuts, chemicals

IRAQ
AREA: 169,235 sq mi (438,317 sq km)
POPULATION: 30,399,572
CAPITAL: Baghdad
LANGUAGES: Arabic, Kurdish, Assyrian, Armenian
GOVERNMENT: Parliamentary democracy
RELIGIONS: Muslim, Christian
LITERACY RATE: 74%
CURRENCY: Iraqi dinar
MAIN EXPORTS: Crude oil and materials

IRELAND
AREA: 27,136 sq mi (70,282 sq km)
POPULATION: 4,670,976
CAPITAL: Dublin
LANGUAGES: English, Irish Gaelic (both official)
GOVERNMENT: Republic
RELIGIONS: Roman Catholic, Church of Ireland
LITERACY RATE: 99%
CURRENCY: Euro
MAIN EXPORTS: Machinery and equipment, computers, chemicals, pharmaceuticals, live animals

ISRAEL
AREA: 8,522 sq mi (22,072 sq km)
POPULATION: 7,473,052
CAPITAL: Jerusalem
LANGUAGES: Hebrew, Arabic (both official), English
GOVERNMENT: Parliamentary democracy
RELIGIONS: Jewish, Muslim, Christian
LITERACY RATE: 97%
CURRENCY: New Israeli shekel
MAIN EXPORTS: Machinery and equipment, software, cut diamonds, agricultural products, chemicals, textiles

ITALY
AREA: 116,348 sq mi (301,340 sq km)
POPULATION: 61,016,804
CAPITAL: Rome
LANGUAGES: Italian (official), German, French, Slovene
GOVERNMENT: Republic
RELIGIONS: Roman Catholic, Protestant, Jewish, Muslim
LITERACY RATE: 99%
CURRENCY: Euro
MAIN EXPORTS: Engineering products, textiles, production machinery, motor vehicles, transport equipment, chemicals, food, beverages, tobacco, minerals

JAMAICA
AREA: 4,244 sq mi (10,992 sq km)
POPULATION: 2,868,380
CAPITAL: Kingston
LANGUAGES: English, English patois
GOVERNMENT: Constitutional parliamentary democracy
RELIGIONS: Protestant, Roman Catholic
LITERACY RATE: 88%
CURRENCY: Jamaican dollar
MAIN EXPORTS: Alumina, bauxite, sugar, bananas, rum, coffee, yams, beverages, chemicals, apparel, mineral fuels

JAPAN
AREA: 145,914 sq mi (377,916 sq km)
POPULATION: 126,475,664
CAPITAL: Tokyo
LANGUAGE: Japanese
GOVERNMENT: Constitutional monarchy with a parliamentary government
RELIGIONS: Shintoist, Buddhist
LITERACY RATE: 99%
CURRENCY: Yen
MAIN EXPORTS: Transport equipment, motor vehicles, semiconductors, chemicals

JORDAN
AREA: 34,495 sq mi (89,342 sq km)
POPULATION: 6,508,271
CAPITAL: Amman
LANGUAGES: Arabic (official), English
GOVERNMENT: Constitutional monarchy
RELIGIONS: Sunni Muslim, Christian
LITERACY RATE: 91%
CURRENCY: Jordanian dinar
MAIN EXPORTS: Clothing, fertilizers, potash, phosphates, vegetables, pharmeceuticals

KAZAKHSTAN
AREA: 1,052,090 sq mi (2,724,900 sq km)
POPULATION: 15,522,373
CAPITAL: Astana
LANGUAGES: Russian (official), Kazakh
GOVERNMENT: Republic
RELIGIONS: Muslim, Russian Orthodox, Protestant
LITERACY RATE: 100%
CURRENCY: Tenge
MAIN EXPORTS: Oil and oil products, ferrous metals, chemicals, machinery, grain, wool, meat, coal

KENYA
AREA: 224,081 sq mi (580,367 sq km)
POPULATION: 41,070,934
CAPITAL: Nairobi
LANGUAGES: English, Kiswahili (both official), native languages
GOVERNMENT: Republic
RELIGIONS: Protestant, Roman Catholic, Muslim, native beliefs
LITERACY RATE: 85%
CURRENCY: Kenyan shilling
MAIN EXPORTS: Tea, horticultural products, coffee, petroleum products, fish, cement

KIRIBATI
AREA: 313 sq mi (811 sq km)
POPULATION: 100,743
CAPITAL: Tarawa
LANGUAGES: English (official), I-Kiribati
GOVERNMENT: Republic
RELIGIONS: Roman Catholic, Protestant, Muslim, Baha'i
LITERACY RATE: NA
CURRENCY: Australian dollar
MAIN EXPORTS: Copra, coconuts, fish, seaweed

KOREA, NORTH
AREA: 46,540 sq mi (120,538 sq km)
POPULATION: 24,457,492
CAPITAL: Pyongyang
LANGUAGE: Korean
GOVERNMENT: Communist state one-man dictatorship
RELIGIONS: Buddhist, Confucianist, Christian, Chondogyo (Religion of the Heavenly Way)
LITERACY RATE: 99%

CURRENCY: North Korean won

MAIN EXPORTS: Minerals, fish products

KOREA, SOUTH

AREA: 38,502 sq mi (99,720 sq km)

POPULATION: 48,754,657

CAPITAL: Seoul

LANGUAGE: Korean

GOVERNMENT: Republic

RELIGIONS: Christian, Buddhist

LITERACY RATE: 98%

CURRENCY: South Korean won

MAIN EXPORTS: Semiconductors, motor vehicles, computers, steel, ships

KOSOVO

AREA: 4,203 sq mi (10,886 sq km)

POPULATION: 1,825,632

CAPITAL: Pristina

LANGUAGES: Albanian, Serbian (both official), Bosnian, Turkish, Roma

GOVERNMENT: Republic

RELIGIONS: Muslim, Serbian Orthodox, Roman Catholic

LITERACY RATE: 92%

CURRENCY: Euro

MAIN EXPORTS: Scrap metals, leather products, machinery, appliances, mining and processed metal products

KUWAIT

AREA: 6,880 sq mi (17,819 sq km)

POPULATION: 2,595,628

CAPITAL: Kuwait City

LANGUAGES: Arabic (official), English

GOVERNMENT: Constitutional emirate

RELIGIONS: Muslim, Christian, Hindu, Parsi

LITERACY RATE: 93%

CURRENCY: Kuwaiti dinar

MAIN EXPORTS: Oil and refined products, fertilizers

KYRGYZSTAN

AREA: 77,202 sq mi (199,952 sq km)

POPULATION: 5,587,443

CAPITAL: Bishkek

LANGUAGES: Kyrgyz, Russian (both official), Uzbek

GOVERNMENT: Republic

RELIGIONS: Muslim, Russian Orthodox

LITERACY RATE: 99%

CURRENCY: Kyrgyzstani som

MAIN EXPORTS: Cotton, wool, meat, tobacco, gold, mercury, uranium, shoes

LAOS

AREA: 91,429 sq mi (236,800 sq km)

POPULATION: 6,477,211

CAPITAL: Vientiane

LANGUAGES: Lao (official), French, English, ethnic languages

GOVERNMENT: Communist state

RELIGIONS: Buddhist, animist, Christian

LITERACY RATE: 69%

CURRENCY: Kip

MAIN EXPORTS: Wood products, electricity, tin, copper, gold

LATVIA

AREA: 24,938 sq mi (64,589 sq km)

POPULATION: 2,204,708

CAPITAL: Riga

LANGUAGES: Latvian (official), Lithuanian, Russian

GOVERNMENT: Parliamentary democracy

RELIGIONS: Lutheran, Christian, Orthodox

LITERACY RATE: 100%

CURRENCY: Latvian lat

MAIN EXPORTS: Wood and wood products, machinery and equipment, metals, textiles, foodstuffs

LEBANON

AREA: 4,015 sq mi (10,399 sq km)

POPULATION: 4,143,101

CAPITAL: Beirut

LANGUAGES: Arabic (official), French, English, Armenian

GOVERNMENT: Republic

RELIGIONS: Muslim, Christian

LITERACY RATE: 87%

CURRENCY: Lebanese pound

MAIN EXPORTS: Jewelry, base metals, chemicals, fruit and vegetables, paper

LESOTHO

AREA: 11,720 sq mi (30,355 sq km)

POPULATION: 1,924,886

CAPITAL: Maseru

LANGUAGES: English (official), Sesotho (southern Sotho), Zulu, Xhosa

GOVERNMENT: Parliamentary constitutional monarchy

RELIGIONS: Christian, native beliefs

LITERACY RATE: 85%

CURRENCIES: Loti, South African rand

MAIN EXPORTS: Manufactured clothing, road vehicles, footwear, wool and mohair

LIBERIA

AREA: 43,000 sq mi (111,370 sq km)

POPULATION: 3,786,764

CAPITAL: Monrovia

LANGUAGES: English (official), tribal dialects

GOVERNMENT: Republic

RELIGIONS: Native beliefs, Christian, Muslim

LITERACY RATE: 58%

CURRENCY: Liberian dollar

MAIN EXPORTS: Rubber, timber, iron, diamonds, cocoa, coffee

LIBYA

AREA: 679,362 sq mi (1,759,540 sq km)

POPULATION: 6,597,960

CAPITAL: Tripoli

LANGUAGES: Arabic, Italian, English

GOVERNMENT: Authoritarian state

RELIGION: Sunni Muslim

LITERACY RATE: 83%

CURRENCY: Libyan dinar

MAIN EXPORTS: Natural gas, chemicals

LIECHTENSTEIN

AREA: 62 sq mi (161 sq km)

POPULATION: 35,236

CAPITAL: Vaduz

LANGUAGES: German (official), Alemannic dialect

GOVERNMENT: Constitutional monarchy

RELIGIONS: Roman Catholic, Protestant

LITERACY RATE: 100%

CURRENCY: Swiss franc

MAIN EXPORTS: Parts for motor vehicles, dental products, prepared foodstuffs

LITHUANIA

AREA: 25,212 sq mi (65,299 sq km)

POPULATION: 3,535,547

CAPITAL: Vilnius

LANGUAGES: Lithuanian (official), Polish, Russian

GOVERNMENT: Parliamentary democracy

RELIGIONS: Roman Catholic, Protestant, Russian Orthodox

LITERACY RATE: 100%

CURRENCY: Litas

MAIN EXPORTS: Mineral products, textiles, clothing, machinery and equipment, plastics

LUXEMBOURG

AREA: 998 sq mi (2,585 sq km)

POPULATION: 503,302

CAPITAL: Luxembourg

LANGUAGES: Luxembourgish, German, French

GOVERNMENT: Constitutional monarchy

RELIGIONS: Roman Catholic, Protestant, Jewish, Muslim

LITERACY RATE: 100%

CURRENCY: Euro

MAIN EXPORTS: Machinery and equipment, steel products, chemicals, rubber products

MACEDONIA

AREA: 9,928 sq mi (25,713 sq km)

POPULATION: 2,077,328

CAPITAL: Skopje

LANGUAGES: Macedonian, Albanian, Turkish, Serb, Roma

GOVERNMENT: Parliamentary democracy

RELIGIONS: Macedonian Orthodox, Muslim

LITERACY RATE: 96%

CURRENCY: Macedonian denar

MAIN EXPORTS: Food, beverages, tobacco, iron and steel, textiles

MADAGASCAR

AREA: 226,657 sq mi (587,039 sq km)

POPULATION: 21,926,221

CAPITAL: Antananarivo

LANGUAGES: French, Malagasy (both official), English

GOVERNMENT: Republic

RELIGIONS: Native beliefs, Christian, Muslim

LITERACY RATE: 69%

CURRENCY: Malagasy ariary

MAIN EXPORTS: Coffee, vanilla, shellfish, sugar, cotton, cloth, petroleum products

MALAWI

AREA: 45,745 sq mi (118,479 sq km)

POPULATION: 15,879,252

CAPITAL: Lilongwe

LANGUAGES: Chichewa (official), Chinyanja, Chiyao, Chitumbuka, others

GOVERNMENT: Multiparty democracy

RELIGIONS: Christian, Muslim

LITERACY RATE: 63%

CURRENCY: Malawian kwacha

MAIN EXPORTS: Tobacco, tea, sugar, cotton, coffee, peanuts, wood products, clothing

MALAYSIA

AREA: 127,355 sq mi (329,848 sq km)

POPULATION: 28,728,607

CAPITAL: Kuala Lumpur

LANGUAGES: Bhasa Malaysia (official), English, Chinese, Malayalam, others

GOVERNMENT: Constitutional monarchy

RELIGIONS: Muslim, Buddhist, Taoist, Hindu, Christian, Confucianist

LITERACY RATE: 89%

CURRENCY: Ringgit

MAIN EXPORTS: Electronic equipment, petroleum and liquefied natural gas, wood and wood products, palm oil, rubber

MALDIVES

AREA: 115 sq mi (298 sq km)

POPULATION: 394,999

CAPITAL: Male

LANGUAGES: Dhivehi (official), English

GOVERNMENT: Republic

RELIGION: Sunni Muslim

LITERACY RATE: 94%

CURRENCY: Maldivian rufiyaa

MAIN EXPORT: Fish

MALI

AREA: 478,841 sq mi (1,240,192 sq km)

POPULATION: 14,159,904

CAPITAL: Bamako

LANGUAGES: French (official), Bambara

GOVERNMENT: Republic

RELIGIONS: Muslim, native beliefs, Christian

LITERACY RATE: 46%

CURRENCY: Communauté Financière Africaine franc

MAIN EXPORTS: Cotton, gold, livestock

MALTA

AREA: 122 sq mi (316 sq km)

POPULATION: 408,333

CAPITAL: Valletta

LANGUAGES: Maltese, English (both official)

GOVERNMENT: Republic

RELIGION: Roman Catholic

LITERACY RATE: 93%

CURRENCY: Euro

MAIN EXPORTS: Machinery, fish

MARSHALL ISLANDS

AREA: 70 sq mi (181 sq km)

POPULATION: 67,182

CAPITAL: Majuro

LANGUAGES: Marshallese, English (both official), Japanese

GOVERNMENT: Constitutional government

RELIGION: Christian

LITERACY RATE: 94%

CURRENCY: U.S. dollar

MAIN EXPORTS: Copra cake, coconut oil, handcrafts, fish

MAURITANIA

AREA: 397,955 sq mi (1,030,700 sq km)

POPULATION: 3,281,634

CAPITAL: Nouakchott

LANGUAGES: Arabic (official), Pulaar, Soninke, Wolof, French, Hassaniya

GOVERNMENT: Military junta

RELIGION: Muslim

LITERACY RATE: 51%

CURRENCY: Ouguiya

MAIN EXPORTS: Iron ore, fish and fish products, gold, copper, petroleum

MAURITIUS

AREA: 788 sq mi (2,041 sq km)

POPULATION: 1,303,717

CAPITAL: Port Louis

LANGUAGES: English (official), Creole, Bhojpuri, French

GOVERNMENT: Parliamentary democracy

RELIGIONS: Hindu, Roman Catholic, Protestant, Muslim

LITERACY RATE: 84%

CURRENCY: Mauritian rupee

MAIN EXPORTS: Clothing and textiles, sugar, cut flowers, molasses, fish

MEXICO

AREA: 758,449 sq mi (1,964,374 sq km)

POPULATION: 113,724,226

CAPITAL: Mexico City

LANGUAGES: Spanish, Mayan, Nahuatl and other native languages

GOVERNMENT: Federal republic

RELIGIONS: Roman Catholic, Protestant

LITERACY RATE: 91%

CURRENCY: Mexican peso

MAIN EXPORTS: Manufactured goods, oil and oil products, silver, fruit, vegetables

MICRONESIA

AREA: 271 sq mi (702 sq km)

POPULATION: 106,836

CAPITAL: Palikir

LANGUAGES: English (official), others

GOVERNMENT: Constitutional government

RELIGIONS: Roman Catholic, Protestant

LITERACY RATE: 89%

CURRENCY: U.S. Dollar

MAIN EXPORTS: Fish, garments, bananas, black pepper, saku (kava), betel nut

MOLDOVA

AREA: 13,067 sq mi (33,843 sq km)

POPULATION: 4,314,377

CAPITAL: Chisinau

LANGUAGES: Moldovan (official), Russian, Gagauz

GOVERNMENT: Republic

RELIGIONS: Eastern Orthodox, Jewish, Baptist

LITERACY RATE: 99%

CURRENCY: Moldovan leu

MAIN EXPORTS: Foodstuffs, textiles, machinery

MONACO

AREA: .75 sq mi (1.94 sq km)

POPULATION: 30,539

CAPITAL: Monaco

LANGUAGES: French (official), English, Italian, Monégasque

GOVERNMENT: Constitutional monarchy

RELIGION: Roman Catholic

LITERACY RATE: 99%

CURRENCY: Euro

MAIN EXPORTS: NA

MONGOLIA

AREA: 603,909 sq mi (1,564,117 sq km)

POPULATION: 3,133,318

CAPITAL: Ulaanbaatar

LANGUAGES: Khalkha Mongol, Turkic, Russian

GOVERNMENT: Parliamentary

RELIGIONS: Buddhist Lamaist, Muslim, Shamanist, Christian
LITERACY RATE: 98%
CURRENCY: Togrog/tugrik
MAIN EXPORTS: Copper, livestock, animal products, cashmere, wool, hides, fluorspar

MONTENEGRO
AREA: 5,333 sq mi (13,812 sq km)
POPULATION: 661,807
CAPITAL: Podgorica
LANGUAGES: Serbian, Bosniak, Albanian, Montenegrin
GOVERNMENT: Republic
RELIGIONS: Orthodox, Muslim, Roman Catholic
LITERACY RATE: NA
CURRENCY: Euro
MAIN EXPORTS: NA

MOROCCO
AREA: 172,413 sq mi (446,550 sq km)
POPULATION: 31,968,361
CAPITAL: Rabat
LANGUAGES: Arabic (official), Berber dialects, French
GOVERNMENT: Constitutional monarchy
RELIGIONS: Muslim, Christian, Jewish
LITERACY RATE: 52%
CURRENCY: Moroccan dirham
MAIN EXPORTS: Clothing, fish, inorganic chemicals, transistors, crude minerals, fertilizers, petroleum products, fruit

MOZAMBIQUE
AREA: 308,642 sq mi (799,379 sq km)
POPULATION: 22,948,858
CAPITAL: Maputo
LANGUAGES: Portuguese (official), Bantu languages
GOVERNMENT: Republic
RELIGIONS: Catholic, Muslim, Zionist Christian
LITERACY RATE: 48%
CURRENCY: Metical
MAIN EXPORT: Bulk electricity

MYANMAR (BURMA)
AREA: 261,228 sq mi (676,577 sq km)
POPULATION: 53,999,804
CAPITAL: Nay Pyi Taw
LANGUAGES: Burmese, minority languages
GOVERNMENT: Military regime
RELIGIONS: Buddhist, Baptist, Roman Catholic, Muslim, animist
LITERACY RATE: 90%
CURRENCY: Kyat
MAIN EXPORTS: Natural gas, wood products, beans, fish, rice, clothing, jade, gems

NAMIBIA
AREA: 318,261 sq mi (824,292 sq km)
POPULATION: 2,147,585
CAPITAL: Windhoek
LANGUAGES: English (official), Afrikaans, German, native languages
GOVERNMENT: Republic
RELIGIONS: Christian, native beliefs
LITERACY RATE: 84%
CURRENCIES: Namibian dollar, South African rand
MAIN EXPORTS: Diamonds, copper, gold, zinc, lead, uranium, cattle, processed fish

NAURU
AREA: 8 sq mi (21 sq km)
POPULATION: 9,322
CAPITAL: Yaren District
LANGUAGES: Nauruan, English
GOVERNMENT: Republic
RELIGIONS: Protestant, Roman Catholic
LITERACY RATE: NA
CURRENCY: Australian dollar
MAIN EXPORT: Phosphates

NEPAL
AREA: 56,827 sq mi (147,181 sq km)
POPULATION: 29,391,883
CAPITAL: Kathmandu
LANGUAGES: Nepali, English
GOVERNMENT: Federal democratic republic
RELIGIONS: Hindu, Buddhism, Muslim
LITERACY RATE: 49%
CURRENCY: Nepalese rupee
MAIN EXPORTS: Clothing, carpets, textiles, juice, jute goods

NETHERLANDS
AREA: 16,040 sq mi (41,543 sq km)
POPULATION: 16,847,007
CAPITAL: Amsterdam
LANGUAGES: Dutch, Frisian (both official)
GOVERNMENT: Constitutional monarchy
RELIGIONS: Roman Catholic, Protestant, Calvinist, Dutch Reformed
LITERACY RATE: 99%
CURRENCY: Euro
MAIN EXPORTS: Machinery and equipment, chemicals, fuels, foodstuffs

NEW ZEALAND
AREA: 103,363 sq mi (267,709 sq km)
POPULATION: 4,290,347
CAPITAL: Wellington
LANGUAGES: English, Maori, sign language (all official)
GOVERNMENT: Parliamentary democracy
RELIGIONS: Protestant, Roman Catholic
LITERACY RATE: 99%
CURRENCY: New Zealand dollar
MAIN EXPORTS: Dairy products, meat, wood and wood products, fish, machinery

NICARAGUA
AREA: 50,306 sq mi (130,292 sq km)
POPULATION: 5,666,301
CAPITAL: Managua
LANGUAGE: Spanish (official)
GOVERNMENT: Republic
RELIGIONS: Roman Catholic, Protestant
LITERACY RATE: 68%
CURRENCY: Gold cordoba
MAIN EXPORTS: Coffee, shrimp, lobster, tobacco, beef, sugar, gold, peanuts

NIGER
AREA: 489,189 sq mi (1,266,994 sq km)
POPULATION: 16,468,886
CAPITAL: Niamey
LANGUAGES: French (official), Hausa, Djerma
GOVERNMENT: Republic
RELIGIONS: Muslim, native beliefs, Christian
LITERACY RATE: 29%
CURRENCY: Communauté Financière Africaine franc
MAIN EXPORTS: Uranium ore, livestock, cowpeas, onions

NIGERIA
AREA: 356,669 sq mi (923,768 sq km)
POPULATION: 155,215,573
CAPITAL: Abuja
LANGUAGES: English (official), Hausa, Yoruba, Igbo, Fulani
GOVERNMENT: Federal republic
RELIGIONS: Muslim, Christian, native beliefs
LITERACY RATE: 68%
CURRENCY: Naira
MAIN EXPORT: Petroleum and petroleum products, cocoa, rubber

NORWAY
AREA: 125,021 sq mi (323,803 sq km)
POPULATION: 4,691,849
CAPITAL: Oslo
LANGUAGE: Norwegian (official)
GOVERNMENT: Constitutional monarchy
RELIGIONS: Protestant, Roman Catholic
LITERACY RATE: 100%
CURRENCY: Norwegian krone
MAIN EXPORTS: Petroleum and petroleum products, machinery and equipment, metals, chemicals, ships, fish

OMAN
AREA: 119,499 sq mi (309,501 sq km)
POPULATION: 3,027,959
CAPITAL: Muscat
LANGUAGES: Arabic (official), English, Indian languages
GOVERNMENT: Monarchy
RELIGIONS: Ibadhi Muslim, Sunni Muslim, Shia Muslim, Hindu
LITERACY RATE: NA
CURRENCY: Omani rial
MAIN EXPORTS: Petroleum, fish, metals, textiles

PAKISTAN
AREA: 307,374 sq mi (796,095 sq km)
POPULATION: 187,342,721
CAPITAL: Islamabad
LANGUAGES: Urdu (official), Punjabi, Sindhi, Siraiki, Pashtu, others
GOVERNMENT: Federal republic
RELIGIONS: Muslim, Christian, Hindu
LITERACY RATE: 49%
CURRENCY: Pakistani rupee
MAIN EXPORTS: Textiles, rice, leather, sports goods, carpets

PALAU
AREA: 177 sq mi (458 sq km)
POPULATION: 20,956
CAPITAL: Melekeok
LANGUAGES: English, Palauan, Sonsoralese, Tobi, others
GOVERNMENT: Constitutional government
RELIGIONS: Roman Catholic, Protestant
LITERACY RATE: 92%
CURRENCY: U.S. Dollar
MAIN EXPORTS: Shellfish, tuna, copra, garments

PANAMA
AREA: 29,120 sq mi (75,420 sq km)
POPULATION: 3,460,462
CAPITAL: Panama City
LANGUAGES: Spanish (official), English
GOVERNMENT: Constitutional democracy
RELIGIONS: Roman Catholic, Protestant
LITERACY RATE: 93%
CURRENCIES: Balboa, U.S. dollar
MAIN EXPORTS: Bananas, shrimp, sugar, coffee, clothing

PAPUA NEW GUINEA
AREA: 178,703 sq mi (462,839 sq km)
POPULATION: 6,187,591
CAPITAL: Port Moresby
LANGUAGES: Tok Pisin, English, Hiri Motu (all official), native languages

GOVERNMENT: Constitutional monarchy with parliamentary democracy
RELIGIONS: Roman Catholic, Protestant, native beliefs
LITERACY RATE: 57%
CURRENCY: Kina
MAIN EXPORTS: Oil, gold, copper ore, logs, palm oil, coffee, cocoa, crayfish, prawns

PARAGUAY
AREA: 157,046 sq mi (406,747 sq km)
POPULATION: 6,459,058
CAPITAL: Asunción
LANGUAGES: Spanish, Guarani (both official)
GOVERNMENT: Constitutional republic
RELIGIONS: Roman Catholic, Protestant
LITERACY RATE: 94%
CURRENCY: Guaraní
MAIN EXPORTS: Soybeans, feed, cotton, meat, edible oils, electricity

PERU
AREA: 496,223 sq mi (1,285,212 sq km)
POPULATION: 29,248,943
CAPITAL: Lima
LANGUAGES: Spanish, Quechua (both official), Aymara
GOVERNMENT: Constitutional republic
RELIGIONS: Roman Catholic, Evangelical
LITERACY RATE: 93%
CURRENCY: Nuevo sol
MAIN EXPORTS: Copper, gold, zinc, coffee, potatoes, asparagus, textiles, fish meal

PHILIPPINES
AREA: 115,830 sq mi (299,998 sq km)
POPULATION: 101,833,938
CAPITAL: Manila
LANGUAGES: Filipino, English (both official), others
GOVERNMENT: Republic
RELIGIONS: Roman Catholic, Muslim
LITERACY RATE: 93%
CURRENCY: Philippine peso
MAIN EXPORTS: Copper products, petroleum products, coconut oil, fruits

POLAND
AREA: 120,727 sq mi (312,682 sq km)
POPULATION: 38,441,588
CAPITAL: Warsaw
LANGUAGE: Polish
GOVERNMENT: Republic
RELIGIONS: Roman Catholic, Eastern Orthodox, Protestant
LITERACY RATE: 100%
CURRENCY: Zloty
MAIN EXPORTS: Machinery and transport equipment, manufactured goods, food

PORTUGAL
AREA: 35,556 sq mi (92,090 sq km)
POPULATION: 10,760,305
CAPITAL: Lisbon
LANGUAGE: Portuguese, Mirandese
GOVERNMENT: Parliamentary democracy republic
RELIGIONS: Roman Catholic, Protestant
LITERACY RATE: 93%
CURRENCY: Euro
MAIN EXPORTS: Wood and cork, wood pulp and paper, oil products, skin and leather, plastics and rubber, agricultural products, food products, optical instruments

QATAR
AREA: 4,473 sq mi (11,585 sq km)
POPULATION: 848,016
CAPITAL: Doha
LANGUAGES: Arabic (official), English
GOVERNMENT: Emirate
RELIGIONS: Muslim, Christian
LITERACY RATE: 89%
CURRENCY: Qatari rial
MAIN EXPORTS: Petroleum products, fertilizers, steel, liquefied natural gas

ROMANIA
AREA: 92,043 sq mi (238,390 sq km)
POPULATION: 21,904,551
CAPITAL: Bucharest
LANGUAGES: Romanian, Hungarian, Romany
GOVERNMENT: Republic
RELIGIONS: Eastern Orthodox, Protestant, Catholic
LITERACY RATE: 98%
CURRENCY: Leu
MAIN EXPORTS: Textiles and footwear, metals and metal products, machinery and equipment, minerals, fuels, chemicals

RUSSIA
AREA: 6,601,668 sq mi (17,098,241 sq km)
POPULATION: 138,739,892
CAPITAL: Moscow
LANGUAGES: Russian, others
GOVERNMENT: Federation
RELIGIONS: Russian Orthodox, Muslim
LITERACY RATE: 100%
CURRENCY: Russian ruble
MAIN EXPORTS: Petroleum and petroleum products, natural gas, wood and wood products, metals, chemicals

RWANDA
AREA: 10,169 sq mi (26,338 sq km)
POPULATION: 11,370,425

CAPITAL: Kigali
LANGUAGES: Kinyarwanda, French, English (all official), Bantu, Kiswahili
GOVERNMENT: Republic
RELIGIONS: Roman Catholic, Protestant, Muslim, native beliefs
LITERACY RATE: 70%
CURRENCY: Rwandan franc
MAIN EXPORTS: Foodstuffs, steel

SAINT KITTS AND NEVIS
AREA: 101 sq mi (262 sq km)
POPULATION: 50,314
CAPITAL: Basseterre
LANGUAGE: English
GOVERNMENT: Parliamentary democracy
RELIGIONS: Protestant, Roman Catholic
LITERACY RATE: 98%
CURRENCY: East Caribbean dollar
MAIN EXPORTS: Machinery, food, electronics, beverages, tobacco

SAINT LUCIA
AREA: 238 sq mi (616 sq km)
POPULATION: 161,557
CAPITAL: Castries
LANGUAGES: English (official), French patois
GOVERNMENT: Parliamentary democracy
RELIGIONS: Roman Catholic, Protestant
LITERACY RATE: 90%
CURRENCY: East Caribbean dollar
MAIN EXPORTS: Bananas, clothing, cocoa, vegetables, fruit, coconut oil

SAINT VINCENT AND THE GRENADINES
AREA: 150 sq mi (388 sq km)
POPULATION: 103,869
CAPITAL: Kingstown
LANGUAGES: English, French patois
GOVERNMENT: Parliamentary democracy
RELIGIONS: Protestant, Roman Catholic, Hindu
LITERACY RATE: 96%
CURRENCY: East Caribbean dollar
MAIN EXPORTS: Bananas, taro, arrowroot starch, tennis rackets

SAMOA
AREA: 1,093 sq mi (2,831 sq km)
POPULATION: 193,161
CAPITAL: Apia
LANGUAGES: Samoan (Polynesian), English
GOVERNMENT: Parliamentary democracy
RELIGIONS: Protestant, Roman Catholic
LITERACY RATE: 100%
CURRENCY: Tala
MAIN EXPORTS: Fish, coconut oil and cream, copra, taro, garments, beer

SAN MARINO
AREA: 24 sq mi (62 sq km)
POPULATION: 31,817
CAPITAL: San Marino
LANGUAGE: Italian
GOVERNMENT: Independent republic
RELIGION: Roman Catholic
LITERACY RATE: 96%
CURRENCY: Euro
MAIN EXPORTS: Building stone, lime, wood, chestnuts, wheat, wine, hides

SAO TOME AND PRINCIPE
AREA: 349 sq mi (904 sq km)
POPULATION: 179,506
CAPITAL: São Tomé
LANGUAGE: Portuguese
GOVERNMENT: Republic
RELIGION: Christian
LITERACY RATE: 85%
CURRENCY: Dobra
MAIN EXPORTS: Cocoa, copra, coffee, palm oil

SAUDI ARABIA
AREA: 830,000 sq mi (2,149,690 sq km)
POPULATION: 26,131,703
CAPITAL: Riyadh
LANGUAGE: Arabic
GOVERNMENT: Monarchy
RELIGION: Muslim
LITERACY RATE: 79%
CURRENCY: Saudi riyal
MAIN EXPORTS: Petroleum and petroleum products

SENEGAL
AREA: 75,955 sq mi (196,723 sq km)
POPULATION: 12,643,799
CAPITAL: Dakar
LANGUAGES: French (official), Wolof, Pulaar, Jola, Mandinka
GOVERNMENT: Republic
RELIGIONS: Muslim, indigenous beliefs, Christian
LITERACY RATE: 40%
CURRENCY: Communauté Financière Africaine franc
MAIN EXPORTS: Fish, groundnuts (peanuts), petroleum products, phosphates, cotton

SERBIA
AREA: 29,913 sq mi (77,474 sq km)
POPULATION: 7,310,555
CAPITAL: Belgrade
LANGUAGES: Serbian (official), Romanian, Hungarian, Slovak, Ukrainian, Croatian, Albanian
GOVERNMENT: Republic
RELIGIONS: Serbian Orthodox, Muslim, Roman Catholic, Protestant
LITERACY RATE: 96%
CURRENCY: Serbian dinar
MAIN EXPORTS: Iron, steel, clothes, wheat, fruit and vegetables, nonferrous metals

SEYCHELLES
AREA: 176 sq mi (456 sq km)
POPULATION: 89,188
CAPITAL: Victoria
LANGUAGES: Creole, English (official)
GOVERNMENT: Republic
RELIGIONS: Roman Catholic, Anglican, other Christian
LITERACY RATE: 92%
CURRENCY: Seychelles rupee
MAIN EXPORTS: Canned tuna, frozen fish, cinnamon bark, copra, petroleum products

SIERRA LEONE
AREA: 27,699 sq mi (71,740 sq km)
POPULATION: 5,363,669
CAPITAL: Freetown
LANGUAGES: English (official), Mende, Temne, Krio
GOVERNMENT: Constitutional democracy
RELIGIONS: Muslim, native beliefs, Christian
LITERACY RATE: 35%
CURRENCY: Leone
MAIN EXPORTS: Diamonds, rutile, cocoa, coffee, fish

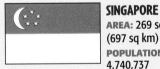

SINGAPORE
AREA: 269 sq mi (697 sq km)
POPULATION: 4,740,737
CAPITAL: Singapore
LANGUAGES: Chinese (Mandarin), English, Malay, Hokkien, others
GOVERNMENT: Parliamentary republic
RELIGIONS: Buddhist, Muslim, Taoist, Hindu, Catholic, Protestant
LITERACY RATE: 93%
CURRENCY: Singapore dollar
MAIN EXPORTS: Machinery and equipment (including electronics), consumer goods, chemicals, mineral fuels

SLOVAKIA
AREA: 18,933 sq mi (49,036 sq km)
POPULATION: 5,477,038
CAPITAL: Bratislava
LANGUAGES: Slovak (official), Hungarian
GOVERNMENT: Parliamentary republic

RELIGIONS: Roman Catholic, Protestant, Orthodox

LITERACY RATE: 100%

CURRENCY: Euro

MAIN EXPORTS: Machinery and electrical equipment, vehicles, base metals, plastics

SLOVENIA
AREA: 7,827 sq mi (20,272 sq km)

POPULATION: 2,000,092

CAPITAL: Ljubljana

LANGUAGES: Slovenian, Serbo-Croatian

GOVERNMENT: Parliamentary republic

RELIGIONS: Roman Catholic, Lutheran, Muslim

LITERACY RATE: 100%

CURRENCY: Euro

MAIN EXPORTS: Manufactured goods, machinery and transport equipment, chemicals, food

SOLOMON ISLANDS
AREA: 11,157 sq mi (28,896 sq km)

POPULATION: 571,890

CAPITAL: Honiara

LANGUAGES: English (official), Melanesian pidgin, native languages

GOVERNMENT: Parliamentary democracy

RELIGIONS: Church of Melanesia, Roman Catholic, Protestant

LITERACY RATE: NA

CURRENCY: Solomon Islands dollar

MAIN EXPORTS: Timber, fish, copra, palm oil, cocoa

SOMALIA
AREA: 246,199 sq mi (637,652 sq km)

POPULATION: 9,925,640

CAPITAL: Mogadishu

LANGUAGES: Somali (official), Arabic, English, Italian

GOVERNMENT: Transitional parliamentary

RELIGION: Sunni Muslim

LITERACY RATE: 38%

CURRENCY: Somali shilling

MAIN EXPORTS: Livestock, bananas, hides, fish, charcoal, scrap metal

SOUTH AFRICA
AREA: 470,693 sq mi (1,219,090 sq km)

POPULATION: 49,004,031

CAPITAL: Pretoria (administrative); Cape Town (legislative); Bloemfontein (judicial)

LANGUAGES: IsiZulu, IsiXhosa, Africaans, Sepedi, English, Setswana, others

GOVERNMENT: Republic

RELIGIONS Christian, Muslim, Hindu, native beliefs, animist

LITERACY RATE: 86%

CURRENCY: Rand

MAIN EXPORTS: Gold, diamonds, platinum, machinery and equipment, metals and other minerals

SPAIN
AREA: 195,124 sq mi (505,369 sq km)

POPULATION: 46,754,784

CAPITAL: Madrid

LANGUAGES: Castilian Spanish, Catalan, Galician, Basque

GOVERNMENT: Parliamentary monarchy

RELIGION: Roman Catholic

LITERACY RATE: 98%

CURRENCY: Euro

MAIN EXPORTS: Machinery, motor vehicles, foodstuffs, other consumer goods

SRI LANKA
AREA: 25,332 sq mi (65,610 sq km)

POPULATION: 21,283,913

CAPITAL: Colombo

LANGUAGES: Sinhala (official), Tamil, English

GOVERNMENT: Republic

RELIGIONS: Buddhist, Hindu, Christian, Muslim

LITERACY RATE: 92%

CURRENCY: Sri Lankan rupee

MAIN EXPORTS: Textiles, tea and spices, diamonds, emeralds, rubies, fish

SUDAN
AREA: 967,503 sq mi (2,505,821 sq km)

POPULATION: 45,047,502

CAPITAL: Khartoum

LANGUAGES: Arabic, English (both official), Nubian, Ta Bedawie

GOVERNMENT: Authoritarian regime

RELIGIONS: Sunni Muslim, native beliefs, Christian

LITERACY RATE: 61%

CURRENCY: Sudanese dinar

MAIN EXPORTS: Oil and petroleum products, cotton, sesame, livestock, sugar

SURINAME
AREA: 63,251 sq mi (163,819 sq km)

POPULATION: 491,989

CAPITAL: Paramaribo

LANGUAGES: Dutch (official), Surinamese, English

GOVERNMENT: Constitutional democracy

RELIGIONS: Hindu, Muslim, Roman Catholic, Protestant, native beliefs

LITERACY RATE: 90%

CURRENCY: Surinamese guilder

MAIN EXPORTS: Alumina, crude oil, gold, lumber, shrimp and fish, rice, bananas

---

SWAZILAND
AREA: 6,704 sq mi (17,363 sq km)

POPULATION: 1,370,424

CAPITAL: Mbabane

LANGUAGES: siSwati, English (both official)

GOVERNMENT: Monarchy

RELIGIONS: Zionist, Roman Catholic, Muslim, Anglican, Baha'i, Methodist

LITERACY RATE: 82%

CURRENCY: Emalangeni

MAIN EXPORTS: Refrigerators, citrus, canned fruit

SWEDEN
AREA: 173,731 sq mi (449,961 sq km)

POPULATION: 9,088,728

CAPITAL: Stockholm

LANGUAGE: Swedish

GOVERNMENT: Constitutional monarchy

RELIGIONS: Lutheran, Roman Catholic, Orthodox, Baptist, Muslim, Jewish

LITERACY RATE: 99%

CURRENCY: Swedish krona

MAIN EXPORTS: Iron and steel products, chemicals

SWITZERLAND
AREA: 15,937 sq mi (41,277 sq km)

POPULATION: 7,639,961

CAPITAL: Bern

LANGUAGES: German, French, Italian, Romansch (all official)

GOVERNMENT: Federal republic

RELIGIONS: Roman Catholic, Protestant

LITERACY RATE: 99%

CURRENCY: Swiss franc

MAIN EXPORTS: Machinery, chemicals, metals, watches, agricultural products

SYRIA
AREA: 71,498 sq mi (185,179 sq km)

POPULATION: 22,517,750

CAPITAL: Damascus

LANGUAGES: Arabic (official), Kurdish, Armenian, Aramaic, Circassian

GOVERNMENT: Republic under military regime

RELIGIONS: Sunni Muslim, Alawite, Druze, and other Muslim sects, Christian, Jewish

LITERACY RATE: 80%

CURRENCY: Syrian pound

MAIN EXPORTS: Crude oil, petroleum products, fruit and vegetables, cotton fiber, clothing, meat and live animals, wheat, minerals

TAIWAN
AREA: 13,892 sq mi (35,980 sq km)

POPULATION: 23,071,779

CAPITAL: Taipei

LANGUAGES: Chinese (Mandarin), Taiwanese, Hakka dialects

GOVERNMENT: Multiparty democracy

RELIGIONS: Buddhist, Taoist, Christian

LITERACY RATE: 96%

CURRENCY: New Taiwan dollar

MAIN EXPORTS: Electronics, machinery, textiles, metals, plastics, chemicals, optical, photographic, and medical instruments

TAJIKISTAN
AREA: 55,251 sq mi (143,099 sq km)

POPULATION: 7,627,200

CAPITAL: Dushanbe

LANGUAGES: Tajik (official), Russian

GOVERNMENT: Republic

RELIGIONS: Sunni Muslim, Shia Muslim

LITERACY RATE: 99%

CURRENCY: Tajikistani somoni

MAIN EXPORTS: Aluminum, electricity, cotton, fruit, vegetable oil, textiles

TANZANIA
AREA: 365,755 sq mi (947,301 sq km)

POPULATION: 42,746,620

CAPITAL: Dar es Salaam (commercial); Dodoma (political)

LANGUAGES: Kiswahili, English (both official), Arabic

GOVERNMENT: Republic

RELIGIONS: Christian, Muslim, native beliefs

LITERACY RATE: 69%

CURRENCY: Tanzanian shilling

MAIN EXPORTS: Gold, coffee, cashew nuts, manufactures, cotton

THAILAND
AREA: 198,117 sq mi (513,121 sq km)

POPULATION: 66,720,153

CAPITAL: Bangkok

LANGUAGES: Thai, English

GOVERNMENT: Constitutional democracy

RELIGIONS: Buddhism, Muslim, Christian, Hindu

LITERACY RATE: 93%

CURRENCY: Baht

MAIN EXPORTS: Computers, transistors, seafood, clothing, rice

TOGO
AREA: 21,925 sq mi (56,785 sq km)

POPULATION: 6,771,993

CAPITAL: Lomé

LANGUAGES: French (official), Ewé, Mina, Kabyé, Dagomba

GOVERNMENT: Republic under transition to democratic rule

RELIGIONS: Native beliefs, Christian, Muslim

LITERACY RATE: 61%

CURRENCY: Communauté Financière Africaine franc

MAIN EXPORTS: Cotton, phosphates, coffee, cocoa

TONGA
AREA: 289 sq mi (749 sq km)

POPULATION: 105,916

CAPITAL: Nuku'alofa

LANGUAGES: Tongan, English

GOVERNMENT: Constitutional monarchy

RELIGION: Christian

LITERACY RATE: 99%

CURRENCY: Pa'anga

MAIN EXPORTS: Squash, fish, vanilla beans, root crops

TRINIDAD AND TOBAGO
AREA: 5,384 sq mi (13,945 sq km)

POPULATION: 1,227,505

CAPITAL: Port-of-Spain

LANGUAGES: English (official), Hindi, French, Spanish, Chinese (Mandarin)

GOVERNMENT: Parliamentary democracy

RELIGIONS: Roman Catholic, Hindu, Anglican, Baptist, Pentecostal, Muslim, others

LITERACY RATE: 99%

CURRENCY: Trinidad and Tobago dollar

MAIN EXPORTS: Petroleum and petroleum products, chemicals, steel products, sugar, cocoa, coffee, citrus, vegetables, flowers

TUNISIA
AREA: 63,170 sq mi (163,610 sq km)

POPULATION: 10,629,186

CAPITAL: Tunis

LANGUAGES: Arabic (official), French

GOVERNMENT: Republic

RELIGION: Muslim

LITERACY RATE: 74%

CURRENCY: Tunisian dinar

MAIN EXPORTS: Textiles, mechanical goods, phosphates and chemicals, agricultural products, hydrocarbons

TURKEY
AREA: 302,535 sq mi (783,562 sq km)

POPULATION: 78,785,548

CAPITAL: Ankara

LANGUAGES: Turkish (official), Kurdish

GOVERNMENT: Republican parliamentary democracy

RELIGION: Muslim

LITERACY RATE: 87%

CURRENCY: Turkish lira

MAIN EXPORTS: Clothing, foodstuffs, textiles, metal manufactures

TURKMENISTAN
AREA: 188,455 sq mi (488,096 sq km)

POPULATION: 4,997,503

CAPITAL: Ashgabat

LANGUAGES: Turkmen, Russian, Uzbek, others

GOVERNMENT: Republic

RELIGIONS: Muslim, Eastern Orthodox

LITERACY RATE: 98%

CURRENCY: Turkmen manat

MAIN EXPORTS: Gas, oil, cotton, textiles

TUVALU
AREA: 10 sq mi (26 sq km)

POPULATION: 10,544

CAPITAL: Funafuti

LANGUAGES: Tuvaluan, English, Samoan, Kiribati

GOVERNMENT: Constitutional monarchy with a parliamentary democracy

RELIGION: Protestant

LITERACY RATE: NA

CURRENCIES: Australian dollar, Tuvaluan dollar

MAIN EXPORTS: Copra, fish

UGANDA
AREA: 93,065 sq mi (241,037 sq km)

POPULATION: 34,612,250

CAPITAL: Kampala

LANGUAGES: English (official), Ganda, other native languages

GOVERNMENT: Republic

RELIGIONS: Roman Catholic, Protestant, Muslim, native beliefs

LITERACY RATE: 67%

CURRENCY: Ugandan shilling

MAIN EXPORTS: Coffee, fish and fish products, tea, gold, cotton, flowers

UKRAINE
AREA: 233,032 sq mi (603,550 sq km)

POPULATION: 45,134,707

CAPITAL: Kiev

LANGUAGES: Ukrainian (official), Russian

GOVERNMENT: Republic

RELIGIONS: Ukrainian Orthodox, Ukrainian Catholic, Protestant, Jewish, Roman Catholic

LITERACY RATE: 100%

CURRENCY: Hryvnia

MAIN EXPORTS: Fuel and petroleum products, chemicals, machinery and transport

UNITED ARAB EMIRATES
AREA: 32,278 sq mi (83,600 sq km)

POPULATION: 5,148,664
CAPITAL: Abu Dhabi
LANGUAGES: Arabic (official), Persian, English, Hindi, Urdu
GOVERNMENT: Federation
RELIGIONS: Shia Muslim, Christian, Hindu
LITERACY RATE: 78%
CURRENCY: Emirati dirham
MAIN EXPORTS: Crude oil, natural gas, dried fish, dates

UNITED KINGDOM
AREA: 94,058 sq mi (243,609 sq km)
POPULATION: 62,698,362

CAPITAL: London
LANGUAGES: English, Welsh, Scottish Gaelic
GOVERNMENT: Constitutional monarchy
RELIGIONS: Anglican, Roman Catholic, Protestant, Muslim, Hindu
LITERACY RATE: 99%
CURRENCY: British pound
MAIN EXPORTS: Manufactured goods, fuels, chemicals, food, beverages, tobacco

UNITED STATES
AREA: 3,794,100 sq mi (9,826,675 sq km)
POPULATION: 313,232,044

CAPITAL: Washington, D.C.
LANGUAGES: English, Spanish
GOVERNMENT: Federal republic
RELIGIONS: Protestant, Roman Catholic, Jewish, others
LITERACY RATE: 99%
CURRENCY: U.S. dollar
MAIN EXPORTS: Soybeans, fruit, corn, capital goods, automobiles, medicines

URUGUAY
AREA: 68,038 sq mi (176,218 sq km)
POPULATION: 3,308,535

CAPITAL: Montevideo
LANGUAGES: Spanish, Portunol, Brazilero
GOVERNMENT: Constitutional republic
RELIGIONS: Roman Catholic, Protestant, Jewish, others
LITERACY RATE: 98%
CURRENCY: Uruguayan peso
MAIN EXPORTS: Meat, rice, leather products, wool, fish, dairy products

UZBEKISTAN
AREA: 172,740 sq mi (447,395 sq km)
POPULATION: 28,128,600

CAPITAL: Tashkent
LANGUAGES: Uzbek, Russian, Tajik
GOVERNMENT: Republic
RELIGIONS: Muslim, Eastern Orthodox
LITERACY RATE: 99%
CURRENCY: Uzbekistani sum
MAIN EXPORTS: Cotton, gold, energy products, mineral fertilizers, automobiles

VANUATU
AREA: 4,706 sq mi (12,188 sq km)
POPULATION: 224,564

CAPITAL: Port-Vila
LANGUAGES: English, French, Bislama (all official), others
GOVERNMENT: Parliamentary repubulic
RELIGIONS: Protestant, Roman Catholic, native beliefs
LITERACY RATE: 74%
CURRENCY: Vatu
MAIN EXPORTS: Copra, beef, cocoa, timber, kava, coffee

VATICAN CITY (HOLY SEE)
AREA: .17 sq mi (.44 sq km)
POPULATION: 832
CAPITAL: None

LANGUAGES: Latin, Italian, French, others
GOVERNMENT: Ecclesiastical
RELIGION: Roman Catholic
LITERACY RATE: 100%
CURRENCY: Euro
MAIN EXPORTS: NA

VENEZUELA
AREA: 352,141 sq mi (912,041 sq km)
POPULATION: 27,635,743

CAPITAL: Caracas
LANGUAGES: Spanish (official), native dialects
GOVERNMENT: Federal republic
RELIGIONS: Roman Catholic, Protestant, others
LITERACY RATE: 93%
CURRENCY: Bolivar
MAIN EXPORTS: Petroleum, bauxite and aluminum, steel, chemicals, agricultural products

VIETNAM
AREA: 127,881 sq mi (331,210 sq km)
POPULATION: 90,549,390

CAPITAL: Hanoi
LANGUAGES: Vietnamese (official), English, French, Chinese, Khmer, others
GOVERNMENT: Communist state
RELIGIONS: Buddhist, Hoa Hao, Cao Dai, Roman Catholic, Protestant, others
LITERACY RATE: 90%
CURRENCY: Dong
MAIN EXPORTS: Crude oil, marine products, rice, coffee, rubber, tea, garments, shoes

YEMEN
AREA: 203,848 sq mi (527,964 sq km)
POPULATION: 24,133,492

CAPITAL: Sanaa
LANGUAGE: Arabic
GOVERNMENT: Republic
RELIGION: Muslim
LITERACY RATE: 50%
CURRENCY: Yemeni rial
MAIN EXPORTS: Crude oil, coffee, dried and salted fish, liquefied natural gas

ZAMBIA
AREA: 290,586 sq mi (752,614 sq km)
POPULATION: 13,881,336

CAPITAL: Lusaka
LANGUAGES: Bemba, Nyanja, Tonga, Lozi, Lunda, Kaonde, Luvale, English (all official)
GOVERNMENT: Republic
RELIGIONS: Christian, Muslim, Hindu, native beliefs
LITERACY RATE: 81%
CURRENCY: Zambian kwacha
MAIN EXPORTS: Copper, cobalt, electricity, tobacco, flowers, cotton

ZIMBABWE
AREA: 150,872 sq mi (390,757 sq km)
POPULATION: 12,084,304

CAPITAL: Harare
LANGUAGES: English (official), Shona, Sindebele, native languages
GOVERNMENT: Parliamentary democracy
RELIGIONS: Syncretic, Christian, Muslim
LITERACY RATE: 91%
CURRENCY: Zimbabwean dollar
MAIN EXPORTS: Tobacco, gold, ferroalloys, textiles and clothing

Index

Photo Credits

Regional Maps and Updates: Joe LeMonnier
Original Continent Maps: Joe Lertola

Front Cover: Rubberball Productions (boy standing in center); Shutterstock.com (all other photos). **1–77:** Shutterstock.com (all). **78–79:** Shutterstock.com (railroad, mine, lake); National Geographic/Getty Images (Nenet woman). **80–106:** Shutterstock.com (all). **107:** ©Photobulb/Dreamstime.com (kente cloth). **108–109:** Shutterstock.com (elephants); National Geographic/Getty Images (boy). **110:** ©David Gomez/iStockphoto.com (giraffe). **111–120:** Shutterstock.com (all). **121:** Time Life Pictures/Mansell/Time Life Pictures/Getty Images (Amundsen). **Back Cover:** Shutterstock.com (all).